Distributed Agency

FOUNDATIONS OF HUMAN INTERACTION

General Editor: N. J. Enfield, The University of Sydney

This series promotes new interdisciplinary research on the elements of human sociality, in particular as they relate to the activity and experience of communicative interaction and human relationships. Books in this series explore the foundations of human interaction from a wide range of perspectives, using multiple theoretical and methodological tools. A premise of the series is that a proper understanding of human sociality is only possible if we take a truly interdisciplinary approach.

Series Editorial Board:

Recently published in the series:

DISTRIBUTED AGENCY

Edited by N. J. Enfield

and

Paul Kockelman

OXFORD
UNIVERSITY PRESS

OXFORD
UNIVERSITY PRESS

Oxford University Press is a department of the University of Oxford. It furthers
the University's objective of excellence in research, scholarship, and education
by publishing worldwide. Oxford is a registered trade mark of Oxford University
Press in the UK and certain other countries.

Published in the United States of America by Oxford University Press
198 Madison Avenue, New York, NY 10016, United States of America.

© Oxford University Press 2017

Library of Congress Cataloging-in-Publication Data
Names: Enfield, N. J., 1966– editor. | Kockelman, Paul.
Title: Distributed Agency / [edited by] N. J. Enfield and Paul Kockelman.
Description: Oxford ; New York : Oxford University Press, [2017] |
Series: Foundations of human interaction | Includes bibliographical references and index.
Identifiers: LCCN 2016022303 (print) | LCCN 2016038875 (ebook) |
ISBN 9780190457211 (paperback) | ISBN 9780190457204 (cloth) |
ISBN 9780190457228 (pdf) | ISBN 9780190457235 (Online Content)
Subjects: LCSH: Semiotics—Psychological aspects. | Communication—Psychological aspects. |
Human behavior. | Cognition. | Psycholinguistics. | BISAC: LANGUAGE
ARTS & DISCIPLINES / Linguistics / General. | SOCIAL SCIENCE / Anthropology / Cultural. |
SOCIAL SCIENCE / General.
Classification: LCC P99.4.P78 D47 2017 (print) | LCC P99.4.P78 (ebook) | DDC 128/.4—dc23
LC record available at https://lccn.loc.gov/2016022303

CONTENTS

SERIES EDITOR PREFACE

The human capacity for distributed agency allows us to dissociate social units from the borders of the individual. Our social units—the "agents" who operate in people's worlds—can morph and shift in shape and size and constitution. From fleeting moments of cooperation to historical movements of community, people extend beyond the bounds of individuals. The case studies presented in this volume provide a wide-ranging set of entry points into this captivating area of study. Together they show that when we look at distributed agency we are looking at the cognitive and cultural dynamics of human sociality.

N. J. E.
Sydney, September 2016

EDITORS' PREFACE

We never really act alone. Our agency is enhanced when we cooperate with others, and when we accept their help. We benefit when we take credit for people's achievements, or when we free-ride on their ideas and their strengths. And not only is our agency shared through action in these ways, but we often have agency without having to engage in action at all. Even when at rest, we are bound up in networks of cause and effect, intention and accountability. The distribution of agency, for better or worse, is everywhere, and our species has perfected its arts.

This book presents an interdisciplinary inroad into the latest thinking about the distributed nature of agency: what it's like, what are its conditions of possibility, and what are its consequences. The book's 26 chapters are written by a wide range of scholars, from anthropology, biology, cognitive science, linguistics, philosophy, psychology, geography, law, economics, and sociology. While each chapter takes up different materials using different methods, they all chart relations between the key elements of agency: intentionality, causality, flexibility, and accountability. Each chapter seeks to explain how and why such relations are distributed—not just across individuals, but also across bodies and minds, people and things, spaces and times. To do this, the authors work through empirical studies of particular cases, while also offering reviews and syntheses of key ideas from the authors' respective research traditions.

IDEAS AND QUESTIONS GUIDING THIS BOOK

All creatures have some form of agency, but agency in humans is arguably unique. Humans have a special capacity to share agency through joint commitment and cooperation toward common goals, as well as through coercive and parasitic practices by which we co-opt the capacities, and take credit for the consequences, of others. We are the most flexible and creative actors of all species, as shown by our formidable and complex technologies, from levers, swords, and printing presses, to bridges, drones, and the internet. Culture is itself the exemplar of relatively unconscious collective creativity. (Or at least many human agents like to think!)

We can think of agency as having two key components. First, there is *flexibility*. This is about who (or what) has a hand or say in the creation of some effect, object, idea, or action: from theorems and inventions to floods and revolutions, from commodities and crimes to conversations and crises. In most cases, many "hands" contribute, at different degrees of remove, with more or less effort and effect, and with greater or lesser visibility. These hands are social as much as material; cognitive as much as somatic; individual as much as collective; natural as much as artificial; flexibly creative as much as rigidly causal. Indeed, as soon as one starts tracking such connections, the distinctions often break down. It is hard to see where cognition ends and embodiment begins; where the divide between nature and artifice is to be drawn; where to cut off an individual from a collectivity.

The second component of agency is *accountability*. We must ask how those with agency are held accountable (usually by other kinds of agents) for their contribution. Who realizes the cost of a product, or garners the right to use it? Who is blamed for the failure of an action? Who is praised for the genesis of an idea? Who or what benefits from a new adaptation? Who berates themselves over an imagined sin? Through what mechanisms? Accountability is identified in different ways, using judgments with varying degrees of justness, rationality, and depth of vision. Accountability is both moral and economic, causal and normative, grounded in natural selection and cultural evaluation.

Current understandings of human agency suggest that our flexibility and accountability are often not located in the individual alone, but are radically *distributed*. This suggests a number of questions, which guided the discussions that have shaped the contributions to the book.[1] Among these are the following:

- Why and how do we excerpt agents at certain scales, and how do different understandings of agency alter such scales?
- When we cooperate with others, when is our agency weakened, and when is it enhanced?
- In what ways is material culture an extension of the person?
- While artifacts and technologies increase our flexibility in obvious ways, how do they affect our accountability?
- What are the causal forces that determine the scope and constraints of our agency? How are these forces related to norms?

- Why is it often considered appropriate to punish or reward a person for something that someone else did?
- How is it that multiple individuals can behave as one?
- What is the role of distributed agency in human evolution, and in ontogeny?

In short, who or what contributes to some action, idea, object, or outcome? And who or what is held accountable? In what ways, and to what degrees? With what conditions, and with what consequences? These are the questions we ask in this book.

CONTENTS

The ten parts of the book each group together essays that overlap in regard to their empirical topics and analytic commitments. Part One, "Agency as Flexible and Accountable Causality," introduces key themes through four interrelated chapters. In the first two chapters, Enfield theorizes some elements of agency, broadly understood as flexible and accountable causality; and then describes how agency, thus framed, is distributed across actors and activities. In the second two chapters, Kockelman reviews and synthesizes some classic texts that lead to such an understanding of agency; and then describes a variety of other possible ways of framing it.

The next nine parts take up interrelated questions from a variety of stances, partly deriving from the cross-disciplinary commitments of authors, and partly from the empirical contents they analyze and the theoretical questions they answer.

In Part Two, "The Agency of Institutions and Infrastructure," Bernstein takes up agency in actual state agencies—in particular, legal and political institutions that promulgate laws and regulations shaping the actions of citizens—and Elyachar takes up agency in the context of political revolutions, when critical energies are used to create, use, and destroy key forms of infrastructure.

Part Three presents perspectives on "Language and Agency." While much previous work on language and agency has focused on the representational and meta-representational capacities of humans, these four chapters take us into the trenches of interaction: talk-in-interaction as it unfolds in real-time practices, in face-to-face encounters. Dingemanse uses the science fiction fantasy of brain-to-brain interfaces to shed light on the natural distribution of agency in human communication; Floyd focuses on requests as a key means for instigating and negotiating the sharing of agency; also on this theme, Rossi and Zinken focus in more closely on the fine-grained grammatical categories that languages provide as tools for mobilizing other people; and Sidnell focuses on a particularly important but overlooked element of the shared construction of action in interaction, namely the accountability that comes with our impositions on others.

In Part Four, "Economy and Agency," Guyer examines the ethics of debt as a way of distributing agency both across people and through time, and Maurer looks at the infrastructures of monetary accounting, where the act of "recording" an exchange can in fact be seen as effecting the very exchange itself. In Part Five, "Distributing Agency within Selves and Species," Parry explores the distribution of agency in moving the human body in professional therapy sessions, and d'Ettorre—on a very different scale—shows how agency is distributed across masses of individual bodies in the case of eusocial organisms such as ants.

In Part Six, "Social Bonding Through Embodied Agency," the theme of agency in human groups is further developed, with an overview by Cohen of some elements of social bonding through group exercise in humans, and a focus by Tarr on the same in dance and music. And in Part Seven, "Agency and Infancy," Rączaszek-Leonardi highlights the importance of different timescales in an exploration of the understanding of agency between infants and caregivers, and Tunçgenç stresses the importance of close temporal coordination in the bodily movements of infants and caregivers as a crucial step on the path from individual to collective agency in the lifespan.

Part Eight, "The Agency of Materiality," presents three studies of how agency gets into, and out of, inanimate objects: Crossland discusses the agency of human remains, as understood through forensic anthropology; Smith considers the agentive role of marbles in the lives of children; and Wilf explores how computerized algorithms can be a source of contingencies that are harvested to cultivate artistic creativity. In Part Nine, "The Place of Agency," Adams takes up agency through the eyes of a geographer focused on spatially distributed selves, and Lahlou looks at it through the lens of installations—or spatially arranged ensembles of affordances that shape the activities of those who act and think inside them. And in Part Ten, "From Cooperation to Deception and Disruption," Schweikard outlines the central importance of intentionality and normativity in the cooperative framework of joint action, while Umbres turns our attention to deception—a decidedly antisocial form of distributed agency—and Zuckerman delves further into the dark side of agency, with a study of attempts to sabotage others' courses of action, and the post hoc framings and attributions of agency that then emerge.

ENVOI

Human agency concerns the fundamental conditions and constraints under which we pursue our goals, from the simplest everyday actions to the greatest uses and abuses of power in society. But a deep understanding of human agency is elusive because the concept of agency has been understood and examined in such different ways. The meaning of the term *agency* is often radically simplified, reduced to or conflated with that of other terms: compare *free will, choice, language, power, generativity, imagination, self-consciousness.* There have been important advances in separate disciplines, but there has been little opportunity to combine and build on the collective achievements of research on human agency carried out using sometimes radically different approaches. Our goals with this collection of essays are to assemble insights from new research on the anatomy of human agency, to address divergent framings of the issues from different disciplines, and to suggest directions for new debates and lines of research. We hope that it will be a resource for researchers working on allied topics, and for students learning about the elements of human-specific modes of shared action, from causality, intentionality, and personhood to ethics, punishment, and accountability.

NOTE

1. The forum for most of these discussions was a retreat held at Ringberg Castle, Tegernsee/Kreuth, Germany, April 13–17, 2014, attended by most of the book's contributors, and several others. The retreat was funded by a European Research Council grant "Human Sociality and Systems of Language Use" (Grant number 240853, to Enfield). The discussion continued by correspondence and led to the further invitation and inclusion of several authors whose work was important to the project. We are grateful to all participants and contributors for their invaluable input. We thank Angela Terrill at Punctilious Editing (http://www. punctilious.net/) for first-class indexing. Please note the following conventions for transcripts in a number of chapters: underline = stress; [= beginning of overlap;] = end of overlap; (4.4) = 4.4 seconds of silence; text in ((double brackets)) refers to visible bodily behavior; text in (single brackets) = not clearly audible.

CONTRIBUTORS

Paul C. Adams, Department of Geography and the Environment, University of Texas at Austin

Anya Bernstein, Law School, SUNY Buffalo

Emma Cohen, Institute of Cognitive and Evolutionary Anthropology, University of Oxford

Zoë Crossland, Department of Anthropology, Columbia University

Patrizia d'Ettorre, Laboratory of Experimental and Comparative Ethology, University of Paris 13, Sorbonne Paris Cité

Mark Dingemanse, Max Planck Institute for Psycholinguistics

Julia Elyachar, Department of Anthropology, Princeton University

N. J. Enfield, Department of Linguistics, The University of Sydney

Simeon Floyd, SENESCYT (National Science Ministry), Ecuador; Radboud University Nijmegen, and Max Planck Institute for Psycholinguistics

Jane I. Guyer, Department of Anthropology, Johns Hopkins University

Paul Kockelman, Department of Anthropology, Yale University

Saadi Lahlou, London School of Economics and Political Science

Bill Maurer, Department of Anthropology, University of California at Irvine

Ruth H. Parry, Faculty of Medicine and Health Sciences, University of Nottingham

Joanna Rączaszek-Leonardi, Faculty of Psychology, University of Warsaw

Giovanni Rossi, University of Helsinki

David P. Schweikard, Department of Philosophy, Europa-Universität Flensburg

Jack Sidnell, Departments of Anthropology and Linguistics, University of Toronto

Benjamin Smith, Department of Anthropology, Sonoma State University

Bronwyn Tarr, Social and Evolutionary Neuroscience Research Group, University of Oxford

Bahar Tunçgenç, Institute of Cognitive and Evolutionary Anthropology, University of Oxford

Radu Umbres, Faculty of Political Sciences, National School of Political and Administrative Sciences, Bucharest

Eitan Wilf, Department of Sociology and Anthropology, Hebrew University

Jörg Zinken, Institute for the German Language (IDS), Mannheim

Charles H. P. Zuckerman, Department of Anthropology, University of Michigan

PART ONE

Agency as Flexible
and Accountable Causality

CHAPTER 1

Elements of Agency

N. J. ENFIELD

On October 15, 1965, on Whitehall Street in Lower Manhattan, David J. Miller burned his draft card in protest at the Vietnam War (Miller 2001):

The expectant crowd fell hush in front of me. The hecklers across the street ceased their ranting and watched silently. An eerie stillness settled upon our canyon as the last rays of the fall sun clung to the tops of the buildings. I said the first thing that came to my mind. "I am not going to give my prepared speech. I am going to let this action speak for itself. I know that you people across the street really know what is happening in Vietnam. I am opposed to the draft and the war in Vietnam."

I pulled my draft classification card from my suit coat pocket along with a book of matches brought especially for the occasion since I did not smoke. I lit a match, then another. They blew out in the late afternoon breeze. As I struggled with the matches, a young man with a May 2nd Movement button on his jacket held up a cigarette lighter. It worked just fine.

The draft card burned as I raised it aloft between the thumb and index finger of my left hand. A roar of approval from the rally crowd greeted the enflamed card. This awakened the momentarily mesmerized hecklers and they resumed their shouts.

As the card burned, I discovered that I had made no preparation for the card to be completely consumed. I dropped the card as the flame reached my finger-tips. At my trial in federal court, the unburnt corner of my draft card, with a bit of my signature, was introduced into evidence. The FBI had been Johnny-on-the-spot in retrieving the charred remains of my card so as to assist in their prosecution even though I never denied that I burned my card. Future card burners used tongs or cans in order to complete the job.

... Three days later the FBI swooped in on me in Manchester, New Hampshire.... I made bail the next day. I remained free till June 1968 when the draft-card burning case finally lost in the U.S. Supreme Court. I served 22 months in federal prison in Pennsylvania from 1968 to 1970.

Miller's story of publicly burning his draft card as a means of protesting against the US government's program of conscription during the Vietnam War illustrates the core elements of agency: he had a degree of flexibility in carrying out the behavior, and a degree of accountability. What does this mean? Let us start with the elements of flexibility:[1]

(1) Agents have *flexibility* over meaningful behavior, insofar as:
    (a) to some degree they *control* or determine that the behavior is done at a certain place and time (thus, to some degree Miller determined that his draft card would be burned at that place and time; though with minor delays due to his malfunctioning matches);
    (b) to some degree they *compose* or design the behavior as a means for a particular end; a thing to be done and a way to do it (thus, Miller at some level had the plan to destroy this draft card as a protest against the war, and he determined sub-plans as means to that greater end);
    (c) to some degree they *subprehend*[2] or anticipate how others could view and react to the behavior; for instance to some extent they may be prepared for certain interpretants—in other words, rational responses—by others; they may be surprised or disposed to sanction non-anticipated interpretants (thus, Miller was not surprised when hecklers tried to disrupt him, when FBI agents took his burned card as evidence, or when they arrested him in the following days; nor when he was praised as a hero by members of the antiwar movement).

These elements of flexibility are understood in terms of the semiotic process that underlies an agent's behavior (Kockelman 2007, 2013). Thus, controlling (1a) is about the production of perceptible behavior—potential signs—without respect to what that perceptible behavior may be taken to mean, or to what interpretants it might so elicit. In Miller's case, controlling simply had to do with instigating an event of fire destroying a piece of paper.

Composing (1b) is about the relation between an agent and an overall semiotic process that this agent instigates. Composing in this sense concerns the degree to which an agent selects that behavior for a function, as a means to an end, and the degree to which her carrying out of the behavior is responsible for success in achieving her goal. Miller's goal was to protest against the war; as an agent, he played a role in determining which behavior would be produced and what that behavior may stand for. His selection of tools (draft card, fire) as means toward a local end (destroying the physical manifestation of a government order) determined the conditions for success in his venture: without the card actually catching fire and burning up, the planned action would not have been consummated. As Miller describes, there were minor obstacles to the execution of the card-burning behavior, related to the affordances of fire and paper: for one thing, the wind blew out his matches on his first attempts, and for another, the heat of the burning paper caused him to let go of the card and in the end not succeed in fully destroying it. For the behavior to succeed as Miller composed it, the effective destruction of a specific piece of paper was necessary to the consummation of a specific political act.

Within composing, we can distinguish between execution and planning. Differences in the manner of execution of a sign, which may be functions of the skill or conditions of an agent, will have consequences for how effectively a sign will succeed in standing for a particular object. While execution is the degree to which one's physical production of the relevant sign is done in such a way as to determine that the sign should be taken to stand for a certain object, planning is deciding which sign-object relations are to be created in the first place. Miller planned to put fire to paper, but his execution was lacking. In the end his plan was carried out, executed with the help of a bystander with a lighter.

Subprehending (1c) is about the relation between the agent and the overall semiotic process. Subprehension concerns the degree to which an individual effectively foresees the interpretants—in other words, the reactions and responses—that the sign event may evince. One way to measure this would be in the ways a person might reveal that they have prepared for a certain interpretant and not others. For example, if I ask *What's his address?* while at the same time pulling out a pen and paper to write the address down, by pulling out the pen and paper I am showing evidence of having subprehended that your interpretant (your answer) of my sign (my question) will be to tell me the person's address, which I will then be already prepared to write down. Another way to measure subprehension in this sense is to monitor the accountability involved. Is a person surprised by or disposed to sanction certain interpretants? If I ask *What's his address?* and you look at me and say nothing, I might repeat the question or say *Hey I asked you something.* An agent subprehends interpretants of a sign event to some degree (especially the potential accountability): being prepared for some interpretants and not others; being surprised by, or disposed to sanction, some interpretants and not others. As noted above, Miller was surely not surprised by the heckling, the arrest, the conviction; nor was he presumably surprised by the praise, support, and imitation from other activists. This indicates that his degree of agency on the measure of subprehension was high.

With an agent's flexibility comes accountability, as Miller anticipated or at least subprehended:

(2) Agents have *accountability* for meaningful behavior, insofar as:
   (a) they may be subject to public *evaluation* by others for their behavior, where this evaluation—in the form of interpretants like praise, blame, or demand for reasons—may focus on any of the distinct components of flexibility given in (1), above (thus, Miller's actions were evaluated by many people from onlookers at the scene to federal judges in the US Supreme Court);
   (b) they may be regarded as having some degree of *entitlement* to carry out the behavior, and give reasons for it, and they or others may invoke this entitlement; this may relate to any of the distinct components of flexibility given in (1), above (thus, Miller's behavior was precisely designed to give him an opportunity to state his reasons for action, with the intention to publicize those reasons for action);
   (c) they may be regarded by others as having some degree of *obligation* to carry out the behavior, and give reasons for it, and they or others may invoke this obligation; this may relate to any of the distinct components of flexibility laid out in (1), above (thus, Miller's behavior could be used as a basis for motivating others, possibly through a sense of moral obligation, to do the same).

Another way of framing accountability in relation to behavior in the sense just defined is *ownership* of the behavior. Thinking in terms of accountability foregrounds the possibility of blame or praise, while ownership foregrounds rights and obligations.

So, in sum, agency is the relation between a person and a course of action and its effects. To summarize it in the leanest terms possible:

(3) With regard to some goal-directed controlled behavior, agency consists of the following:
  (A) Flexibility
    1. Controlling (determining that a perceptible/physical behavior occurs)
    2. Composing (selecting the behavior, its function, and execution)
    3. Subprehending (effectively anticipating interpretants of the behavior)
  (B) Accountability
    1. Being evaluated (by others, on any of [A1–3])
    2. Being entitled (a right to do the behavior can be recognized and invoked)
    3. Being obligated (a duty to do the behavior can be recognized and invoked)

There is a special relation between flexibility and accountability. Flexibility is regimented both by natural laws and by social norms, and often by these two in combination. One's accountability is lower when one's behavior is more heavily constrained by natural laws, because less choice is involved. Supporters of Miller are unlikely to sanction him for having delayed the burning of the card before he was given the cigarette lighter; they would recognize that his flexibility was at that moment thwarted by natural causes, and not by, say, some form of hesitation in anticipation of likely sanctions.

And so we arrive at Kockelman's definitive equation: Agency equals flexibility plus accountability. How flexible you are depends on how freely you can determine the elements of a course of behavior and its outcomes, in multiple senses: the physical carrying out of the behavior, the planning and design of the behavior, the placing of the behavior in an appropriate context, the anticipation or subprehension of likely effects of the behavior—including, especially, the reactions of others—in that context. How accountable you are depends on how much it can be expected or demanded that other people will interpret what you do in certain ways, for example, by responding, asking for reasons, sanctioning, praising, or blaming you. With these elements distinguished, we begin to understand why the concept of agency is far from simple or primitive, and why it has resisted easy definition. With the elements of agency distinguished, we may begin to understand the many subtleties of the agency problem, something that is especially needed when we want to take the next step and ask how agency is distributed.

ACKNOWLEDGMENTS

Thanks go to Paul Kockelman for his significant input to this work. Note that this chapter draws partly on sections of my 2013 book *Relationship Thinking* (Oxford University Press). I gratefully acknowledge support from the Max Planck Society (through MPI Nijmegen), the European Research Council (through grant 240853, "Human Sociality and Systems of Language Use"), and the University of Sydney (through Bridging Grant ID 176605).

NOTES

1. This analysis of flexibility in agency is due to Kockelman (2007, 2013), though I take one liberty with the terminology (Enfield 2013:104–117). Kockelman's term for (1c) is "commitment," defined as "the degree to which one may anticipate an interpretant, where this anticipation is evinced in being surprised by and/or disposed to sanction unanticipated interpretants" (Kockelman 2007:380). I propose "subprehension," to avoid confusion with other dominant meanings of the word "commitment" (for example, in Kockelman 2007:153 and passim, "commitment" has a technical meaning in the domain of accountability, referring to "deontic obligation," something one is obliged to do). On agency and language specifically, see Ahearn (2010), Duranti (2004).

2. *Subprehend* may be defined as follows. If you subprehend something, it is as if you anticipate or expect it, but not in any active or conscious way; rather, if you subprehend something, when it happens you cannot say later that you had not anticipated or expected it. Subprehension is thus close to the notion of habitus (Bourdieu 1977).

REFERENCES

Ahearn, Laura M. 2010. "Agency and Language." *Society and Language Use* 7: 28.

Bourdieu, Pierre. 1977. *Outline of a Theory of Practice.* Cambridge: Cambridge University Press.

Duranti, Alessandro. 2004. "Agency in Language." In *A Companion to Linguistic Anthropology*, edited by D. Alessandro, 451–473. Malden, MA: Blackwell.

Enfield, N. J. 2013. *Relationship Thinking: Agency, Enchrony, and Human Sociality.* Oxford: Oxford University Press.

Kockelman, Paul. 2007. "Agency: The Relation Between Meaning, Power, and Knowledge." *Current Anthropology* 48(3): 375–401.

Kockelman, Paul. 2013. *Agent, Person, Subject, Self: A Theory of Ontology, Interaction, and Infrastructure.* Oxford: Oxford University Press.

Miller, David. 2001. "Reclaiming Our History: Memoirs of a Draft-Card Burner." *Reclaiming Quarterly* (82). http://www.reclaimingquarterly.org/82/rq-82-draftcard.html Retrieved March 12, 2011.

CHAPTER 2
Distribution of Agency

N. J. ENFIELD

It is easy to think that "an agent" should coincide exactly with an individual. But this is seldom, if ever, the case. One reason agents do not equal individuals is that the elements of agency can be divided up and shared out among multiple people in relation to a single course of action. When I get you to pass the salt, it is me who plans the behavior but you who executes it. Or when I report what a candidate said in yesterday's speech, it is me who speaks the words but the candidate who is accountable for what was expressed. With distributed agency, multiple people act as one, sharing or sharing out the elements of agency.

One person may provide the flexibility needed for meeting another person's ends—as in slavery, factories, and armies—or for meeting shared ends—as in team sports, co-authorship, and joint enterprise. Similarly, one person may bear the accountability entailed by another person's flexibility. It is hardly rare for a person to inherit the blame for someone else's punishable actions. Howitt (1904), writing on Aboriginal Australia, "mentions the case of an accused man pointing to his elder brother to take the blame, because an elder brother stands for and should, ideally, protect a younger" (Berndt and Berndt 1964:299). In law of this kind, "people are categorized in units the members of which are interdependent ... [and] relations both within and between those units may not be framed only, or predominantly, in kinship terms" (Berndt and Berndt 1964:303). This nonmodern approach has difficulty fitting into today's world. In 2009, there was a campaign in the Australian Aboriginal community at Lajamanu in

the Northern Territory to find a solution to persistent social problems arising from the incompatibility of indigenous and government law. Here was
the problem. If people who committed crimes were jailed and thus separated from their community before they could face traditional punishment
(known as payback) then this payback would be meted out on family members of the transgressors, often leading to continuing feuds. The campaign
called for official recognition of traditional punishment, allowing that bail
be granted to indigenous offenders so that they might face punishment
(for example, being speared through the thigh) and thus resolve the matter
to the satisfaction of the community before being taken to jail.

Distributed accountability of the kind that the Lajamanu campaign
sought to avoid is the essence of *the feud*, a universal phenomenon. Take
for example the *gjakmarrja*—or blood feuds—of rural Albania. Blood feud-
ing was largely dormant during the communist period, but with the fall
of communism in the early 1990s, old feuds were rekindled, and people
found themselves being held accountable for things that were done before
they were born, sometimes by people they had never met. Here is a case
(Mustafa and Young 2008:99–100):

> A family living in a village outside *Bajram Curri* ... came under a new threat,
> even though the man from their family who had committed a blood feud killing
> had himself died seventeen years ago. The perpetrator's death did not satisfy
> the indebted family who sent a warning that they expected "blood payment" in
> the form of the life of a male member of the remaining family. The family under
> threat consisted of a widow living with her two sons, their wives, and several
> children. The family had already adjusted to the threatening situation: the eldest
> son had gone into hiding elsewhere, and the younger remained indoors, unable
> to leave the house. Obviously this situation had a drastic effect on the earning
> capacity of the family.

Cases like this take us to the heart of distributed agency. One man commits
a misdeed against another, and yet revenge is taken years later between
the two men's grandchildren, neither of whom was involved in the original
transgression. Here, someone is held to account for something that someone else chose to do. Here, agency, with its components of flexibility and
accountability, is divided and shared out among multiple individuals while
still being anchored in a single, sometimes decades-long course of action.
Cases like this highlight one of the key reasons why agents do not equal
individuals: the locus of agency is the social unit, and social units are not
confined to individual bodies.

This is another, related reason agents do not equal individuals: social units are often compound persons. People are able to merge together to form single units of motivation, flexibility, and accountability. If you and I agree to make sauce, we commit to a common course of behavior, which means that we have joint reasons for action. We act as one. We may carry out different subcomponents of the job of preparation—you pour; I stir—but normally in the end we will agree to share the praise or blame for success or failure. So just as an individual may act as a distinct unit of social action and accountability, so may she be part of a larger unit, a unit that incorporates other people.

The fission or dividing of agency between people is familiar from examples like speechwriters and messengers: two individuals own two parts of the agency involved. Joint action is the inverse of this. Joint action is the fusion or unifying of individuals into single, compound units of agency. People can become socially fused in common action, especially with regard to their accountability. But to define joint action, it is not enough to say that two or more people do the action together. Because we are talking about agency, we must work in terms of agency's distinct elements. A comprehensive examination of joint action must distinguish joint agency at its logically distinct levels: joint controlling, joint composing, joint subprehending, joint evaluability, joint entitlement, joint obligation. Multiple individuals may together inhabit a single social unit with reference to any of these elements of agency.

Numerous species display fission-fusion social organization, "chang[ing] the size of their groups by means of the fission and fusion of subunits . . . according to both their activity and the availability and distribution of resources" (Aureli et al. 2008:627). These social dynamics arise naturally from the fact that we live in large and intensive social groups yet we are separate individuals. The fission-fusion dynamic in humans can be fast-paced. Through the course of any day we move in and out of membership of transient, often momentary pairs or groups. These changes may occur at fine time scales, such as when we switch in conversation from the status of speaker versus addressee and back again, or in a chess game when we alternatively have the status of being the one whose turn it is. Or the changes may occur at longer time scales, less frequent in the life span and typically with greater ceremony, such as when we change from single to married, or from lay to initiated. Fission-fusion dynamics in human social life must be understood not just in terms of group size and location but also in terms of the numerous if not innumerable relationship types that ultimately define a society. These relationships may be called statuses, as defined originally by the anthropologist Ralph Linton: sets of rights and duties that hold with respect to certain others. Much of social life is about managing changes of status. The navigation of status often involves moving in and out of membership in composite units of agency. Changes of status, at all levels of grain, are closely associated with fission-fusion agency.

For joint action, there needs to be joint commitment (Clark 2006). In the philosopher John Searle's terms, joint commitment might be defined as a status function declaration of one's acceptance of some form of shared accountability (Searle 2010). Psychologist Herb Clark uses this notion to reanalyze the notorious experiments conducted by Stanley Milgram in New Haven in the 1960s (Milgram 1974). Volunteers in an experimental setting were instructed to administer electric shocks to another volunteer whenever he made an error in a memory task. They were surprisingly willing to inflict harm in this experiment, a fact that has been analyzed as having to do with obedience to authority. Clark reinterprets the finding, suggesting that joint commitment is what really accounts for why volunteers in these experiments ended up behaving in ways they would otherwise have abhorred. These volunteers were not merely doing what they were told. By agreeing to participate in the experiment in the first place, they had made a pact with the experimenter, and people are—evidently—deeply reluctant to withdraw from social pacts. Clark uses Milgram's extreme example of joint commitment for illustration, but his point is that these pacts are being made by all of us, all the time. They are a constant and essential part of social life and they are implicit in our every move. But when you jointly commit, what are you committing to? The answer is that you are agreeing to merge, on some level, with another individual in carrying out a single course of action. Clark's point is that you then become socially and morally accountable for reneging on that agreement. This is cognitively underpinned by what students of human sociality, from philosophy (e.g., John Searle, Raimo Tuomela) to biology (e.g., Michael Tomasello, Josep Call), refer to as shared intentionality (Tomasello et al. 2005).

Distributed cognition (Hutchins 2006) is a type of distributed agency in the sense meant here. Often, distributed cognition encompasses physical action and not just cognitive processes like reasoning. But since cognition is more generally a kind of goal-directed flexible behavior, then distributed cognition can also be analyzed in terms of the three elements of flexibility in agency: animating, authoring, and subprehending (and their interpreter corollaries: perceiving, ascribing, and interpreting). We should be able to improve our accounts of distributed cognition by exploring implications of the ideas that sometimes the distribution of cognition is in the realm of what we do with our bodies (controlling and executing);

sometimes it is in the planning or authoring of what is to be done and how it is to be done (composing); sometimes it is in the figuring out of why to do it or what will result (subprehending, anticipating, projecting); and sometimes it is in associated aspects of accountability: evaluation, entitlement, obligation.

People fission and fuse not just with other people but also with artifacts: scallops, mosquitoes, and furniture can have agency too (Latour 2005). When the anthropologist Alfred Gell used the term "distributed personhood," he was pointing out that the locus of individuals' agency is not confined to the borders of their bodies (Gell 1998). His example was of the soldiers who laid land mines in Pol Pot's Cambodia. "The soldier's weapons are *parts* of him which make him what he is," Gell wrote (1998:20–21). "As agents, they were not just where their bodies were, but in many different places (and times) simultaneously. Those mines were components of their identities as human persons, just as much as their fingerprints or the litanies of hate and fear which inspired their actions." Accountability, too, can be materially extended, but with limits. If a land mine has agency, it is surely less than a man's, and different in kind. At least, an inanimate object may play a role in a causal chain of events with social consequences. Laidlaw (2010) gives the example of a vase that falls off your apartment window ledge, hurting a passerby. You, and not the vase, become accountable for this "act." You and the vase are not equal members of a fused unit of accountability. Suppose you are caught stealing money and hiding it in a vase. Could you propose to the court that your vase be held to account, requesting that the vase be punished instead of you? While it is clear that agency is radically distributed, extending to objects and artifacts, examples like this show that there are strong asymmetries.

A large part of social interaction is about solving a me/us problem, in real time: Who is doing this, me or us? This requires us to navigate the fission and fusion by which we exit and enter units of social agency together with others. We need to do this because there is a persistent mismatch between the immutable separateness of our physical bodies, on the one hand, and the constant malleability of the units of social agency that we inhabit from moment to moment, on the other. Am I acting on my behalf alone? Or are my current goals, my current reasons for action, shared with others as well? Is this behavior by me or by us? Social interaction is a fission-fusion affair involving constant navigation of separateness and boundedness, affiliation and disaffiliation, and a tacking back and forth between inhabiting different social units. This has always-relevant consequences for our social relationships, both fleeting and enduring, and for the rights, duties, and mutual dispositions that define these relationships.

ACKNOWLEDGMENTS

Thanks go to Paul Kockelman for his significant input to this work. Note that this chapter draws partly on sections of my 2013 book *Relationship Thinking* (Oxford University Press). I gratefully acknowledge support from the Max Planck Society (through MPI Nijmegen), the European Research Council (through grant 240853 "Human Sociality and Systems of Language Use"), and the University of Sydney (through Bridging Grant ID 176605).

REFERENCES

Aureli, F., C. M. Schaffner, C. Boesch, S. K. Bearder, J. Call, C. A. Chapman, R. Connor, A. Di Fiore, R. I. M. Dunbar, and S. P. Henzi. 2008. "Fission-Fusion Dynamics." *Current Anthropology* 49(4): 627–654.

Berndt, Ronald M., and Catherine H. Berndt. 1964. *The World of the First Australians*. Sydney: Ure Smith.

Clark, Herbert H. 2006. "Social Actions, Social Commitments." In *Roots of Human Sociality: Culture, Cognition, and Interaction*, edited by N. J. Enfield and Stephen C. Levinson, 126–152. London: Berg.

Gell, Alfred. 1998. *Art and Agency*. Oxford: Clarendon Press.

Howitt, Alfred William. 1904. *The Native Tribes of South-East Australia*. Cambridge: Cambridge University Press.

Hutchins, Edwin. 2006. "The Distributed Cognition Perspective on Human Interaction." In *Roots of Human Sociality: Culture, Cognition and Interaction*, edited by N. J. Enfield and Stephen C. Levinson, 375–398. Oxford, UK: Berg.

Laidlaw, James. 2010. "Agency and Responsibility: Perhaps You Can Have Too Much of a Good Thing." In *Ordinary Ethics: Anthropology, Language, and Action*, edited by Michael Lambek, 143–164. New York: Fordham University Press.

Latour, Bruno. 2005. *Reassembling the Social: An Introduction to Actor-Network-Theory*. Oxford: Oxford University Press.

Milgram, Stanley. 1974. *Obedience to Authority: An Experimental View*. New York: Harper & Row.

Mustafa, Mentor, and Antonia Young. 2008. "Feud Narratives: Contemporary Deployments of *Kanun* in Shala Valley, Northern Albania." *Anthropological Notebooks* 14(2): 87–107.

Searle, John R. 2010. *Making the Social World: The Structure of Human Civilization*. New York: Oxford University Press.

Tomasello, Michael, Malinda Carpenter, Josep Call, Tanya Behne, and Henrike Moll. 2005. "Understanding and Sharing Intentions: The Origins of Cultural Cognition." *Behavioral and Brain Sciences* 28(5): 664–670.

CHAPTER 3
Gnomic Agency

PAUL KOCKELMAN

There are many different ways of framing agency, and thereby fore-
grounding different kinds of agents. My point in what follows is not to
endorse any particular frame, but merely to sketch some of the key features
of several pervasive frames. Such frames—as ways of understanding and
interrelating flexibility, causality, and accountability—have grounded the
intuitions of many influential thinkers. And so it is useful to understand, if
only to undermine, their characteristic assumptions.

ARISTOTELIAN AGENCIES

Aristotle (2001) famously described four kinds of causes that may underlie
any entity. There is the material cause (the substance something is composed of, however heterogeneous), the formal cause (the way this substance
has been shaped, organized, or patterned), the final cause (the functions
such a formed substance may serve), and the efficient cause (that which
gives form to substance, often for the sake of some function). Aristotle's
word for cause was *aition*, which is closely linked to notions of responsibility. In some sense, such causes are responsible for the existence of an
entity. This is not to say that they should be held accountable in any legal
or moral sense, but only to say that we may make reference to such causes
when we try to account for such entities.

Such causes, broadly construed, provide one useful way of framing
agency. In particular, we might define (Aristotelian) agents as causes that

we can take account of. Acting alone, or in concert, they are a salient condition of possibility for the existence of entities, or the occurrence of events. Natural selection is thus an agent. A worker is an agent. A tool is an agent. An enzyme is an agent. Oxidation is an agent. Even lightning bolts, and chance phenomena more generally, are agents. Note, then, that while it is easy to make a splash by calling some non-intentional actor an "agent" (a land mine, dust, concrete, continental drift, worms, the trade winds, a comet, etc.), this is only because so many people have a limited sense of what an agent is. In this Aristotelian framing, in contrast, anything of causal account is an agent and, indeed, interestingly so. Such a framing is thus not limited to the kinds of causes enumerated by Aristotle, but may include whatever causes are (deemed) worthy of account: ghosts and gravity, sieving and serendipity, witches and wishes, global warming and political apathy, semiotic practices and thermodynamic processes, and much else besides.

Needless to say, most entities and events have many causes (each of which can itself be an entity or event with many causes, and so on, ad infinitum). And so agency is necessarily distributed in depth (each cause of some effect is itself the effect of some cause), and necessarily distributed in breadth (each effect has many causes; each cause has many effects). This is not to say that all such causes are salient enough to show up in some account: causal accounting, as the figuring (out) of agency, tends to focus on those causes that are particularly relevant to the agents who are doing the accounting: for example, those causes that are least expected; those causes most easy or difficult to intervene in; those causes that are most powerful, marketable, or useful; those causes most amenable to our intuitions; those causes that seem most intentional; those causes with the most dire effects; and so forth. To study agency is to study causal understandings, and imaginings, of the world: not just the conditions for, and consequences of, entities and events; but also the conditions for, and consequences of, particular accountings (of such conditions and consequences). *There is no interesting account of agency that is not simultaneously an account of those agents who are trying to account for agency.*

BACONIAN AGENCIES

We may extend this framing, and get a better sense of its stakes, by applying some categories of Bacon (2000) to those of Aristotle. If knowledge turns on the discovery of causes, power turns on the directing of causes. Knowledge and power are thus necessarily coupled: in directing known causes, we may discover new causes; and we may use such discoveries in our subsequent directings. From this standpoint, a Baconian agent exhibits a kind of meta-agency: whatever has knowledge about, or power over, the sorts of causes described above. Such an agent can offer an account of such causes, so far as it can discover them; and it may make such causes count, so far as it can direct them. Indeed, for such agents, we can often invoke accountability in the strong sense. That is, not only can we account for such agents (e.g., thematize them, characterize them, reason about them), but we can also hold such agents accountable for their actions and effects (e.g., hinder them or hasten them, reward them or punish them, praise them or shame them). Finally, and reflexively, it is often the case that such Baconian agents have yet to discover all the causes that direct them. Such "blind spots" constitute one key sense of the unconscious: we often have limited knowledge over precisely those causes that have power over us.

This way of framing agency foregrounds not only the recursive and reflexive nature of agency, but also the relative nature of agency. In particular, different agents have different degrees of knowledge and power, and so different degrees of agency. But, that said, because there are so many different kinds of causes, most kinds of power and knowledge are incommensurate, so that it makes little sense to contrast them by degree. For example, while we might compare the strength of two men, it is difficult to compare the strength of one man with the speed of another. Similarly, while we might compare how much you know about chemistry with how much I know, it is difficult to compare your factual knowledge (know that) with my practical knowledge (know how). And so on, and so forth. That is, it only really makes sense to talk about different degrees of agency when we can isolate out a shared dimension of agency (for example, how much money, or credit, one has at one's disposal). And for many, if not most, kinds of agents, with their potentially heterogeneous suites of context-specific and event-contingent causal capacities, that is impossible. Modes of agency are as heterogeneous and incommensurate as the causes they direct and discover, as the entities such causes enable, and as the events such causes occasion.

INSTRUMENTAL AGENCIES

Returning to Aristotle, it is sometimes useful to set aside material causes and formal causes, and instead focus on efficient causes (understood as "means") and final causes (understood as "ends"). In this more restricted framing, agents are relatively instrumental: they wield a variety of means to achieve a variety of ends. Philosophers like James and Peirce went so far as to define "lively agents" and "mindful agents" in related terms. For example, James stated, "The pursuance of future ends and the choice of means for their attainment are thus the mark and criterion of the presence of mentality" (1918:8). Indeed, in some sense, the Baconian framing treats knowledge and power in terms of instrumental reasoning: to what extent does an agent understand which causes lead to which effects; to what extent can an agent create such causes (as means) in order to bring about such effects (as ends).

Such agents might be considered more or less agentive as a function of the range of means they have at their disposal, and as a function of the variety of ends they may seek to achieve. That is, from the standpoint of this particular framing, the more open or flexible an agent (in regard to its means and ends), the more agentive that agent. Such means may include tools, utterances, paths, forces, compositions, signs, representations, affects, traps, goods, and so forth. Such ends may include any kind of resource or value potentially securable through such means: money, food, sex, reputation, freedom, enlightenment, power, security, certainty, information, territory, transcendence, immortality, revenge, and even agency itself. And such openness or flexibility is often imagined to be causally grounded in some putative human-specific capacity: imagination, generativity, cognition, metaphor, displacement, the symbolic, language, mind, choice, meta-representations, culture, reason, and so forth.

That said, any number of distinctly "non-lively" and "non-mental" entities exhibit characteristics of instrumental agency: they are means that may be used to pursue ends (e.g., a rock used as a weapon); and they may even have been made for the sake of achieving such ends (e.g., a bowl made for holding soup). While such made or used agents reflect the purposes of those agents who make them or use them, they don't seem to undertake purposeful actions themselves. For this reason, they are sometimes understood as derivative agents, as opposed to originary agents. Note, then, that from the standpoint of the first framing of agency, they would be agents without qualification. But once we restrict ourselves to focusing on means and ends, as a particular subset of Aristotle's causes, such agents are thereby demoted, showing up in causal accounts as "less than" fully agentive. By way of contrast, the mindful or lively agents introduced above often seem to exhibit a kind of reflexive agency: they are auto-technic (using themselves as a means) and they are auto-telic (having themselves as an end). Indeed, it is often useful to unitize agency (and thereby enclose "agents") by reference to such modes of reflexive coherence.

Just as any effect may itself be a cause that gives rise to another effect, any end may itself be a means to a further end. And so we again find a relatively recursive pattern: a means-ends chain that stretches on indefinitely in two directions at once. Or does it? We just saw how many affordances, like the branch one uses to climb a tree, are means (insofar as one may use them to undertake an action), but not themselves ends (insofar as the branches were not made for the sake of climbing). Nature is often romantically understood to be constituted by this bottoming out of instrumentality. Conversely, Aristotle argued that such means-ends chains had to stop somewhere, and thus "top in." In particular, there must be some end that is not itself the means for further ends. He called such a final end *eudaimonia*, which is often translated as human flourishing, or happiness. And he thought that this highest good, or supreme value, was of utmost importance to philosophy and politics.

Whether or not such higher goods are crucial to philosophy and politics, they are certainly crucial to many understandings of agency, which are just as prone to promote value-oriented agents as they are to demote derivative agents. In particular, a related tradition understands each of us instrumental agents as having too many ends, in that we have more desires than we might ever hope to attain (given our finite time on this earth, and the finite means at our disposal). And so a key question arises: how do we decide which desire we want to act upon, or which end we hope to achieve? To which final end, or at least more distal end, should our intermediate ends be oriented? Such a question presumes that we are not just instrumental agents, who have some flexibility in regard to our means and ends, but that we are also selecting and/or economizing agents. That is, not only is there more than one way to skin a cat, but there are more ways to spend our time than skinning cats; and so we need to choose not just *how* to do things, but *what* things to do. And so the question of evaluating agents arises: agents who not only act instrumentally, but also evaluate instrumental acts in reference to values and, in particular, in reference to values that could be otherwise.

Such values are often understood to constitute some kind of relatively shared standard that allows us to order means and ends according to their relative desirability (Taylor 1989). Such standards help us determine which course of action is more just, honorable, or efficient—and hence which course of action we should pursue if we are to be a just, honorable, or efficient actor. Such a process is also recursive: one kind of agent may be relatively flexible in regard to the means and ends it has at its disposal; another kind of agent, a kind of meta-agent, may be relatively flexible in regard to the standards of values it has at its disposal (to decide which means and ends are best); and so on. That is, just as one can order desires relative to a standard, one can order standards relative to a meta-standard (and so on, recursively). In such a situation, the question is not so much *Which route through life should I take*, but rather *Which map should I use to assess which routes there are, how should these routes be weighted, and what constitutes the terrain in the first place?*

Such agents are often held accountable to a large degree: not only can they account for their own values (in the sense of being able to thematize, characterize, and reason about them), but they can also be held accountable for upholding certain values (in the sense of being praised or punished as a function of whether or not they follow them). Indeed, quite crucially, they can often be praised for pursuing the "correct" end, or punished for pursuing the "incorrect" end, even if they fail to achieve it. And many such agents often hold themselves reflexively accountable in precisely these ways, feeling pride or shame (if not "indebtedness" or "guilt") as a function of whether or not they did, or at least tried to do, the right thing. For these reasons, agents that can internalize standards, and/or the character judgments such standards license, are often understood to be particularly agentive kinds of agents. Conversely, and somewhat pessimistically, many such agents are understood to have less agency than they might otherwise have. In a critical tradition most forcibly articulated by Marx, while such agents may freely choose among a range of possibilities (or relative to a standard), they did not get to choose the range of possibilities (nor the standard). To return to our notion of the unconscious, we often seem to have little agency over the wellsprings of our agency.

Crucially, just like Aristotelian agents, many such evaluative agents are inherently distributed: while it may be a single human actor who undertakes an action, the choice of which action to undertake, and the reasoning underlying why that's the best choice, is usually done in interaction with others (you and me in this conversation), by reference to shared values (we in this community, with some shared history), and more or less implicitly or unconsciously. Such values and, in particular, disputes over such values, often lead to collective actions in which a collective "we" not only determines what to do, and why it should be done, but also actually does it (however hierarchical, and often unfair, the distributed divisioning of this determination). And so, at issue are not just collective behaviors like working and playing, communing and communicating, but also wars and revolutions, invasions and insurgencies.

The foregoing tradition tends to focus on a certain class of final causes: those that turn on the relatively self-conscious strivings of intentional agents, and hence teleological processes of a stereotypic sort. Just as interesting are what philosophers like Mayr (1992) calls teleonomic agents: instincts, traits, organs, and automata. For present purposes, teleonomic agents are adaptive agents: they not only exhibit means-ends behaviors (or characteristics), but they were also selected, and thus shaped, for the sake of those behaviors. Such agents that are selected (but cannot themselves select, or "choose," in the strong sense just described) are also considered derivative agents—insofar as their key characteristics are understood as having been imposed by another agent (and not just by seemingly intentional agents such as artists and engineers, but also by seemingly unintentional agents like natural selection). Mayr thought that such teleonomic processes were guided by an internal program (such as DNA, an algorithm, or some kind of intricate engineering mechanism). And he characterized such programs as being more or less "open" insofar as they were more or less sensitive to contextual inputs. In this tradition, universal Turing machines are radically open (in that they can run any program you give them); and members of the species *homo sapiens* are radically open (in that they have the capacity to inhabit any culture they inherit, with each such culture having distinctive suites of means and ends, distinctive modes of knowledge and power, and distinctive causal capacities and evaluative rationalities). The relative "openness" of such agents is, of course, yet another way of imagining their relative agentiveness. And again, such an agentiveness is not necessarily agentive in any stereotypic sense insofar as it might have been "programmed" by an external agent—your parents or teachers, your culture or society, a particular religion or ideology, and so forth. (Recall the admonishments of Marx.)

This sense of agency usefully points to another sense of accountability. All of the products of natural selection can be held accountable in the first sense: we can account, if only partially, for their coming to be. The world itself, in the sense of an "environment," can hold organisms accountable for their adaptations—selecting the most fit from the least fit, and thereby changing the adaptiveness of a population of organisms over time. And a few such organisms, which like to think of themselves as being on the top of a ladder, are uniquely accountable in the moral sense (or so they tell themselves, in their self-accounts). Of course, many try to offer evolutionary accounts (and, perhaps more often, non-evolutionary accounts, often by reference to some kind of god, qua meta-meta-agent) of the origins of that seemingly unique kind of moral accountability. But, that said, many will argue that teleological processes (that undergird moral accountability) are themselves the products of teleomatic processes (which are distinctly non-intentional), which are themselves the products of non-telic processes of various kinds (such as sieving and serendipity). In other words, it is not clear, once various forms of selection have been properly understood (from selecting among different values, qua choice, to natural selection of different variants, qua evolution), that all agents are not derivative agents somehow—so far as their own agency is causally distributed in such ways. There seems to be an enormous contingency underlying the complex, non-intentional causalities that lead to reflexively-instrumental, meta-evaluational, and self-accounting modes of agency.

AGENCY ENCLOSED

Given all these different ways of framing agency, and thereby figuring different kinds of agents, we may ask why human agents are so prone to frame and figure in particular ways. Why do they ascribe agency along specific dimensions—the causal, the flexible, the reflexive, the evaluative, the teleological, the moral? Why do they order (along such dimensions) by reference to particular degrees—more or less causal, flexible, reflexive, evaluative, teleological, moral, and so forth? Why is it so easy to excerpt agentive figures from multi-causal backgrounds? Look, there is an agent, qua figure (all else becoming background, and so of "no account"). Why do they excerpt and enclose particular units—drawing figures within particular boundaries: skin, self, team, society, and so forth?

Different collectivities, with different histories and cultures, frame and figure in different ways; and, indeed, are framed and figured in different ways by themselves and others. To some degree, a large chunk of politics turns on who gets to determine the relevant dimensions and degrees of agency, what causes and capacities are considered important, what orderings are appropriate, what units can be excerpted, where to draw boundaries between figures and grounds. In some sense, the most consequential forms of agency reside in who or what determines what counts as agency, and thus who or what should be held accountable as an agent.

When we stress these kinds of inherently reflexive, political, and genealogical concerns alongside the foregoing and more canonical kinds of questions and commitments regarding teleonomic processes, and their conditions and consequences, we are opening up inquiry into what might best be called "teleognomic agency," or simply *gnomic agency*.

REFERENCES

Aristotle. 2001. *Physics. The Collected Works of Aristotle*, edited by Richard McKeon, 214–394. New York: The Modern Library.

Bacon, Francis. 2000. *The New Organon*. Cambridge: Cambridge University Press.

James, William 1918. *The Principles of Psychology*. Vol. 1. New York: Dover.

Mayr, Ernest W. 1992. "The Idea of Teleology." *Journal of the History of Ideas* 53: 117–135.

Taylor, Charles. 1989. *Sources of the Self*. Cambridge, MA: Harvard University Press.

CHAPTER 4

Semiotic Agency

PAUL KOCKELMAN

Semiotic processes are usually understood to have three key components: a sign stands for an object and gives rise to an interpretant. For example, you point (a sign), to something (an object), and I turn to look (an interpretant). In what follows, we will be interested in the semiotic agents that seem to lie at the center of such processes: those entities that do not just signify (by expressing signs of objects) and interpret (by expressing interpretants of signs), but also get signified and interpreted (and thus constitute an object of their own and others' semiotic processes). See Figure 4.1. That is, such agents not only have the capacity to "point" and "look" (broadly construed), they also have the capacity to be "pointed to" and "looked at" by other such agents (which may even include themselves, at some degree of remove).

For a semiotic agent to be an "agent" requires that it is also a semiotic object (from the standpoint of another such agent). In what follows we will look at several different modes of semiotic agency (and hence several different modes of semiotic objectivity). Rather than seeing semiotic agents as simple effects of, or deep conditions for, semiotic processes (such as a Foucauldian subject or a Cartesian ego), we will see them as reflexively constituted creatures, and hence causally concomitant with such processes. Just as you can't understand such agents without reference to semiotic processes, semiotic processes cannot be understood without reference to such agents.

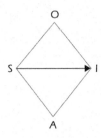

Figure 4.1 Semiotic Processes and Semiotic Agents.

AGENCY THROUGH THE LENS OF SENSATION AND INSTIGATION, SELECTION AND SIGNIFICANCE

Vervet monkeys are semiotic agents. Upon sensing a predator, one such monkey can instigate an alarm call. And upon sensing the call, another such monkey can instigate an escape. Here there are at least two semiotic agents engaged in overlapping semiotic processes. See Figure 4.2. For the first semiotic agent (A1), the object (O1) is the predator (say, an eagle). The sign (S1) is an iconic index of that eagle (say, a characteristic wing shape silhouetted against the sky). And the interpretant (I1) is the alarm call. For the second semiotic agent (A2), the object (O2) is still the eagle, but now at some degree of indexical remove. The sign (S2) is the alarm call. And the interpretant (I2) is the action of running into the underbrush. Instead of one agent simply seeing and running; we have two coupled agents, the first seeing and calling, and the second hearing and running.

Crucially, we may also consider the object (qua predator) to be a relatively derivative agent (A3)—one who is not just seen and pointed to (by the first agent), but also looked at (or "heard") and run from (by the second agent). Such a predatory agent can, of course, also sense and instigate in its own right. Indeed, its ability to see and swoop is one of the key reasons it constitutes such an important object in the semiotic processes of the vervet monkeys.

There is also a fourth agent (A4) in this scenario—one that is inherently distributed, insofar as it is not just composed of the first two agents, but also partially created by the third agent. In particular, the first two agents arguably constitute a genetic unit of accountability, by reference to processes like inclusive fitness, and thus function as a kind of extended organism.

Moreover, so much of the sensing and instigating behavior of this distributed agent (framed as an organism, qua bottom ellipse) makes sense only in reference to the sensing and instigating behavior of the third agent

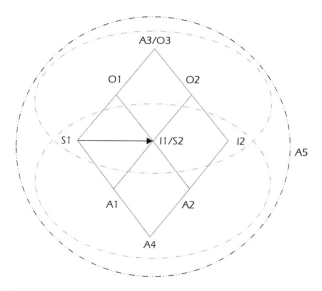

Figure 4.2 Communication Between Conspecifics.

(framed as an environment, qua top ellipse). The capacities and propensities of prey are often best understood in terms of the capacities and propensities of predators. Organism and environment are, indeed, so inseparable when functionally understood that it is tempting to call such a unit an *envorganism*, and to see it as a fifth agent (A5, qua encompassing circle). Such envorganisms, as the locus of those causal processes we must take into account to understand natural selection, might even be considered the originary agents of all evolutionary scenarios (notwithstanding how distributed, emergent, contingent, and confusing they might at first seem).

In short, agency is distributed not only across two cooperative agonists (A1 and A2, together equivalent to A4), but also across such agonists and their antagonist (A3). And it is distributed not only across such interacting agents (framed as waypoints along evolutionary paths), but also across the longue-durée processes (A5) that give rise to such agentive precipitates (such as natural selection).

Let us set aside this larger ensemble of agencies, and focus on the capacities of a single semiotic agent, generically understood. What are its key features? First, such an agent is capable of sensing and instigating. In particular, for something to constitute a sign, it must be able to not just stand out in an environment (be a difference) but also be sensible to an organism. And for something to constitute an interpretant, it must be able to not just stand up in an environment (make a difference) but also be instigatable by an organism. And so we can inquire into the range of qualities and events, practices and processes, relations and interrelations, actions and affects, that an agent can sense or instigate. What kinds of sensory and instigatory capacities does it have? What scales is it sensitive to? How do various kinds of media (from tools to techniques) enable it to extend its capacities or shift its scales? Relatedly, what is the range of semiotic objects such an agent might relate to via its signs and interpretants, its sensations and instigations? Given its current environment, what counts as an object for it? And given its capacities, and the affordances of potential environments, what *could* count as an object for it? Some agents have a wide range of actual, or at least potential, signs, objects, and interpretants; some agents have a relatively small range. What are the conditions for, and consequences of, various ranges?

Second, not only do semiotic agents sense and instigate, and thereby relate to objects via their signs and interpretants, but they are also caught up in selection in a variety of senses. To foreground two extremes, we might say that agents are capable of being selected, and/or capable of selecting, such that their instigations (interpretants) make sense in the context of their sensations (signs), given the features of their objects and their interests as agents. As we saw in the example of vervet monkeys, agents might have been naturally selected to produce certain interpretants (such as calling and fleeing) in the context of certain signs (such as wing shapes and calls), given the objects those signs and interpretants correlate with (such as predators), and given their own interests as agents (say, to survive and reproduce under conditions of predation). And, as we saw in the chapter on gnomic agency, agents might also engage in "choice" in a stereotypic sense: given a range of possible and desirable interpretants (of some sign, correlated with some object, itself critical to the interests of the agent), such an agent can select which one is the most desirable, and thus worthy of instigating (given the agent's evaluative standard).

To be sure, these examples barely scratch the surface of various modes of selecting and being selected. There are agents capable of undergoing, and undertaking, artificial selection. There are agents capable of making and using tools, and being made into or used as tools. There are agents that can write, and run, algorithms. And so on, and so forth. As always, we can argue about whether such agents are more or less "originary" or "derived" (and, indeed, whether they should be called "agents" at all). And we can inquire into the relative "openness" of their processes of selection. This is not so much the question of what range of signs and interpretants they can sense and instigate, but rather the relative flexibility, or contextual sensitivity, of their interpretant-sign relations. What kinds of "learning" or "programming" or "enculturation" or "evolution" are they capable of, or amenable to? What complex adaptations can they (hope to) achieve? What feats of strength and imagination, calculation and communication, sympathy and sociality, caring and killing, are they capable of? To what degree are they capable of distributing, and thereby concatenating and concentrating, their individual agencies? To what degree can they select options that will increase the range of their possible selections?

AGENCY THROUGH THE LENS OF ONTOLOGIES IN TRANSFORMATION

So much for semiotic agents understood through the intersection of sensing and instigating, on the one hand, and significance and selection, on the other. Now let us turn to a relatively overlapping topic, agency through the lens of ontologies in transformation. Table 4.1 characterizes agents in relation to indices, individuals, kinds, and ontologies. The key issue here is the way that ontologies contribute to interpretations. Table 4.2 characterizes several ways that the ontologies of agents might transform over time. The key issue here is the way that interpretations contribute to ontologies.

Suppose, for example, that you are the individual and I am the agent. I watch you engage in some kind of performance, or trial of strength (an index), and infer that you have some kind of competence, or power (a kind). The performance might be a piano recital, a dissertation defense, a conversation in German, a chemical assay, a race, whatever. I could therefore expect other performances from you, as complex indices, that would be keeping with that kind—for example, success at another trials of strength of a similar nature (e.g., if you played that sonata, I bet you can also play this sonata).

Table 4.1 ONTOLOGIES IN TRANSFORMATION

Index	Any quality that is relatively perceivable (to some agent).
Kind	Any projected propensity to exhibit particular indices.
Agent	Any entity that can perceive such an index and project such a kind (itself often an individual).
Individual	Any entity that can evince indices (to an agent) and thereby be a site to project kindedness (by that agent).
Ontology	The assumptions an agent has as to the indices, kinds, and individuals that constitute a particular world.

Table 4.2 TRANSFORMATIONS IN ONTOLOGIES

1. Indices (and signs more generally) may change an individual's kind irrespective of an agent's ontological assumptions.
2. Indices may change an agent's ontological assumptions regarding the kinds that constitute a particular individual.
3. Indices may change an agent's ontological assumptions regarding the indices that constitute a particular kind.
4. Indices may change an agent's ontological assumptions regarding the indices, individuals, kinds, and agents that constitute a particular world.
5. Changes in an agent's ontological assumptions about a world (in the foregoing ways) may change the world about which the agent makes assumptions.

This would be a simple case of transformativity number 2: having seen a connection between an index and an individual, an agent connects an individual to a kind (given a set of ontological assumptions in regard to the behavior of various kinds). Other kinds of transformativity are also possible. For example, in the case of transformativity number 3, the agent might hold fast to its assumption that the individual is of a certain kind and, upon perceiving it behave a certain way, update its understanding of the underlying propensities of such kinds (e.g., I guess babysitters don't always behave as I thought). Inductive reasoning is of this type. In the case of transformativity number 4, the agent might hypothesize a new kind (as a way to make sense of anomalous behavior), or start tracking indices it had never noticed before (perhaps because of the advent of a new medium, such as a microscope), or attend to a novel individual (whose behavioral patterns seem newly relevant and potentially predictable). Or, in the case of transformativity number 5, the individual (itself an agent in another frame) might internalize the assumptions of the perceiving agent and change its behavior accordingly—say, a patient trying, however unconsciously, to fit (or thwart) a doctor's diagnosis. (Indeed, an illness, or diagnostic category, is a quintessential kind.) Lastly, there is transformativity number 1, the fact that individuals are caught up in multiple causal processes that help create them and their kindedness, more or less irrespective of the ontological assumptions of particular agents: chemical reactions (creating kinds like "acid" and "base"), evolutionary processes (creating kinds like "dog" and "raccoon"), socialization processes (creating kinds like "punk" and "mod"), and so forth.

From the standpoint of such an analytic framework, an agent has many basic capacities. It can perceive indices and project kinds. It can hold (or at least exhibit) ontological assumptions (which enable it to project as a function of what it perceives). And these assumptions can themselves transform over time. For example, such agents can be more or less sensitive to the fact that their assumptions are in error and thereby come to update them.

For any such agent, we can thereby inquire into the range of indices it can perceive, the richness of the kinds it can entertain, the diversity of the individuals onto which it can project such kinds, and the number of different worlds it can imagine. Concomitantly, we may inquire into the complexity of the inferences such an agent can engage in, the ease with which it may update its ontological assumptions, the degree to which it can detect and correct errors in its assumptions, and the extent to which its assumptions can change the world. And we can inquire into its access to forms of media that extend such capacities (or buffer itself from the effects or limits on such capacities).

Crucially, such an agent can itself be an individual that exhibits indices that are perceivable to other agents (including itself); and these other agents can project kinds onto it, and thereby come to interact with it in particular ways. That is, such an agent is not just a source of perception and projection; it is also a site of perception and projection. And just as its own ontological assumptions about the world can transform (through its indexical encounters with various individuals), the ontological assumptions that other individuals have about it can transform (via their indexical encounters with it). And, indeed, as per transformativity number 5, such an agent might even be able to internalize the ontological assumptions that other agents have about it, and thereby come to behave according to their beliefs about its various kinds. Note, then, how radically "distributed" such agents can be.

Finally, this whole framework easily scales to a meta-level, for we have just described a particularly important kind in our own ontology—the agent. And we can project such a kind (or power) onto various individuals as a function of the indices they express (as the evincing and exercising of that power). Such agents are a particular kind of kind: one that can perceive and project in ways that conform to ontologies and transform ontologies. In short, and to return to our opening concerns, such agents not only ontologize entities in the world, but they are also ontologized as entities in the world.

AGENCY THROUGH THE LENS OF RESIDENCE IN, AND REPRESENTATIONS OF, THE WORLD

We might characterize comportment as any behavior that involves heeding affordances, wielding instruments, undertaking actions, performing roles, or fulfilling identities. And we might characterize one kind of agent as any entity (process, event, actor, assemblage, etc.) that enables and constrains one's comportment insofar as it makes a difference in regard to: (1) what one does and how one does it; (2) where and when one engages in such a doing; and (3) why one does it, and what effects arise because one does it. From one perspective, an agent is whatever alters the contents (what and how), contexts (where and when), and consequences (why and to what effect) of one's comportment—even if only retroactively. From another perspective, an agent is whatever has some measure of control (where and when), composition (what and how), and commitment (why and to what effect) in regard to its own comportment. See Table 4.3. And just as the latter kind of agent need not be an "individual," the former kind of agent includes imaginaries and institutions as much as interactions and infrastructure. In this framing, agents are not just whatever "has" some degree of control, composition and commitment (semiotically speaking), but also whatever enables and constrains the contents, contexts, and consequences of such "havelings."

Such would be a way of understanding agency as a mode of residence in the world. We would also do well to understand agency as a mode of representing the world (itself always already built on ways of residing in the world). Such agencies enable and constrain the contents of our propositions: not just what we are talking or thinking about (as topics, or referents), but also what we are saying or thinking about such topics (as foci, or predicates). And such agencies enable and constrain our reasoning with such propositions: not just the forms of evidence and inference that lead to such propositions (as roots), but also the forms of evidence and inference that flow from such propositions (as fruits). From one perspective, a representational agent is whatever has some capacity to topicalize, characterize, and reason. From another perspective, a representational agent is whatever enables and constrains the contents of our propositions, the conclusions we draw from them, or the conclusions that drew us to them. See Table 4.4. And again, just as the former kind of agent need not be an "individual," the latter kind of agent includes imaginaries and institutions as much as interactions and infrastructure. In short, both residential and representational

---

Table 4.3 RESIDENTIAL AGENCY

Control the contexts (where and when) of one's behavior
Compose the contents (what and how) of one's behavior
Anticipate the consequences (why and to what effect) of one's
  behavior

Table 4.4 REPRESENTATIONAL AGENCY

Determine Topics (of Representations)

Determine Foci (that Apply to such Topics)

Determine Arguments (that Lead to, or Follow from, such Topic-Focus
  Relations)

modes of agency are inherently multidimensional, graded, embedded, and
distributed phenomena.

AGENCY THROUGH THE LENS OF CAUSAL PROCESSES

As should be clear from both the foregoing perspectives, agents stand at
the center of causal processes—as targets as much as sources. Such causal
processes can, for present purposes, be understood in relatively simple and
stereotypic terms: one event (E1) leads to another event (E2) in the context
of a field of forces. See Figure 4.3a. How such force fields condition such
event sequencing is not of concern here (and, indeed, would take most of
human knowledge to explicate fully). Rather, I am interested in drawing
out the repercussions of such processes for our understanding of semiotic
agents (insofar as such agents "understand" such processes).

Suppose, for example, that an agent is more or less aware of the causal
relation between two such events;[1] and suppose that an agent is more or
less able to sense and/or instigate such events. In regard to instrumental
agency, such an agent might instigate E1 as a means to bring about E2
as an end. In regard to inferential agency, such an agent might predict E2
(having sensed E1), or retrodict E1 (having sensed E2). In other words, to
such an agent, E1 and E2 relate not just as cause and effect, but also—
at least potentially—as means to ends, sign of object, and object of sign.
Instrumental and inferential practices don't just constitute causal processes in their own right, they also depend on them to function and, in
particular, to *mal*function.

Such causal processes (and hence such instrumental and inferential
practices, and hence the semiotic agencies themselves), are subject to various reframings. First, any particular event is caught up in a myriad of force
fields, and so is (partially) causal of many other events, and (partially)
caused by many other events. See Figure 4.3b. Moreover, any causal process may be reframed as one link in a longer causal process; or as a longer
causal process that is made up of many links, each of which is a smaller

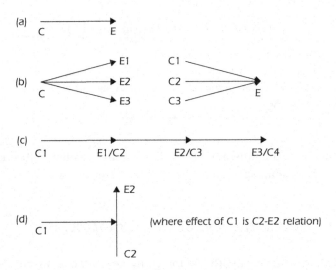

Figure 4.3 Embedding and Enchaining of Causal Processes.

causal process. See Figure 4.3c. Which specific events, force fields, and scales an agent attends to are, in part, a function of what events it can sense and instigate, and what force fields it is aware of. And they are, in part, a function of what it is currently engaged in—either instrumentally or inferentially.

Second, just as semiotic processes can incorporate causal processes (i.e., a sign-object relation, in Figure 4.1, can be a cause-effect relation), causal processes can incorporate semiotic processes (i.e., a sign-interpretant relation, in Figure 4.1, can be a cause-effect relation). As an example of the first case, I can infer fire from smoke (and thereby use a causal process to engage in a semiotic practice). As an example of the second case, I can raise my hand in order to get you to answer my question (and thereby use a semiotic process to engage in a causal practice). Indeed, the key objects of many semiotic processes are precisely causal processes: many semiotic agents can signify and interpret such processes; and thereby communicate, collaborate, and compete in regard to such processes; and thereby help or hinder others in their ability to direct or discover such processes.

Finally, a particularly important kind of effect (E2) is the setting up, removing, or rechanneling of a force field that links two other events (E3 and E4). See Figure 4.3d. In particular, an agent that instigates E1 in order to cause E2 may thereby ultimately govern the instrumental and inferential processes of other agents (who are caught up in E3 and E4). Causing causality is closely linked to conducting conduct, and hence a key mode of power or governance.

In short, to know about the causal, inferential, and instrumental processes that an agent is attentive to (and/or subject to), is to know much of what there is to know about that agent. Agents not only discover and direct such processes, but their own processes can be discovered and directed.

With such points in mind, we can now ask a series of questions about particular semiotic agents. What is the range of causal processes they can sense and instigate (and hence direct and discover)? How do such causal processes allow such agents to have agency over larger or smaller swatches of space-time (insofar as E1 and E2 are spatiotemporally "near" or "far" from each other). In other words, to what degree can such agents both act at a distance and with precision? Which such causal processes are relatively portable, insofar as the relevant force fields can be expected to hold wherever (and whenever) such agents go? To what degree can agents make them more portable—by creating an infrastructure, or built environment, in which such force field can be made relatively reliably present? To what degree can agents make causal chains relatively reflexive insofar as the effects they induce act back on them as causes? To what degree can agents discover, and perhaps come to direct, the causal processes that created them as effects (for example, converting natural selection into artificial selection)? In short, or perhaps more generally, to what degree are semiotic agents, through their causal processes, and hence in regard to their instrumental and inferential practices, relatively flexible—in the sense of self-reflective, framing, governing, displaceable, precise, portable, self-reflexive, and so forth?

SPHERES OF INFLUENCE

We may often usefully distinguish between an agent's relatively immediate and relatively mediate spheres of causal (inferential and instrumental) influence. The immediate sphere (or network, or infrastructure, or context) consists of the range of events they can (more or less) directly sense or instigate. The mediate sphere consists of the range of events they can sense or instigate only indirectly, by tapping into various force fields, and the causal processes these condition and enable. In other words, the mediate sphere consists of all the events an agent can instigate or sense only by way of the causal processes it is caught up in, and attentive to; and hence what they can instrumentally instigate, or inferentially know, at one (or more) degrees of causal remove.

Crucially, the distinction between immediate and mediate spheres, like the notion of causality more generally, is relatively frame-dependent, requiring that we delimit where the agent ends and the environment begins, or where the agent's relatively inalienable media ends (e.g., its eyes and hands) and its relatively alienable media begins (i.e., its telescopes and rocket launchers). In this way, it consists of a flexible and contestable boundary, which may shift whenever new media, new environments, new forms of knowledge, new techniques, new technologies, and so forth come into play. Indeed, to tie together two earlier topics, it may even (and perhaps more often) shift as a function of new ontological assumptions as to where an organism ends and its environment begins, or which capacities are essential to an organism versus ancillary, or which force fields in an environment are crucial versus contingent.

A key limit on the agent is thereby delimited: where its effects (qua instigations) would end without one or more channels versus where its effects can end given such force fields (which take those instigations as causes, and help generate further effects). In some sense, agency is radically distributed for the simple reason that without all those force fields, or channels, an agent is relatively provincial. Its sphere (or rather network) of influence, and hence the agent itself, is only as small, or as large, as the causal processes it can direct and discover.

ACCOUNTABILITY

Those events that an agent can sense and instigate, instrumentally direct or inferentially discover, via the causal processes it is caught up in, do not—by themselves—delimit the agent, or even its sphere of influence. This is because a significant chunk of agency rests in accountability: of all the effects an agent can have in the world, given all the causes it is caught up in, only some are directly attributed to it (by other agencies), such that it can be held accountable for them. We are punished or rewarded only *for* particular events and *through* particular events, even if we are causally (inferentially, instrumentally) entangled in a much wider range of processes. And so such particularly consequential events loom large *in* and *for* our ontology. That is, such events (for which we are accountable) are not just key objects in our ontologies (as part of their contents, so to speak); they are also a key condition of possibility for our ontologies (whatever their particular contents).

A wide range of agents can internalize such consequentiality. That is, they can take into account the way their inferences and instigations have effects back on them, for better or worse, through the regimenting agents that hold them accountable; and they can thereby act (infer and/or instigate) in ways that channel such consequentiality: stopping it, redirecting it, modulating it, minimizing it (and sometimes even fostering it). This ability of an organism to internalize the consequences of its own actions, by means of such regimenting agencies, is one key part of our understanding of self-consciousness. But that said, such agencies need not be intentional: we can internalize the sharpness of knifes and the swiftness of predators as much as the gaze of states and the attitudes of parents. Indeed, not only our learned behavior, on developmental timescales, turns on internalization as such; most of our innate behavior also turns on the internalization of the reliable causal pathways that constitute our environments on evolutionary timescales. Every organism's body/mind/habitus/imaginary is a diagram of the (salient, reliable, pervasive, shocking) force fields of its environment. (That said, what we have internalized (from past environments) may be out of skew with the current environment—so we are not necessarily well fitted to where we find ourselves.)

With this understanding of causality and semiosis in hand, we may now highlight various senses of accountability. Semiotic agents not only count on (or take into account) causal processes, but they also make them count, both inferentially and instrumentally. Some can, to some degree, offer accounts of such causal processes: they can point to them, predicate properties of them, and reason about them. Some can, to some degree, control the when and where of causal unfoldings (qua E1), the what and how (qua field of forces), and the why and to what effect (qua E2). Reciprocally, semiotic agents are themselves the source and target of semiotic processes, so other semiotic agents can count on, and offer accounts of, them. Finally, as a function of all of this, and as just laid out, agents can be held accountable for the causal processes they are caught up in (by other agents)—an accounting that, to some degree, constitutes the agent.

NOTE

1. Not necessarily aware in the sense of "conscious of," but rather in the sense of "has ontological assumptions regarding." For more on each of these accounts of agency, see Kockelman (2012, 2014a, 2014b, 2015). For more on vervet monkeys, see Cheney and Seyfarth (1990). See Gell (1992) for a different take on spheres of influence.

REFERENCES

Cheney, Dorothy L., and Robert M. Seyfarth. 1990. *How Monkeys See the World.*
    Chicago: University of Chicago Press.
Gell, Alfred. 1992. *Art and Agency.* Oxford: Oxford University Press.
Kockelman, Paul. 2012. "The Ground, The Ground, The Ground: Why Archaeology Is
    So 'Hard.'" *Yearbook of Comparative Literature* 58: 176–183.
Kockelman, Paul. 2014a. *Agent, Person, Subject, Self.* Oxford: Oxford University Press.
Kockelman, Paul. 2014b. "The Anthropology of an Equation: Sieving Spam,
    Algorithmic Agents, and Ontologies in Transformation." *Hau: Journal of
    Ethnographic Theory* 3 (3):33–61.
Kockelman, Paul. 2015. "Four Theories of Things: Aristotle, Marx, Heidegger, and
    Peirce." *Signs in Society* 3 (1):153–192.

PART TWO

Agency of Institutions and Infrastructure

CHAPTER 5

Agency in State Agencies

ANYA BERNSTEIN

The democratic state is an administrative state. It is often portrayed, for convenience, as a legislature, a court, or a chief executive. But the actual work of representative governance is done primarily in administrative agencies, which interpret and implement the often vague ambitions inscribed in statutes. Agencies translate legislative pronouncements into rules that set standards and regulate conduct; investigate and ensure compliance; adjudicate disputes and prosecute violators.[1] Agencies, in short, both interpret and implement the laws that legislatures pass. Whether we are interested in consolidated sovereignty or diffuse pathways of power, it is administrative agencies that enact much of the state's effect in the world. When we talk about agency in the state, then, we must primarily be talking about agency in agencies.

That may seem odd. Bureaucracy seems like the absence of agency: just mechanistic gear-grinding continuing things begun by other, distant, powerful actors. Where can agency find a foothold amid the faceless people, the featureless buildings, the infinite red tape, the endless unread files? Few have captured this un-agency more grippingly than Hannah Arendt (1994), who shows in consternating detail how bureaucracy melts individuals into a mass, subordinating them to an unstoppable process set in motion by others elsewhere—actual agents—and negating their accountability for even their most extreme acts. In bureaucratese, the things that happen happen in the passive voice.

Here there is no room for conduct that creates, starting off the uncontrollable iterations of response and reinterpretation that characterizes true political action (Arendt 1958). It would be a travesty to conflate the agonistic, agentive sphere of politics, where any answer is always subject to further contestation, with that of administration, which reduces human activity to a striving for smooth functioning and conclusive answers (Honig 1993).

So, another oddity: administration has world-changing effects, but seems bereft of agents. Infuriatingly—yet conveniently—bureaucracy appears as an undifferentiated entity exerting power that cannot be held to account. It is the decider's enforcer: an implementing thug who carries out orders but lacks any creative abilities of his own.

This common image, it turns out, distorts our understanding of both agencies and agency. It conceals the complex distribution of possibility and responsibility within bureaucracy, which involves individual subjectivities, interpersonal relations, and socially structured decision-making (Blau 1963; Bernstein 2008). And it obscures the varied ways that accountability for bureaucratic action is structured by different social arenas. What kind of accountability is available, it turns out, depends on the position from which one does the accounting. Here, I unpack one administrative process to show how units of agency emerge and blend in the ongoing process of differentiation and subsumption that characterizes bureaucratic action. I then explain how one particular social arena—litigation—provides a scaffolding for bureaucratic accountability that, like all scaffoldings, both enables and constrains.

Bureaucracy's complex distribution of agency and the legal scaffoldings for its accountability have two linked implications. One, bureaucracy may be a paradigmatic case of distributed agency. If we conceive of agency not as a heroic individual exerting power over others, but as an always interdependent social activity, then bureaucracy's subsumption of individual impulses in mass results looks less like agency's nemesis and more like its instantiation. Rather than seeing agency in agencies as an oddity, then, we may see in it an oddly forthright presentation of the nature of agency itself.

Two, identifying legal scaffoldings that enable and constrain bureaucratic accountability suggests that accountability is perspectival not only in agencies, but in general. Whether accountability is available, and what it looks like when it is, depends not on some underlying relation between actor and action, but on the scaffoldings that structure the interpretation of action in particular social arenas. Understanding accountability scaffoldings in particular social realms is thus central to understanding the nature of accountability generally. Indeed, it may be more accurate not to speak of accountability generally, but only of local tropes of accountability.

American administrative agencies are bewilderingly variegated in their mandates, their hierarchical structures, and their operational traditions. Among the most important, and most opaque, things agencies do is to implement the statutes that legislatures pass. They do so largely through rules of conduct that have legally binding force. In the United States, the Administrative Procedure Act and the legal cases interpreting it lay out the public face of this rulemaking power. An agency charged with implementing a statute solicits public comments on a proposed rule and then publishes a final rule, which responds to significant comments, justifies significant choices, and sets out constraints on conduct by those under its purview.

Beyond those constraints, the internal process is up to the people who run the agency. One brief example can demonstrate how different social units—sub-individual, individual, group—emerge and recede as agents at different stages of a bureaucratic process. In the Environmental Protection Agency (EPA), mid-level administrators may convene "workgroups" of scientists, engineers, economists, policy analysis, lawyers, enforcement officers, and political negotiators to develop a regulation. Colleagues from the initiating office gather information and draft primary documents, but workgroups use their range of expertise and perspective to analyze the evidence, design the rule, and resolve conflicts.

Workgroup conveners are advised to avoid "bastards"—participants who pursue goals and grind axes unrelated to the rule production, thereby delaying or derailing the process (McGarity 1991:73). After higher-level administrators allow the proposed rule to be published and public comments have been received, individual workgroup members respond to comments about the parts of the rule they drafted. The convener submits these responses, workgroup recommendations for the final rule, and dissents from those recommendations to higher-level administrators, who resolve remaining conflicts before approving the final rule (McGarity 1991).

Thus, what appears in public as a monologic pronouncement by an undifferentiated organization emerges from ongoing social relations and iterative interactions that both individuate and collectivize human action (Hull 2012). The external world that provides the evidence on which administrators base their rules influences regulatory developments (Bernstein 2016). Particular contributions are attributable to human individuals as they take positions within the workgroup. That individuation is largely erased as the group reaches compromise positions. But the erasure is not complete, since unresolved conflicts move up for resolution at higher levels. The notice of proposed rulemaking briefly presents the proposal as a univocal, undifferentiated text addressed to the public. But it is promptly disaggregated again as administrators respond to comments on the particular pieces of the rule they drafted, and workgroup members stake out positions on emerging conflicts. Those specificities are then gradually erased again as higher-level administrators resolve those conflicts, leading to the final rule—another seemingly univocal text.

Individual contributions thus appear, meld into a mass, and become re-articulated at different stages of the process in ways visible differently to differently situated observers. For a private party, the proposed rule appears to have been produced by the agency as a whole. Agency employees who craft the rule and respond to comments, in contrast, see their colleagues' individual contributions. But neither of these is the only, or the real, agent. Each individual's actions have effects in the world, but only insofar as they pass through the congealing process that undifferentiates them into collective action. At the same time, the collective could not act absent each individual's contributions, which influence the final product. What emerges in public view, naturally, are only the final products of internal differentiation. The image of bureaucracy as an impenetrable morass may thus owe something to bureaucracy's self-presentation in public products—and to observers' sometimes gullible acceptance of it.

Within the agency, similarly, individuals are ascribed professional competencies and characterological proclivities—scientists, bastards—yet also treated as a collective mass—the workgroup. Not quite the ideal arena of Weberian interchangeability, actual bureaucracies take into account how individuals, with their backgrounds and personalities, contribute to or detract from collective action. Yet this also highlights the enduring interdependence of bureaucratic actors, whose individual contributions are irrelevant, uninterpretable, unimplementable without the whole that subsumes them.

This inherent interdependence frustrates both participants and theorists of bureaucracy. Yet interdependence is in the very nature, not just of bureaucracy, but of agency itself. The idea that agencies' agency is undifferentiated masks internal complexity in much the same way as the idea that individuals' agency is indivisible. Bureaucracy, thus, may provide a viable image of how agency works generally—an image that is unusually forthcoming about its distributed nature, building the interdependence of action not only into how it works, but also into what it values.

Who is responsible for agency action? It depends who's asking, and in what way. One very visible way American society assigns accountability for agency action is through litigation. Litigation is not the only route to accountability, of course. On the contrary, it shows how particular, and peculiar, the scaffoldings for accountability in different realms may be. In litigation, the legal status of the action at issue—not the proximal actor or decision-maker—determines who may be accountable and how.

For instance, you can sue a federal employee who violates your rights under the United States Constitution. If you win, the court assigns the defendant responsibility for harming you and usually requires that defendant to pay you money. Such "constitutional tort" lawsuits allow for one particular kind of accountability. It is textually bounded: constitutional tort lawsuits can assign responsibility only for violations of rights guaranteed by the federal Constitution. It is backward-looking and restitutionary, assigning blame and monetary compensation for past action. And it is individualistic. While the *conduct* at issue in a constitutional tort lawsuit may arise from agency policy, the *litigation* can target only individuals, not agencies. Constitutional tort lawsuits enable accountability only for individuals who personally undertake an unconstitutional act, not for the bureaucratic structures underlying their decision to do so.

You can also sue a federal employee who harms you in some more ordinary way, such as by destroying your property, under the Federal Tort Claims Act (FTCA). The FTCA also structures a backward-looking and restitutionary accountability, providing money damages for past action. It provides accountability only for the universe of actions the statute specifies: torts for which private parties would be liable.[2] But in contrast to constitutional tort lawsuits, accountability under the FTCA is collective, not individualistic: the government is the only defendant available. If you sue an individual government employee under the FTCA, the statute requires courts to substitute the United States as defendant.

Finally, you can challenge an agency's rule under the Administrative Procedure Act (APA), which allows lawsuits "seeking relief other than money damages." By prohibiting monetary restitution for past action, the APA provides scaffolding for a future-oriented accountability: courts do not punish agencies for passing bad rules, but can prevent an existing rule from having further effects. APA lawsuits hold neither individuals nor the government as a whole to account, but the agency itself. Accountability here is limited to acts taken in the name of, and held out to represent, the agency. And the consequences it imposes adhere not to an individual person but to a bureaucratic position. The court's judgment addresses whoever leads the agency, whether or not that person had anything to do with the offending rule. Thus the APA's accountability treats the agency as a unitary organism that endures through time irrespective of personnel.

These three legal regimes allow for the construction of accountabilities with different temporal orientations; different consequences; and different units of responsibility. These differences depend neither on the closeness of the actor to the act, nor on the act's organizational complexity. Rather, they depend on how the conduct at issue looks from the perspective of each particular legal regime: constitutional law, tort law, administrative law. Litigation channels legally distinguishable acts into separate structures that define the kinds of legal accountability that can be constructed for them.

This legal accountability enabled by litigation, of course, covers neither all acts undertaken by or in agencies, nor all the forms of accountability available for any particular act. One version of accountability, for instance, is conspicuously missing: this regime provides no way to reward the exercise of agency in agencies, only to punish or limit it. Litigation only works in one direction. But one can hypothesize that accountability scaffoldings will always be constructed with a particular slant. Other social arenas will have their own ways to channel, define, and delimit the accountabilities they enable.

Within the agency, for instance, workgroup members can construct accountabilities that hinge not on the legal status of their acts but on other values and forms of judgment. They may hold one another responsible for the quality of their contributions or their positions in a conflict. Superiors, in turn, will have different avenues for constructing accountability for their subordinates. And so on out. Legislators may impose kinds of public accountability based in political values removed from both legal status, group contribution, and job description. Historians may use altogether different structures to attribute accountability. Who is accountable for agency action, and how they can be held to account, depends on the position from which that accounting is done. Different social arenas offer different scaffoldings for constructing accountability, giving accountability different parameters, consequences, and meanings.

Just as the distributed nature of bureaucratic agency may illuminate a broader characteristic of agency in general, the perspectival nature of bureaucratic accountability may have something to say about accountability elsewhere. Insofar as accountability depends on an attribution of responsibility, what it looks like may always depend on the local structures that make such attributions comprehensible and effective—the social conditions that render a particular attribution of responsibility felicitous (Austin 1962). My brief sketch suggests that even the relatively tightly clustered social realm of litigation provides different scaffoldings that serve as conditions of possibility for, as well as limits on, legal accountability. Such scaffoldings for accountability do not simply allow accountability to be recognized. They allow it to be created in the first place.

NOTES

1. Recent historical work shows that this was the case even in the early United States, generally considered a latecomer to the administrative game (Mashaw 2012).
2. The doctrine of sovereign immunity prevents governments from being sued without their consent. The FTCA provides this consent for the limited circumstances it specifies.

REFERENCES

Austin, John. 1962. *How to Do Things with Words*. Oxford: Oxford University Press.
Arendt, Hannah. (1963) 1994. *Eichmann in Jerusalem: A Report on the Banality of Evil*. New York: Penguin Books.
Arendt, Hannah. 1958. *The Human Condition*. Chicago: University of Chicago Press.
Bernstein, Anya. 2016. "Differentiating Deference." *Yale Journal on Regulation* 33(1): 1–53.
Bernstein, Anya. 2008. "The Social Life of Regulation in Taipei City Hall: The Role of Legality in the Administrative Bureaucracy." *Law and Social Inquiry* 33: 925–954.
Blau, Peter M. (1955) 1963. *The Dynamics of Bureaucracy: A Study of Interpersonal Relations in Two Government Agencies*. Chicago: University of Chicago Press.
Honig, Bonnie. 1993. *Political Theory and the Displacement of Politics*. Ithaca, NY: Cornell University Press.
Hull, Matthew. 2012. *Government of Paper: The Materiality of Bureaucracy in Urban Pakistan*. Berkeley: University of California Press.
Mashaw, Jerry L. 2012. *Creating the Administrative Constitution: The Lost One Hundred Years of American Administrative Law*. New Haven, CT: Yale University Press.
McGarity, Thomas O. 1991. "The Internal Structure of EPA Rulemaking." *Law and Contemporary Problems* 54(4): 57–111.

CHAPTER 6

Upending Infrastructure in Times of Revolt

JULIA ELYACHAR

"We never really act alone," Enfield and Kockelman remind us in the preface to this volume. When millions of people come to the street from their homes and workplaces to fight for a political goal, that fact is easy to see. But who (or what) has agency in situations that seem to be the opposite of "acting alone"? Who (or what) has agency in a revolution forestalled?

Millions of Egyptians took to the street in 2010–11 during the January 25 Revolution in Egypt to overthrow President Hosni Mubarak and to demand bread, freedom, and social justice. They succeeded in forcing Mubarak to resign, with the support of the armed forces. Debates immediately began about whether this was really a revolution and whether it had succeeded or failed. Egyptians called it the January 25th Revolution after Mubarak resigned and continue to do so. Four years later President Morsi of the Muslim Brotherhood had been elected and deposed; chief of the Egyptian armed forces under President Morsi, General Sisi, had become president in turn. Opinions about what had happened, how it had happened, how events should be named, and who was to be credited—and blamed—for the ensuing course of events remain heated and will for years to come. In this brief chapter I do not try to explain these historic events, ask whether the revolution succeeded or failed, or pass judgment on the political agenda or methods of any party. Rather I ask: what can the January 25th Revolution and its aftermath teach us about agency and about distributed agency in particular? I do this by thinking about agency through infrastructure in times of mass revolt. My thinking is informed by Kockelman and Enfield's preface to this volume, by Kockelman's earlier essay on agency (Kockelman 2007), and by a growing body of social science research on infrastructure (for a review, see Larkin 2013).

Agency is often paired with structure. In the simplest of fashion, such pairing allows us to ask, to what degree do we have agency over our own life? Does an "internal self" make us who we are? Or is our social status—our place in social structure—more decisive than a self we only imagine is our own? As scholars, we complicate such questions. As anthropologists, we draw on ethnographic knowledge gained through live interactions with people in determinate settings to think these things through. Anthropology of the Middle East has been a rich place for such debates. The Middle East is a fuzzy geographic concept that became common only during World War II. Many western observers thought of it as a place where individuals (especially women) had little agency. The January 25th Revolution was a surprise to almost all. It showed that agency could overcome structure and tradition after all. Things soon got more complicated. But rather than pursue the terms of this debate, I shift its terms to think about agency together with infrastructure in a time of mass revolt.

Infrastructure long seemed a matter for technocrats, far from concerns about agency or political revolt. Infrastructure usually lies in the background, becoming visible only upon breakdown (Star 1999). Economies cannot function without infrastructure. This commonplace is known in all kinds of economic theory. In Volume II of *Capital*, for example, Marx devotes a great deal of attention to how infrastructure is central to the circulation and realization of value. The creation and maintenance of infrastructure is not itself directly productive of value and yet is essential to the capitalist system of production. Nor, from the standpoint of a neoclassical theory of value, does infrastructure create price. But if you cannot link a product to the market, then that product will spoil and become worthless. If you cannot link a buyer to a seller, then a market cannot function. Infrastructure—roads, airports, ports, and bridges—allows producers to realize the potential economic value of a product. Linking buyers and sellers entails more than physical transportation of goods in space over roads and railroads, as in classic accounts of the role of railroads in 19th-century economic expansion.

Infrastructure is a classic public good, a set of resources available to all and the use of which does not decrease its availability to others. This classic definition of a public good in economics often needs to be fought for in practice. Infrastructure built by colonial states in the 19th century was never available for all. Postcolonial movements held out the promise of infrastructure as a public good for all citizens. Failures of infrastructure in the postcolonial era, in turn, made visible—and came to symbolize—failures of the postcolonial state. Privatization of infrastructure began in postcolonial states under structural adjustment policies in the 1970s. Infrastructure began to be privatized in wealthy countries under neoliberal policies of the 1990s. All this makes infrastructure a terrain and object of political contestation.

Revolts are collective, willed, and condensed events. They are the outcome of many different kinds of social action and political intent. This is different from the kind of hacking into infrastructure on a daily basis that is a normal part of life in poor countries and communities. During mass revolts, infrastructure is repurposed by groups or actively broken down. Roads, phones, subways, and wires become channels through which people are persuaded to act and bodies are motivated to move. Infrastructure is also rendered visible in revolt when people are blocked from moving—when streets are blocked off or squares suffused with people—or when signals cannot be transmitted across computer or mobile phone networks.

Many early commentators on the January 25th Revolution in Egypt gave agency to technological infrastructure. They called it a "Facebook Revolution." This notion went together well with Orientalist stereotypes of the Egyptian people as endlessly and forever patient. Patience is indeed a virtue, as the Egyptian saying goes. But the virtue of patience in popular Egyptian culture had never stopped Egyptians from political action in the past. Years of organizing went into making the January 25th Revolution as well. Many unions, individuals, leaders and parties were involved. Hosni Mubarak and his advisors also thought that the internet had agency—if less than their own agency. They tried to "turn off" the internet during the revolution in an effort to stop social action. While others might have tried in the past to throttle or shut down parts of the internet that reach a particular polity, no government had ever been able to turn off the internet in an entire country and to go off the digital map. Egypt came close, suppressing 91 percent of internet networks and all mobile phones by January 29th (Peterson 2011).

Communications infrastructures had been nationalized in Egypt together with banks and large industry nine years after the 1952 Free Officers Coup. Egypt began to espouse open market policies in the mid 1970s, and free market neoliberal economics in the 1990s and 2000s. Through all of this, Egypt kept tight control over banking and telecommunications. It instituted a private sector telecommunications industry only in the mid-2000s, when it granted mobile phone licenses to two private sector firms to begin operation. Mobile phone use quickly skyrocketed. Signed contracts included a stipulation that telecom and internet service could be shut down at the discretion of authorities in case of national emergency. That stipulation was invoked during the revolution, but the attempt to keep people from communicating, coordinating, and mobilizing backfired.

Egyptians quickly turned to and patched together alternative platforms for communication. These included older platforms such as landlines. Even fifty years after the 1952 Free Officers Coup promised a redistribution of wealth to Egypt's poor, and a remaking of the Egyptian economy, only the wealthy, well connected, or foreigners had access to infrastructure such as landlines. (Lack of landlines on the African continent—including Egypt—made it prime terrain for rapid and deep mobile phone penetration.) Some of those landlines were concentrated in the downtown heart of colonial Egypt, where the most pitched battles of the revolution were fought. Landlines in apartments of activists and their sympathizers became strategic channels—sites around which people visited, gossiped, and planned.

Communicative infrastructures in Egypt were not created by Facebook. But they were crucial in the January 25th Revolution. Efforts to turn off the internet and mobile phones inadvertently made visible the relational and multilayered nature of infrastructures of communicative channels. New communications technologies are integrated moves into existing communications ecologies (Horst and Miller 2006) or communicative infrastructures (Elyachar 2010). Infrastructure always has the "smell of the public" (Robbins 2007), but in times of revolt this is illuminated for all to see.

One image from the revolution shows a group of young men in Tahrir Square at night, crouched over a group of mobile phones, in a tangle of extension cords, wired into stores opened up by owners around Tahrir Square, under spotlights patched by activists into the state grid of streetlights, charging their mobile phones. This captures the way in which poor people in Cairo and elsewhere patch their way into infrastructure of the state on a daily basis (Simone 2004). This kind of slow, long-term, apparently apolitical encroachment of the poor onto land and into infrastructure (Bayat 2009) assumes overt political meaning in times of revolt. Activists also brought out retired technologies like boat phones and satellite communications. They created pirate and alterative infrastructures (Larkin 2013, Simone 2004), patching together whatever worked to keep up contact with one another and with the outside world. They tapped into peer geek networks around the world. With mobile phones turned off, the infrastructure that lay behind them came into view. This included other kinds of communicative channels, those created and reproduced over time through practices of visiting, gossiping, socializing, and strategizing. This multilayered infrastructure of communicative channels jumped out from the background and became part of the action itself.

In such a moment, the politics of platforms becomes clear. Platforms of technologies such as Facebook are neither neutral nor purely technological. Competing models of the market, socio-technologies of market life, technological innovations, engineering dilemmas, and historical layering of infrastructures in Egypt were all wielded together as a communicative infrastructure and functioning platform in which Facebook operated. Platforms themselves became a key terrain of political contestation. Thousands of activists and hackers around the globe got involved in the Egyptian revolution via their concern about platforms and an open internet.

The Muslim Brotherhood was not important in the lead-up to the revolution. They joined in only at the last moment. The Brotherhood had little agency in the revolution in the sense of "the creation of some effect, object ... or action" (Kockelman and Enfield, this volume, p. xii). But when, as the only organized political party able to take the state, their candidate was elected president, it assumed accountability for infrastructure and the public good for which it speaks. Who had agency for the breakdown that ensued? Many insistent answers to that question circulated. Nothing worked. Everyday life had become more precarious. Potholes got bigger; streets were impassible, services were collapsed, infrastructure in even more disrepair. Strikes continued, even in the outskirts of the city, far to the south and the north, in offices even of the most important oil infrastructure companies that generated so much of the country's wealth.

The January 25th Revolution was centered around battles on a few iconic squares. In the year to follow, venders moved onto the street, artists into the squares, and strikers into administrative offices, claiming space for the expression of agency newly emergent in the experience of revolt. Chants from the revolution still rang out: "The people want the downfall of the regime!" "The workers want resignation of the management!" was another common call, such as the call I heard one day in southern Cairo, with workers occupying offices an oil infrastructure firm towards the end of the working day. Along the low brick walls of a telecom company that owned much of the communicative infrastructures of the city splashed graffiti of the Ultras, Egypt's football support clubs who had taken to the streets to support the revolution and paid a high price with their lives. A sign warning the public to stay away merged into drawings of a fist raised high, the image of a martyred young revolutionary, and the phrase "Long live the revolution." That uplifted fist appeared again in graffiti from the Ultras.

That single upended fist is an iconic symbol of resistance. It points up in the air, rather than down toward the ground like a fist wielding tools. This work of upending infrastructure is another, if very different, way of making visible that which was "infra," down below, stand upright for all to see. That which had been *infra*structure becomes another channel along which messages can be run and claims made.

Mass revolts do more than voice resistance to an all-powerful will. They do more than take the state—and then maybe lose it. Mass revolts upend infrastructure and make clear the distributed nature of agency in its different aspects. They leave dramatic traces of collective and often intentional causalities. They create channels for new claims to accountability: who, in fact, did what? Why? To what effect? Who can offer an account of what happened? Which account will hold? Who will be held accountable? Who can be counted on, furthermore, and whose voice counts in the process to come?

Massive revolts upend infrastructure, creating new channels for the conveying of meaning, for dreaming of futures and reclaiming the past. They stand up, as a standard to be reached and a flagpost to be taken. Further kinds of agency—of names to be given, claims to be made, and futures to be dreamed—conjoin around them. To say, then, that the revolution failed—or that it succeeded—is both too easy and too wrong. We cannot find the one place where real agency lies: with the people, with the military, or with Facebook. Agency—in both its components of flexibility and accountability—is always distributed, as we can see so well in the January 25th Revolution and its aftermath.

REFERENCES

Bayat, Asef. 2009. *Life as Politics: How Ordinary People Change the Middle East.* Stanford, CA: Stanford University Press.

Elyachar, Julia. 2010. "Phatic Labor, Infrastructure, and the Question of Empowerment in Cairo." *American Ethnologist* 37(3): 452–464.

Horst, Heather, and Daniel Miller. 2006. *The Cell Phone: An Anthropology of Communication.* Oxford, UK: Berg.

Kockelman, Paul. 2007. "Agency: The Relation Between Meaning, Power, and Knowledge." *Current Anthropology* 48(3): 375–401.

Larkin, Brian. 2013. "The Politics and Poetics of Infrastructure." *Annual Review of Anthropology* 42: 327–343.

Peterson, Mark Allen. 2011. "Egypt's Media Ecology in a Time of Revolt." *Arab Media and Society* 14 (Summer). Accessed August 10, 2016. http://www.arabmediasociety.com/?article=770.

Robbins, Bruce. 2007. "The Smell of Infrastructure: Notes toward an Archive."
    Boundary 2 34(1): 25–33.
Simone, AbdouMaliq. 2004. "People as Infrastructure: Intersecting Fragments in
    Johannesburg." Public Culture 16(3): 407–429.
Star, Susan Leigh. 1999. "The Ethnography of Infrastructure." American Behavioral
    Scientist 43(3): 377–391.

PART THREE

Language and Agency

CHAPTER 7

Brain-to-Brain Interfaces and the Role of Language in Distributing Agency

MARK DINGEMANSE

A VISION OF THE FUTURE

In 1994, Nobel Prize–winning physicist Murray Gell-Mann wrote, "Some day, for better or for worse . . . a human being could be wired directly to an advanced computer, (not through spoken language or an interface like a console), and by means of that computer to one or more other human beings. Thoughts and feelings would be completely shared, with none of the selectivity or deception that language permits" (Gell-Mann 1994:224). Only two decades later, the scientific literature records the first proofs of concept of such brain-to-brain interfaces (Grau et al. 2014; Rao et al. 2014), touting a new era in which brains are directly connected and promising to "revolutionize how humans communicate and collaborate" (Rao et al. 2014:11). This chapter explores some of the assumptions about human interaction implicit in this line of research, and juxtaposes them with a view of language as the ultimate brain-to-brain interface: an interactive, selective, negotiable system that enables individuals with separate bodies to achieve joint agency without giving up behavioral flexibility and social accountability.

A key step on the way to brain-to-brain interfaces has been the development of brain-to-machine interfaces: devices that can be controlled with neural activity. The attraction of such interfaces is that they can bypass some of the constraints of human bodies, a goal that resonates in popular culture but also offers practical applications, for instance in the form of neurally controlled prosthetic devices that enable paralyzed patients to regain limb functions. A more ambitious program is to link such brain-to-machine interfaces together to yield brain-to-brain interfaces (Nicolelis 2013). The applications, medical or otherwise, are somewhat less clear here, but a commonly stated interest is to bypass verbal communication in order to avoid its articulatory bottlenecks and expressive limitations (Rao et al. 2014) or indeed its possibilities for selectivity and deception (Gell-Mann 1994).

Implicit in these ideals of sidestepping the constraints of bodies and language is a narrow view of human agency and communication, and a limited recognition of how material and cultural artifacts have long extended our minds (Clark and Chalmers 1998). "Can information that is available in the brain be transferred directly in the form of the neural code, bypassing language altogether?" ask Rao et al. (2014:1). This reveals a sender-receiver model of communication in which externalization is seen as a mere obstacle to the goal of sharing private processes—the possibility that it may provide much-needed filters and calibration mechanisms is not considered. Rao et al.'s experiment consists of recording brain activity in one person using electro-encephalography and delivering it to another person using a transcranial magnetic stimulation device positioned such that a pulse results in an involuntary upward jerk of the hand. The other has no choice, but is controlled by brute force. This is communication stripped of any possibilities for negotiating joint commitment or shared intentionality (Gilbert 1989). It is akin to pushing someone out of the room rather than persuading him or her to leave.

Current conceptions of brain-to-brain interfaces thus appear to be more about the involuntary unloading of information than about the co-construction of shared understanding, and more about control by brute force than about cooperation by consent—all at a loss of individual agency. Collaboration, of course, always involves some redistribution of individual agency to a larger social unit, creating joint agency. How is this achieved? A brain-to-brain interface implements it physically; language does it socially. The two need not exclude each other. A goal of this chapter is to put forward some insights about human language that may be incorporated in the design of ethically responsible brain-to-brain interfaces (Trimper et al. 2014).

LANGUAGE AND HUMAN AGENCY

To understand how language shapes and constrains distributed agency, there is no better place to look than its primary ecological niche: everyday conversation. The following fragment was recorded in Ghana, but its analysis draws on insights that apply to social interaction everywhere (Sacks 1992). Some family members have just finished processing some newly harvested maize and are now preparing to play a board game. A large metal tub holding the maize is still in the way, making it hard for others to join the game.

Siwu (Neighbours_3093575)

1		((Ben is holding a board game for four; a large metal tub with processed maize stands in the way of others joining))
2	Sesi	kãrãnpɔ laa puta lò yedza ìyo katɔ̃ mmɔ.
		right I'll lift this and put it in storage there
3	Ben	be tè mì puta mì yedza iyo:?
		what are you going to put in storage?
4	Sesi	àtita
		the maize
5	Ben	ta mà ba mà su àtitabi wangbe kɔ̃rɔ̃kɔ̃rɔ̃.
		this maize will be picked up right away
6	Sesi	ã, ma kɛlɛ̀ gu kala
		ah, they're taking it down ((to the lower end of the village))
		((some intervening turns omitted))
12	Sesi	ɛ̀h, nyua bò Afua.
		uh, wait, Afua
13	Afua	((looks up))
14	Sesi	mi mɔɛ gu mɛ̀ si bò su bò sia ngbe.
		grab this with me so we put it right here
15		((1.6 seconds of silence))
16	Sesi	bò su bo yedza i kuruɛ nɛ te mi ba mia sɛ ngbe mi pɛ iraɔ̃ ni.
		let us put this to the side so you can come and play this thing
17		((Sesi & Afua lift tub together and place it one meter to the side))
18	Sesi	kailɛ.
		that's good.
19		((people sit down to play the game))

Sesi offers to put away the tub in the storage room. Ben asks for clarification, and when Sesi makes clear he refers to the maize, Ben notes that it will be taken elsewhere soon. This leads to a slight change of plans. Now all Sesi needs to do is move the tub to the side. He recruits the help of his sibling Afua. Once the obstacle is out of the way, people sit down to play the game. Exchanges like this happen all over the world every day—and it is in this kind of context that we see some of the most fundamental roles of language in social life.

Most importantly, language helps distribute agency. Take Sesi's request for help (lines 12–18): he addresses Afua by name to secure her attention, then produces a first version of the request. When there is no immediate uptake, he reformulates his request, adding a reason which turns it from a mere practical matter into a joint project that may also benefit her ("let's put this to the side so you can come and play this thing," line 16). His actions show that language provides a systematic organization of linguistic resources to interactively manage the many concerns at play when one person asks another to do something. The ultimate effect is that Sesi succeeds in recruiting Afua's body as a "tool" for carrying out a joint action. This is somewhat like the participants in the Rao et al. (2014) experiment, but with the crucial difference that it is jointly negotiated rather than achieved by brute force. Two features in particular help language distribute agency: its selectivity and its negotiability.

The selectivity of language manifests itself in two ways. First, speakers can select the linguistic means for making their ideas public, allowing them to foreground or background certain informational or relational concerns. To this end, language offers a large and renewable supply of words, expressions, and conversational structures. Sesi can refer to the tub of maize with "this" (relying on shared context) or with "the maize" (spelling out the underspecified reference). He can refer to his sister as "Afua" (highlighting her status as an individual) but also include her in the pronoun "us" (highlighting her status as part of a joint social unit created in that very moment). This selectivity makes language highly efficient by enabling it to be underspecified when possible, yet specifiable when necessary (Levinson 2000). A second sense in which language is selective is that speakers can select what to make public and what to keep private. Language provides us with ways to control and filter what we share with whom. Perhaps it is this sense of selectivity that Gell-Mann deplored, as it opens up the possibility for deception. However, this is easily outweighed by the social benefits: some things are better left unsaid. More generally, sharing and withholding information are among the most important ways in which we manage our social relationships. The selectivity of public language means that it offers a set of filters through which we can efficiently and tactfully connect private worlds.

The other key feature of how language distributes agency is its negotiability: the fact that meaning and mutual understanding are always open to negotiation. Mutual understanding between people is built bit by bit in conversation. Every turn at talk is a social action as well as a take on the social action implemented by the prior one. So Sesi's "ah, they're taking it down" displays one possible interpretation of Ben's "this maize will be picked up right away" (lines 5–6) in an instance of the common process of grounding (Clark and Brennan 1991). A more explicit case of the negotiation of understanding is Ben's request for clarification and Sesi's response to it (lines 3–4). This illustrates "conversational repair," the machinery that people use to deal with small but frequent rifts in mutual understanding (Dingemanse et al. 2015).

Don't such misunderstandings exemplify the kind of imperfections that brain-to-brain interfaces aim to rid us of? To the contrary: it is precisely in the tussles of negotiating mutual understanding that language affords a great degree of agency. Here, for instance, conversational repair provides Ben with a way to have a hand in subtly revising Sesi's plans without unilaterally imposing another course of action. In other instances, repair can provide ways to resist something (such as divulging personal information or agreeing with another's statement), empowering people to commit to different degrees of participation without rupturing the social fabric (Sacks 1992). The interactive construction of shared understanding provides people at every turn with opportunities for signaling consent or dissent. This amounts to a set of checks and balances through which people can calibrate and revise the inferences that are constantly made.

People have separate bodies. While brain-to-brain interfaces may somewhat dilute this separateness, language has long bridged it. Never merely individuals, we are always part of a wide range of larger social units, some fleeting and diffuse (like the 4-second long unit of Sesi and Afua moving the tub out of the way, or the more dispersed unit of "readers of this essay") and others more strong and durable (like a close friendship or a kin relation). Language is the main tool through which we are able to navigate this mosaic of social relations, constantly switching frames between "me" and the many different senses of "us" (Enfield 2013). Language allows us to maintain our individual identity and agency while merging and joining forces at other levels.

TOWARD A MORE PRODUCTIVE VIEW OF LANGUAGE FOR BRAIN-TO-BRAIN INTERFACES

Current conceptions of brain-to-brain interfaces strive to connect brains directly, "bypassing language altogether" (Rao et al. 2014), hoping to bring about the complete sharing of thoughts and feelings as Gell-Mann envisioned it. A recurrent dream in this work is the prospect of a "mind meld," in which a super-network of brains may come to be the substrate for something like a meta-consciousness (Nicolelis 2013). From a biological perspective this is not novel. Mind melds —or complex networks in which large numbers of individual agents together achieve a form of sentience—have independently arisen several times in evolution, for instance in eusocial insect societies and in cellular slime molds, the latter capable of impressive feats in maze-solving. The real challenge for brain-to-brain interfaces is not to achieve some inter-linking of brains; it is to harness this technology in a way that does not reduce human participants to the level of amoeba in a slime mold.

Seen in this light, the selectivity and negotiability of language are not bugs, they are features. Thanks to these features of language, we can maintain a complex web of social relations by managing what we share with whom, and we can join forces in larger social units without indefinitely relinquishing individual agency. To throw this into sharper relief, consider what happens when selectivity and negotiability are systematically diminished or punished, as in religious indoctrination or interrogation under torture. Here, the very defining features of individual agency are taken away, and it is no coincidence that we describe such circumstances as dehumanizing or inhumane. Language is what makes us human. It is not merely a conduit for information. We might try exchanging it for a high-throughput physical connection to optimize the flow of some types of information—but we would do so at the tremendous cost of throwing away a rich infrastructure for organizing social agency.

Could brain-to-brain interfaces be designed in a way that incorporates this infrastructure? None of the points made above logically depend on the spoken, face-to-face version of language that is its most prevalent form today. In fact, language is modality-independent to some degree, as shown by the fact that it can be realized wholly visually as in the signed languages of the deaf. So it is not inconceivable that there can be some useful form of social interaction in the substrate of brain-to-brain interfaces. Whatever the modality of communication, the two design features that matter most for creating a truly humane form of brain-to-brain interfaces are: (1) selectivity, giving people control over the relation between public words and private worlds; and (2) negotiability, giving people systematic opportunities for calibrating and revising joint commitments.

CONCLUSIONS

The Hitchhiker's Guide to the Galaxy records the case of the Belcerebon people of Kakrafoon, who were inflicted by a Galactic Tribunal with "that most cruel of social diseases, telepathy" (Adams 2002[1980]:252–3). It was a punishment with unforeseen consequences: "in order to prevent themselves broadcasting every slightest thought that crosses their minds ... they now have to talk very loudly and continuously about the weather, their little aches and pains, the match this afternoon, and what a noisy place Kakrafoon has suddenly become." Current conceptions of brain-to-brain interfaces appear to be on their way to replicating the fate of the Belcerebon people. In contrast, the human condition is enabled by a flexible communication system that saves us from an all too unconstrained sharing of private processes while still helping us to cooperate and achieve shared goals in ways unmatched anywhere in the animal kingdom.

Brain-to-brain interfaces are often presented as a system for sharing information and organizing joint action that is superior to natural language. However, directly connecting one individual's mental life to that of another has the effect of robbing both of a great degree of individual agency. There may be gains in agency elsewhere, but without the checks and balances provided by a system like language, they will likely lie at levels beyond the direct control of the individuals. Language serves as a filter between the private and the public, and as an infrastructure for negotiating consent and dissent. As research into brain-to-brain interfaces matures, it is my hope that it will find ways to incorporate selectivity and negotiability, so as to extend human agency in meaningful ways.

ACKNOWLEDGMENTS

Thanks to Nick Enfield, Steve Levinson, and Paul Kockelman for helping me develop my thinking on the topics raised here. I received helpful comments on draft versions from Nick Enfield and Roel Willems, and I thank other contributors to the Foundations of Social Agency meeting at Ringberg Castle for stimulating interactions. I gratefully acknowledge the support of an NWO Veni grant and of the Max Planck Society for the Advancement of Science.

REFERENCES

Adams, Douglas. 2002. *The Ultimate Hitchhiker's Guide to the Galaxy*.
New York: Del Rey.
Clark, Andy, and David Chalmers. 1998. "The Extended Mind." *Analysis* 58(1): 7–19.
Clark, Herbert H., and Susan E. Brennan. 1991. "Grounding in Communication."
In *Perspectives on Socially Shared Cognition*, edited by Lauren B. Resnick, J. M. Levine, and S. D. Teasley, 13:127–149. Washington, DC: APA Books.

Dingemanse, Mark, Seán G. Roberts, Julija Baranova, Joe Blythe, Paul Drew, Simeon Floyd, Rosa S. Gisladottir, Kobin H. Kendrick, Stephen C. Levinson, Elizabeth Manrique, Giovanni Rossi, N. J. Enfield. 2015. "Universal Principles in the Repair of Communication Problems." *PLOS ONE* 10(9): e0136100. doi:10.1371/journal.pone.0136100.

Enfield, N. J. 2013. *Relationship Thinking: Agency, Enchrony, and Human Sociality*. Oxford: Oxford University Press.

Gell-Mann, Murray. 1994. *The Quark and the Jaguar: Adventures in the Simple and the Complex*. New York: W. H. Freeman.

Gilbert, Margaret. 1989. *On Social Facts*. London/New York: Routledge.

Grau, Carles, Romuald Ginhoux, Alejandro Riera, Thanh Lam Nguyen, Hubert Chauvat, Michel Berg, Julià L. Amengual, Alvaro Pascual-Leone, and Giulio Ruffini. 2014. "Conscious Brain-to-Brain Communication in Humans Using Non-Invasive Technologies." *PLOS ONE* 9(8): e105225. doi:10.1371/journal.pone.0105225.

Levinson, Stephen C. 2000. *Presumptive Meanings: The Theory of Generalized Conversational Implicature*. Cambridge, MA: MIT Press.

Nicolelis, Miguel. 2013. *Beyond Boundaries: The New Neuroscience of Connecting Brains with Machines—and How It Will Change Our Lives*. New York: Henry Holt and Company.

Rao, Rajesh P. N., Andrea Stocco, Matthew Bryan, Devapratim Sarma, Tiffany M. Youngquist, Joseph Wu, and Chantel S. Prat. 2014. "A Direct Brain-to-Brain Interface in Humans." *PLOS ONE* 9(11): e111332. doi:10.1371/journal.pone.0111332.

Sacks, Harvey. 1992. *Lectures on Conversation*. 2 vols. London: Blackwell.

Trimper, John B., Paul Root Wolpe, and Karen S. Rommelfanger. 2014. "When 'I' Becomes 'We': Ethical Implications of Emerging Brain-to-Brain Interfacing Technologies." *Frontiers in Neuroengineering* 7: 4. doi:10.3389/fneng.2014.00004.

CHAPTER 8

Requesting as a Means for Negotiating Distributed Agency

SIMEON FLOYD

REQUESTING ASSISTANCE FROM OTHERS IN SOCIAL INTERACTION

People frequently achieve goals that they are unable (or sometimes unwilling) to accomplish alone by requesting assistance from others. This possibility for distributing agency across multiple individuals, some expressing the goals and others accomplishing the actions, is a basic ingredient of human sociality. It makes possible all types of collective action, from the macro-level of large-scale institutions to the micro-level of face-to-face interaction. Much of our collective action is managed by pre-existing arrangements; for example, nobody needs to be specifically asked to report to work on a given day if there is already a contract establishing the required activities over a period of time. However, at the micro level of co-present social coordination, it is often necessary for a person to use some explicit semiotic means, linguistic or otherwise, to tell another that he or she wishes for something to be done at a given time (see Dingemanse, chapter 7 in this volume). In such cases, people make requests. A "request sequence"[1] in face-to-face interaction can be identified on the basis of two moves[2] involving two participants:

MOVE A: Participant A does something participant B can perceive.
    e.g., *Pass the salt. ((points at salt))*
MOVE B: Participant B does something for participant A.
    e.g., *Here you go. ((passes salt to A))*

Practices of requesting have been studied under a number of frameworks,[3] not all of which look at them in situ to see how they work in natural speech or, importantly, how they are responded to. This chapter discusses the distribution of social agency in light of findings from a study of requesting in a corpus of video recordings of everyday household and community interaction among the indigenous Chachi people of northwest Ecuador (with a sample of 205 request sequences), part of a cross-linguistic project including fieldworkers working all over the world.[4] Specifically, it discusses the tension between a characterization of requesting practices as prosocial and cooperative, in that people step in to help one another, and a characterization of request sequences as inherently unequal, in that one person gives the command and another acts.[5]

MAKING REQUESTS

One common way that people formulate requests is by using the morphosyntactic resources made available to them by the different languages they speak. While grammatical systems vary to some degree, they usually organize the types of formulations they make possible into "sentence types" that are useful for cross-linguistic comparison.[6] Languages tend to distinguish making a statement ("declarative"), asking a question ("interrogative"), and making a command ("imperative"). This last type is primarily dedicated to expressing a desire to direct the actions of others, and as such it is the most frequently used sentence type for requests in many languages (e.g., "Pass the salt"). Speakers also use the other major sentence types for requests: interrogatives ("Can I have the salt?"), declaratives ("I need the salt"), and sometimes other formats including utterances with no verb and thus no sentence type, strictly speaking ("Salt!"). Languages commonly allow for different sentence types to be used flexibly for requesting, often with relation to more "indirect" interrogative and declarative strategies of requesting that may be considered more polite,[7] but languages may also vary greatly with respect to the different frequencies with which the different sentence types are used for requests. The types of indirect request strategies that have been observed for English are also seen in Cha'palaa, but are relatively rare, and imperatives are the most common format (71% of cases).

(1) Imperative request

    A inu jayu kude aamama shipijcha   M1

        i-nu   jayu   ku-**de**   aamama shipijcha

        me-to   a.little give-**IMPERATIVE** grandma madroña.fruit

        Give me a little madroña grandma ((reaches toward B))

    B ((turns toward A; begins passing fruit))   M2

(2) Interrogative request

    A serruchu tsutyuu   M1

        serruchu tsu-tyu-**u**

        saw   lie-NEGATIVE-**INTERROGATIVE**

        Is (your) saw not there?

    B enku (.) tanami ibain (.)   M2

        enku ta-na-mi   i-bain

        here have-POSITION-DECLARATIVE me-also

        Here, I have it. ((goes to get saw))

(3) Declarative request

    A tu- tu'pushujuntsaa kanu juaa   M1

        tu- tu'pu-shujunsta-ya   ka-nu   ju-ya

        nail nail-that.part-FOCUS grab-to be(**DECLARATIVE**)-FOCUS

        It is necessary to grab the part that was nailed.

    B ((grabs and moves board))   M2

Based on their predicates, the examples above represent imperative (1), interrogative (2) and declarative (3) request types. Other spoken material added to the main sentence types may include "vocatives" ("hey"), "mitigators" ("a little salt"), "strengtheners" ("the damn salt"), accounts or explanations ("the soup is not salty enough"), among other elements.

In addition to spoken material, people also frequently combine speech with visual bodily practices, most frequently reaching out to receive objects, holding out objects relevant for the request, and pointing to places

Figure 8.1 Different types of multimodal request formats. *Left:* Holding out the hand (16%). *Middle:* Holding out an object (27%). *Right:* Pointing (42%).

or things involved in the request. Under certain conditions, people are also able to successfully accomplish requests entirely nonverbally, such as when there is an already agreed upon joint activity.[8]

RESPONDING TO REQUESTS

How people formulate their requests is only half of the issue, however. While most work on requesting has focused on request formats in isolation, cues from work in conversation analysis points toward seeing requesting as a sequence of moves in which the initial move provides an opportunity for a subsequent, responsive move. One important aspect of these contingent moments is that they are socially delicate, as the addressee is in a position to potentially reject the request. Work on politeness and "face" in interaction notes how people actively avoid and mitigate this type of face-threatening act.[9] Indeed, looking at the different ways Cha'palaa speakers responded to requests, fulfilling the request is by far the most frequent type of response while rejection is the least frequent.

One way to interpret this finding, which is surely appropriate to some degree, is that people share a generally cooperative stance, and so they maximize the potential for affiliative interactions with no "face-threatening" consequences. People aim for request sequences like those in (1), (2), and (3), above, in which the next move is B accomplishing the requested action, and avoid sequences like (4), in which A's request is not fulfilled.

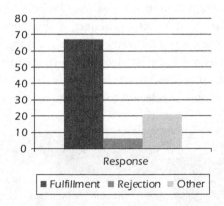

Figure 8.2 Types of responses to requests in Cha'palaa that received sequence-closing responses. Fulfillment was 71%, rejection was 6%, and other actions (i.e., initiating repair: e.g., "What?") represented 22%.

(4) Rejection of a request

    1 A   lemu tsutyuu, lemu deii   M1
            lemu tsu-tyu-u   lemu de-i-i
            lime lie-NEG-Q lime CMPL-become-Q
            Are there no limes? Are the limes gone? ((turns toward B))

    2 B   lemu jutyu kaa ruku   M2
            lemu ju-tyu   kaa-ruku
            lime be-NEG DIM-man
            There are no limes little husband.
            ((reaching into basket to check))

The few rejections that do occur are often, like this one, managed through indirect requests and mitigating, polite answers (in this case, with the use of a diminutive), and rarely is there any overt contention. However, there may be more behind this surface of apparent pervasive cooperative, affiliative behavior. One of the options in Brown and Levinson's original formulation of how people manage face in social interaction is to avoid the face-threatening act in the first place, if there are potential negative consequences.[10] For the study of requesting, this means that in addition to reflecting a cooperative stance, the low rate of overt rejection may also reflect the fact that in most instances people only make requests that have a high chance of success.

Not all members of a society have equal rights to request others to do things in any given time or place, and these rights are tied to the nature of the activity at hand, the setting, and the participants involved.[11] In the context of everyday interaction under discussion here, the different rights and duties expected of individuals are in part structured by their household and community roles. In the collaborative project that the investigation of Cha'palaa requests was part of, each field researcher, based on long-term experience in the communities where the natural speech data was recorded, was asked to provide ethnographically grounded information about the social (a)symmetry of each dyad involved in a given request sequence, when possible. These rationales for identifying such asymmetries varied. In Chachi households in Ecuador, where men often rest in hammocks while women attend to cooking, cleaning, and childcare, husband-wife dyads often show dynamics of gender inequality. Children and adolescents are also expected to take orders from adults to do different household tasks. In other cultural contexts, gender or age might not be as relevant in community contexts as status as host versus guest, for example, or the birth order

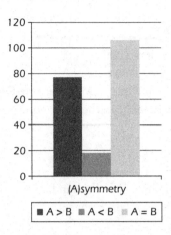

Figure 8.3 Social (a)symmetry in dyads involved in request sequences in Cha'palaa. Most requests in dyads of equal status (53%), but a further 38% are from higher-status to lower-status individuals, compared to only 9% for lower-status to higher-status individuals.

of siblings, in places where this is held as important. When it was possible to characterize dyads as asymmetrical based on knowledge of Chachi society more generally, there were always more cases of a higher-status individuals requesting from lower-status individuals than vice versa.

These findings add another layer to the simple interpretation of high success rates of requests as straightforward cooperation. One important aspect of the apparent tendency toward cooperation is that people tend to ask others to do things when they have more social rights to do so, and so cases of outright rejection are rare since people may not even make socially inappropriate requests in the first place. This perspective leads to the apparently paradoxical conclusion that the cooperative principles that allow individuals to share collective agency also introduce the possibility of social asymmetry, when some actors more frequently take the role of the command-giver and others more frequently accomplish the action requested.

REQUESTING AS COOPERATIVE OR ASYMMETRICAL?

Human behavioral and evolutionary sciences have made much of prosocial, altruistic types of practices seen in the behavior of humans and sometimes in other social species. Some researchers debate how altruistic traits may represent evolutionary fitness through the benefits that individuals obtain by being parts of social collectives.[12] Others focus on understanding human capacities for intersubjective-type thinking, in which people consider the perspectives and desires of others in their own behavior.[13] Such basic properties of humans are no doubt significant, but research on altruism and prosociality sometimes seems to portray an overly rosy view of social relations.

In the social sciences, researchers have long attempted to understand social inequality, focusing as much as on how people dominate each other as on how they assist each other. For example, a situation like that in the Chachi communities under discussion here in which members of society perform labor and receive benefits of labor disproportionately resonates with the type of inequalities emphasized in Marxian analysis. However, Marx was mainly interested in broad social stratification based on economic class and had much less to say about everyday community- or family-internal inequalities.[14] Weberian analysis of social stratification introduces more varied intersecting planes beyond economic class, one of which being the more local social status of the individuals involved.[15] The types of social asymmetries most relevant in the everyday contexts under discussion here mainly concern people's status in terms of age, gender, and kinship relations, although these planes interact with others at different levels of scale. When Weber defined social domination as "the probability that a command with a given specific content will be obeyed by a given group of persons"[16] he may not have been thinking of commands so mundane as "Pass the salt," but these types of requests are in some senses fundamental to larger scale issues. It is a bit of a jump to move from a man in an indigenous Chachi community in Ecuador telling his wife to bring him salt to, say, a mining company requesting access to ancestral Chachi territory to extract minerals. Yet Weber's definition includes terms like "command" and "obey" that seem amenable to being applied to both levels of scale.

Analysts of mundane everyday interaction have resisted the imposition of abstract categories to micro-interactional instances unless there is direct evidence for them in the data, as seen in Schegloff's classic critiques of social scientists' use of abstract concepts like power and social identity without showing empirical evidence based on social interaction.[17] However, given the interactionally grounded finding that the labor and benefits involved in requesting are not shared equally in everyday interaction in Chachi communities, it is perhaps possible to link such findings to broader social issues beyond specific interactions.[18] Indeed, if we look at how Foucault, one of the social sciences' most influential theorists of power, formulates power not as a static relationship but as a way in which certain actions modify others,[19] it seems to fit quite well with conversation analysts' conception of the social as emergent from successive sequential actions:

> In effect, what defines a relationship of power is that it is a mode of action which does not act directly and immediately on others. Instead, it acts upon their

actions: *an action upon an action*, on existing actions or on those which may arise in the present or the future. . . .[A] power relationship can only be articulated on the basis of two elements which are each indispensable if it is really to be a power relationship: that "the other" (the one over whom power is exercised) be thoroughly recognized and maintained to the very end as a person who acts; and that, faced with a relationship of power, a whole field of responses, reactions, results, and possible inventions may open up.[20]

While perhaps it is a more micro-level context than is usually considered in current, more processual understandings of inequality in the social sciences more broadly, a response in a request sequence is one place where we can directly observe at least some of the kinds of responsive actions Foucault refers to. Addressees are in a position to make the request socially meaningful by responding to it, either by fulfilling the request or contesting it. When looking at peoples' overwhelming tendency to fulfill requests, we can see this as a (possibly evolved) trait of altruism and prosociality, but we can also complicate this understanding by showing how this tendency may also reflect asymmetrical social relations in terms of who requests and who responds. While seeming to generate a paradox of concurrent cooperation and inequality, the introduction of this complication does not make humans' social capacity for cooperation any less remarkable. Instead, it highlights this capacity's complex relation to other, sometimes more contested dimensions of sociality.

NOTES

1. Current research on requesting places such practices in a broader context of "recruitments," practices for "making an immediate physical need, problem or wish overt and publicly available, thereby providing an opportunity for a co-participant to assist in meeting the need, resolving the problem, or fulfilling the wish" (Drew and Couper-Kuhlen 2014:28). In this chapter, the more familiar term "request" is used instead of "recruitment," but it is meant in a broad sense that encompasses "requesting" in a narrow sense as well as related practices of "recruiting" assistance from others in interaction. Comparable cases of request/recruitment sequences are identified using the "natural" or "sequential control" method (Dingemanse and Floyd 2014).
2. In conversation analysis, a basic unit is the "adjacency pair," consisting of two "turns" fitted to each other (Sacks, Schegloff, and Jefferson 1974). Request sequences are in many ways an example of an adjacency pair, although since the "turn-taking" rules are formulated for speech and not for the types of practical actions involved in such sequences, here the term "move" can help capture broader type of multimodal "composite" sequential actions (Enfield 2009), so "move" will be employed instead of the traditional "turn" in this chapter.

3. There has been a great deal of research on requests in pragmatics, sociolinguistics, psychology, and related fields. Conversation analysis has put the most emphasis on requesting as part of a request-response; see Drew and Couper-Kuhlen (2014) for a review in a recent collected volume.

4. This study of Cha'palaa was conducted in the context of the Recruitments Subproject (2010–2014), part of the European Research Council project "Human Sociality and Systems of Language Use," directed by Nick Enfield and hosted by the Language and Cognition Department (Stephen Levinson, director) of the Max Planck Institute for Psycholinguistics. While this chapter specifically discusses Cha'palaa, some of the ideas stem from group collaborations with Julija Baranova, Joe Blythe, Mark Dingemanse, Paul Drew, Nick Enfield, Kobin Kendrick, Giovanni Rossi, and Jörg Zinken, and will be further elaborated on in future collective publications. As a coordinator of this subproject, the author would like to acknowledge the contributions of all project members to expanding our understanding of the domain of requests/recruitments.

5. See Rossi and Zinken, chapter 9 in this volume, on the different roles of parties involved in request sequences.

6. Sentences types, which are discussed in a huge array of literature, including one well-known summary by Sadock and Zwicky (1985), are also sometimes referred to with the term "clause types."

7. Indirect (non-explicit, non-imperative, off-record, etc.) requests have long been a topic of research concerning speech acts, politeness and inferential processes in social interaction (Grice 1975, Searle 1975, Clark 1979, Brown and Levinson 1987, among many others).

8. See Rossi (2014) for a detailed account of the conditions of fully nonverbal requesting based on data from Italian. The rate of fully nonverbal requests in the Cha'palaa sample was low (4%).

9. Goffman 1955; Brown and Levinson 1987.

10. Brown and Levinson 1987:69.

11. Curl and Drew 2008 refer to an orientation assuming a high probability that a request will be fulfilled as "entitlement." One factor that relates to whether people take such stances in request sequences (among others, like the cost or "contingency" of the activity, in Curl and Drew's terms) is the relative social (a)symmetry of a dyad in a given context.

12. Wilson 1975, Sober and Wilson 1999, Bowles and Gintis 2011, and many others.

13. See, for example, Tomasello 2009.

14. After Marx's death, Engels applied Marx's analysis to some more family-internal and community-internal dynamics in his 1884 work *The Origin of the Family, Private Property and the State*, and researchers have gone on to find more connections to current understandings of multiple intersecting planes of social identity beyond economic class.

15. For Weber (1978), "status" was one of three major dimensions of social stratification, along with economic class and "party" (i.e., religious-type affiliations).

16. Weber 1978:53.

17. This line is expressed in much of Schegloff's work (e.g., Schegloff 1993).

18. Some work has taken up Schegloff's challenge to seek to empirically ground social categories like gender in interactional analysis; see, for example, Kitzinger 2013.

19. Here is the full quote: "The exercise of power is not simply a relationship between partners, individual or collective; *it is a way in which certain actions*

modify others. Which is to say, of course, that something called Power, with or without a capital letter, which is assumed to exist universally in a concentrated or diffused form, does not exist. Power exists only when it is put into action, even if, of course, it is integrated into a disparate field of possibilities brought to bear upon permanent structures." Foucault 1982:788, author's emphasis.

20. Foucault 1982:789, author's emphasis.

REFERENCES

Bowles, Samuel, and Herbert Gintis. 2011. *A Cooperative Species: Human Reciprocity and Its Evolution*. Princeton, NJ: Princeton University Press.

Brown, Penelope, and Stephen C. Levinson. 1987. *Politeness: Some Universals in Language Usage*. Cambridge: Cambridge University Press.

Clark, Herbert H. 1979. "Responding to Indirect Speech Acts." *Cognitive Psychology* 11(4): 430–477.

Curl, Traci S., and Paul Drew. 2008. "Contingency and Action: A Comparison of Two Forms of Requesting." *Research on Language & Social Interaction* 41(2):129–153.

Dingemanse, Mark, and Simeon Floyd. 2014. "Conversation across Cultures." In *The Cambridge Handbook of Linguistic Anthropology*, edited by N. J. Enfield, Paul Kockelman, and Jack Sidnell, 447–480. Cambridge: Cambridge University Press.

Drew, Paul, and Elizabeth Couper-Kuhlen. 2014. "Requesting—From Speech Act to Recruitment." In *Requesting in Social Interaction*, edited by Paul Drew and Elizabeth Couper-Kuhlen, 1–34. Amsterdam/Philadelphia: John Benjamins.

Enfield, N. J. 2009. *The Anatomy of Meaning: Speech, Gesture, and Composite Utterances*. Cambridge: Cambridge University Press.

Foucault, Michel. 1982. "The Subject and Power." *Critical Inquiry* 8(4): 777–795.

Goffman, Erving. 1955. "On Face-Work: An Analysis of Ritual Elements in Social Interaction." *Psychiatry* 18(3): 213–231.

Grice, H. Paul. 1975. "Logic and Conversation." In *Syntax and Semantics*, edited by Peter Cole and Jerry L. Morgan, 3:41–58. New York: Academic Press.

Kitzinger, Celia. 2013. "Conversation Analysis and Gender and Sexuality." In *The Encyclopedia of Applied Linguistics*, edited by Carol A. Chapelle, 996–1000. Oxford, UK: Wiley-Blackwell.

Rossi, Giovanni. 2014. "When Do People Not Use Language to Make Requests?" In *Requesting in Social Interaction*, edited by Paul Drew and Elizabeth Couper-Kuhlen, 301–332. Amsterdam: John Benjamins.

Sacks, Harvey, Emanuel A. Schegloff, and Gail Jefferson. 1974. "A Simplest Systematics for the Organization of Turn-Taking for Conversation." *Language* 50(4): 696–735.

Sadock, Jerrold M., and Arnold Zwicky. 1985. "Speech Act Distinctions in Syntax." In *Language Typology and Syntactic Description*, edited by Timothy Shopen, 155–196. Cambridge: Cambridge University Press.

Schegloff, Emanuel. 1993. "Reflections on Talk and Social Structure." In *Talk and Social Structure*, edited by Deirdre Boden and Don H. Zimmerman, 44–70. Cambridge, UK: Polity Press.

Searle, John R. 1975. "A Taxonomy of Illocutionary Acts." In *Language, Mind, and Knowledge*, edited by K. Günderson, 344–369. Vol. 7, Minneapolis Studies in the Philosophy of Science. Minneapolis: University of Minneapolis Press.

Sober, Elliott, and David Sloan Wilson. 1999. *Unto Others: The Evolution and Psychology of Unselfish Behavior*. Cambridge, MA: Harvard University Press.

Tomasello, Michael. 2009. *Why We Cooperate*. Cambridge, MA: MIT Press.

Weber, Max. (1922) 1978. *Economy and Society: An Outline of Interpretive Sociology*. Berkeley: University of California Press.

Wilson, Edward O. 1975. *Sociobiology: The New Synthesis*. Cambridge, MA: Belknap Press of Harvard University Press.

CHAPTER 9

Social Agency and Grammar

GIOVANNI ROSSI AND JÖRG ZINKEN

One of the most everyday and conspicuous moments in which human
agency is distributed is when we ask others for help. This happens
all the time in daily life: we constantly rely on others for small and big
practicalities such as getting the salt, moving a sofa, or cooking a meal.
Requests have long been a topic of interest in the social and behavioral sciences, including research concerned with the distribution of human agency
(see Floyd, chapter 8, this volume; Dingemanse, chapter 7. this volume).
Some of our everyday requests are motivated by an individual goal (e.g.,
"can I have a glass of water? I'm so thirsty"), others by a common goal ("give
me the cards so I can deal them to everyone"). Some requests are isolated
from whatever else is going on at the moment, while others are bound up
in ongoing activities. What is common to all actions of requesting is that
a person's behavior is recruited by another to achieve a certain goal. In the
domain of practical action, this typically involves manipulating the material environment or changing the course of one's bodily conduct.

Research on requesting has documented a variety of strategies that
people of different cultures use to get another person's help (see Drew and
Couper-Kuhlen 2014, Rossi 2015, for recent reviews). Not surprisingly,
these strategies often involve language (Floyd, Rossi, and Enfield under
review). Language has a number of properties that aid in making requests.
One is the facility to encode symbolic meaning, which allows a speaker to
specify the action requested with a verb (e.g. "pass") and the object implicated in the action with a noun (e.g. "salt"). Language can also specify who

is to participate in the action requested by means of person marking. Since requests are typically made by an individual to another, linguistic forms like imperatives (e.g., "pass the salt") and recurrent types of interrogatives (e.g., "can you move over a little?") either encode or conventionally imply a second person as the requestee. Second person marking has obvious consequences for the distribution of agency in a requesting event, in that it designates another person as the *animator* of the action requested—the participant who will physically carry it out—while the speaker usually maintains the role of *author* and possibly *principal* of the action—the participant who decides what is to be done and who is responsible for its effects (see Goffman 1981: ch. 3; Enfield, chapter 2, this volume). This is the typical way in which agency is distributed in a requesting event. But it's not the only one. In this chapter, we show that languages offer grammatical structures that afford alternative ways of distributing the agency of an action. We focus in particular on impersonal deontic declaratives like "it is necessary to x," which are used in several languages to express the need for an action without tying it to any particular individual (see Malchukov and Siewierska 2011).

From a grammatical point of view, impersonal deontic declaratives have three core components. One is deontic meaning, which invokes a social obligation that makes relevant the doing of something. Another is declarative form, which—unlike an imperative or an interrogative—doesn't constrain how people should respond to it (Vinkhuyzen and Szymanski 2005). Third, and most important, the statement doesn't specify the agent of the necessary action. In languages like Italian and Polish, this can be done by using either an impersonal verb, such as Italian *bisogna* or Polish *trzeba* ("it is necessary to"), or an intransitive construction with a nonhuman subject (e.g. "the rubbish has to be thrown out").

From an interactional point of view, the grammatical makeup of an impersonal deontic declarative has two main consequences. One is that the same statement can be used to accomplish actions as different as (1) a *request* for someone to do something or (2) an *account* of the speaker's doing that something. In these two scenarios, while the action is formulated as necessary for anyone in the current situation, only one person becomes involved in it (see Rossi and Zinken in press for an analysis of how these alternatives come about). The second property is that, at other times, the participation in the necessary action can be negotiated or avoided. These are cases in which the distribution of agency emerges interactionally and can be observed in vivo. This will be our focus in the rest of the chapter. Consider a first case from Italian. Sergio, Greta, and Dino are chatting in a kitchen while Sergio dyes Greta's hair. Just before the fragment begins,

Greta has asked Sergio to remove a "thingy" from her forehead, which he identifies as a wisp of hair (line 1). Sergio realizes that the hair has glued up because some dye has run down on Greta's forehead. This leads him to state that: "it is necessary also to wipe away the dye from the forehead."

Fragment 1	Tinta_ 2051380 (Italian)
1 Sergio	[questo- ((gets hold of wisp of hair)) **this-**
2 Greta	[(eh non lo so) c'ho un coso (PCL not 3S.A know-1S) EX=have-1S a thingy **(well dunno) I've got a thingy**
3 Sergio	scusa sì bisogna pu[lire:: anche la crema dalla fronte sorry yes necessitate-3S clean-INF also the cream from- the forehead **sorry yes it is necessary also to wipe away:: the dye from the forehead**
4 Dino	[((turns and reaches)) faccio io do.1S 1S.N **I'll do it**
5 Greta	[((reaches out for kitchen paper))

Sergio's statement presents wiping away the dye as the right thing to do for anyone in the current situation. Here, the action could be done by any of the three participants, including Sergio himself. He is the person who is most directly involved in the dyeing process, and who is responsible for having let the dye drip on Greta's forehead, for which he apologizes ("sorry"). While saying *bisogna* "it is necessary to," Sergio moves his hand in the direction of the table, possibly toward the kitchen paper, but then hesitates. At the same time, he gazes at Dino, and in so doing prompts him to get involved. Dino is arguably in a better position to wipe Greta's forehead, because Sergio's hands are stained with dye. Also, Dino has already assisted Sergio more than once earlier in the interaction. Here again, Dino volunteers his help ("I'll do it," line 4). But, as he reaches for the kitchen paper, Greta gets to it before him and goes on to wipe her own forehead.

In this case, two recipients of an impersonal deontic declarative find themselves "competing" for the animatorship of the necessary action. Although Dino makes an explicit bid for it ("I'll do it"), it is Greta who eventually takes it on without much explanation—after all, it is her own body.

The indeterminacy of animatorship left by an impersonal deontic declarative is shown even more clearly in cases where this becomes a matter of explicit negotiation. In fragment 2, from Polish, the family are beginning their lunch. After wishing everyone an enjoyable meal, Jacek (the father) moves to sit down, while Ilona (the mother) surveys the laid table (line 3). She then says something to get Jacek's attention ("eh you know what," line 4) and begins an impersonal deontic statement about the need of doing something with the juice.

Fragment 2   PP2-4 00:19 (Polish)

1   Ilona   smacznego
              tasty-G
              enjoy your meal

2   Jacek   smacznego ( )
              tasty-G
              enjoy your meal ( )

3   (1.2)/((Ilona touches gravy jug and napkin holder, then
                    raises left arm))

4   Ilona   y wiesz co kom[potu¿   (.)
              PCL know-2S what juice-G
              eh you know what, juice

5   [((reaches right arm across the table for the
                                juice jug))

6   Ilona   trzeba ((touches jug))
              necessitate
              it is necessary

7   Jacek   już [ja naleję]
              already 1S.N PF-pour-1S
              right now, I'll pour it

8   [((Ilona lifts the jug))]

9   Ilona   [wziąć] dob[rze
                      take-INF   good
                      to take   good

10   [((Ilona puts the jug down))

11	Jacek	[ty nalejesz¿ ja
		you PF-pour-2S 1S.N
		you'll pour it? I'll

12		na[leję
		PF-pour-1S
		pour it

13	Ilona	[to weź już to nalej
		then take-IMP already then PF-pour-IMP
		then go ahead already, pour then

14		(.)/((Jacek takes the jug))

15	Jacek	będzie mi wygodniej ((picks up jug))
		be.FUT-3S 1S.D convenient-CMPR
		it will be more convenient for me

16	Jacek	((pours juice into everyone's glasses))

As Ilona begins the statement ("juice . . . I"), she reaches across the table toward the juice jug, thus making a bid to take charge of the need she is in the process of formulating. As Ilona continues the statement (" . . . it is necessary . . . ") and her hand reaches the jug (line 6), Jacek begins responding by saying that he will do the necessary action "right now" (line 7). Immediately after this, while Ilona lifts the jug and completes the statement (" . . . to take"), Jacek continues his response by explicitly volunteering to pour the juice ("I'll pour it," line 7). Ilona then accepts the offer ("good," line 9) and puts the jug back down (line 10). Meanwhile, Jacek has started to retract ('you pour it?," line 11), but after Ilona's acceptance he repeats his offer ("I'll pour it," line 12), which is then ratified by Ilona (line 13). While proceeding to pour the juice, Jacek adds an explanation for why he is taking over the job from Ilona: "it will be more convenient for me" (line 15).

An impersonal deontic declarative doesn't constrain participation in the necessary action, but leaves it open to any relevant contributor. In fragment 2, the interaction initially favors a certain individual to take on the action (Ilona), but its subsequent development leads to a change of animatorship. When Ilona begins the statement, she is projectably engaged in pouring the juice. At the same time, however, the preface to her statement "you know what" (line 4) marks it as relevant for Jacek and calls for his attention to what is happening. This complex configuration leads to an explicit negotiation of who will pour the juice. The result is that the animatorship of the necessary action is eventually taken over by the participant who is best positioned to do it.

The last case to be discussed illustrates a reverse situation from the first two, one in which, instead of competing for the animatorship of the necessary action, people try to avoid becoming involved. Michele and Remo are looking for a utensil to pour tea into mugs. In line 1, Michele notices a soup ladle in the sink, immersed in a dirty pot ("well there is this one"). As Michele gets hold of the ladle and inspects it, Remo states that "it would be necessary to wash it."

Fragment 3   Camillo_1241239 (Italian)

1   Michele   cè ci sarebbe questo
              PCL EX be-CND-3S this
              well there is this one

2   (2.4)/((reaches towards soup ladle in the sink))

3   Michele   c'è un po' di pizzoccheri (nel recipiente) però ((grabs ladle))
              EX=be.3S a bit of NAME (in-the container) but
              there's some *pizzoccheri* (in the container) but

4   Remo   allora bisognerebbe lavarlo
              then necessitate-CND-3S wash-INF=3P.A
              then it would be necessary to wash it

5   (2.6)/((Michele shakes ladle and lifts it out of pot))

6   (0.5)/((Remo walks to kitchen door))

7   Michele   ma vuoi farlo tu ((turns to Remo))
              but want-2S do-INF=3S.A 2S.N
              do you want to do it?

8   (0.3)

9   Remo   come
              how
              sorry?

10   Michele   ( ) lavarlo (volevi lavarlo)
              wash-INF=3S.A (want-IPF-2S wash-INF=3S.A)
              ( ) wash- (you wanted to wash it)?

11   Remo   no no no ( ) perché stavo ( ) perché io ho un impegno
              no no no because stay-IPF-1S because 1S.N have-1S one commitment
              no no no ( ) because I was ( ) because I've got something to do

As in the two cases above, before the impersonal deontic statement is made, none of the participants is particularly responsible for the action in question. One element that may at first glance tilt the balance is that, at the time of the statement, Michele is holding the ladle (line 3), which puts him in a better position to go ahead and wash it. But note that this manipulation is motivated by his just-prior noticing and doesn't imply any commitment to wash it. Also, Remo is standing just beside Michele (up until line 6), with visibly nothing to do. This appears to warrant a negotiation of animatorship. In line 6, Remo walks away from the sink, making a bid to leave Michele in charge. Michele then attempts to devolve the washing to him ("do you want to do it?"), bringing into the open the matter of designating the agent. After giving a rather opaque excuse (line 11), Remo dodges becoming involved, and Michele is left to do the washing.

Negotiations of animatorship such as those we have examined in this chapter generally do not occur with forms that designate another person as the animator of an action (e.g. "pass the salt" or "can you move over a little?"). An impersonal deontic declarative, on the other hand, affords such negotiations by virtue of its grammatical design, which doesn't restrict animatorship to a single individual. Although there are a number of cases in which the responsibility for the action in question falls on a specific person (see Rossi and Zinken in press), impersonal deontic declaratives have the potential to generate complex interactions in which the identity of the animator must be sorted out. The three cases we have examined also illustrate the kinds of reasons at play in these interactions, including the presence of obstacles or concurrent commitments, the relative easiness of the action for different people, the rights over one's body.

The case of impersonal deontic statements demonstrates the importance of grammatical detail for social action. What may at first glance appear only subtle, differences of expression turn out to put constraints on what people can or should do in a given situation. Moreover, given the great diversity among languages, grammatical variation will be consequential also for social interaction across cultures. Studying grammar as a resource for social action, and in particular for the distribution of agency, is therefore a crucial piece of the science of human cooperation and sociality.

REFERENCES

Drew, Paul, and Elizabeth Couper-Kuhlen. 2014. "Requesting—From Speech Act to Recruitment." In *Requesting in Social Interaction, Studies in Language and Social Interaction*, edited by P. Drew and E. Couper-Kuhlen, 1–34. Amsterdam/Philadelphia: John Benjamins.

Floyd, Simeon, Giovanni Rossi, and N. J. Enfield, eds. Under review. *Getting Others to Do Things: A Pragmatic Typology of Recruitments*. Berlin: Language Science Press.

Goffman, Erving. 1981. *Forms of Talk*. Philadelphia: University of Pennsylvania Press.

Malchukov, Andrej Lvovich, and Anna Siewierska, eds. 2011. *Impersonal Constructions: A Cross-Linguistic Perspective*. Amsterdam/Philadelphia: John Benjamins.

Rossi, Giovanni. 2015. "The Request System in Italian Interaction." Ph.D. dissertation, Radboud University, Nijmegen, the Netherlands.

Rossi, Giovanni and Jörg Zinken. 2016. "Grammar and Social Agency: The Pragmatics of Impersonal Deontic Statements." *Language* 92(4).

Vinkhuyzen, Erik, and Margaret H. Szymanski. 2005. "Would You Like to Do It Yourself? Service Requests and Their Non-Granting Responses." In *Applying Conversation Analysis*, edited by K. Richards and P. Seedhouse, 91–106. New York: Palgrave Macmillan.

CHAPTER 10

Distributed Agency and Action under the Radar of Accountability

JACK SIDNELL

Communicative, purposive social action is semiotic and involves one person getting another to recognize her intention.[1] As Sidnell and Enfield (2014) write, "A social action's effect is an interpretant of someone's sign, not a mere effect of someone's cause. Social actions only bring about effects by virtue of someone recognizing what is intended, and reacting appropriately." Along these lines, conversation analysts have shown that much of what gets done in interaction is accomplished by the use of "practices of speaking," which, when deployed in some specific sequential context, are recognizable as implementing a particular action. So when, for instance, in the course of a telephone call, Janet says, speaking of her daughter who is at Ann's house, "Do you want me to come and get her?" this is understood, by Ann, to implement an offer rather than as merely asking about her wants and so on. In this [[practice of speaking in context] -> [recognizable action] -> [interactional goal]] scenario, speakers are understood as *accountable* for having done whatever action is so effected. This accountability is realized in various ways. In perhaps the most basic case, a next speaker produces a turn that treats the previous speaker as having done the action for which this turn is an appropriately fitted response (e.g., next speaker produces an acceptance to an "offer," or an answer to a "question"). So for instance in the example mentioned, Ann eventually accepts Janet's offer. Alternatively, a next speaker may name the action he or she understands the first speaker to have done, saying, for instance, "thank you for offering" and so on.[2]

So by making it recognizable to a recipient what action(s) one intends to accomplish, a speaker thereby necessarily becomes accountable for having done that action. But are there ways to achieve some interactional goal without having to do the action that would lead to that outcome by virtue of a recipient's recognition? Relatedly, is there a way to achieve an interactional goal without, in the process, becoming accountable as the agent who effected it? In what follows I will describe three kinds of cases that suggest an affirmative answer to these questions—there are indeed methods by which a participant in interaction can accomplish interactional goals while flying beneath the radar of accountability.[3]

GETTING A CALLER'S NAME BY GIVING ONE'S OWN

First, let us consider a case, described by Sacks (1995), in which institutional call-takers want to get a caller's name. Sacks noted that in calls to a suicide prevention hotline requests for the caller's name were often met with suspicious resistance and questions such as "Why do you need to know?" In order to avoid this eventuality, call-takers would routinely adopt a different strategy, introducing themselves as, for example, "Mr. Smith" and thereby eliciting reciprocal name identifications without going on record as having asked for this information.

Sacks noticed, then, that there was a "fittedness" relation between the two parts of an adjacency pair, so that if the first person says "Hello," then so does the second; if the first person says "This is Mr. Smith," then the second tends to say "This is Mr. Brown," and so on. If there is a tendency to fit the form of the return to the form of the initiating action in any of these greeting ("hello") or introduction ("This is Mr. Smith") pairs, then there exists a way of getting someone's name without asking for it. Rather than asking "What is your name?" one can say "This is Mr. Smith," and this will establish the relevance of the other giving his or her name.

Sacks goes on to note that if the staff member asks "Would you give me your name?" the caller can reply "Why?" or "What for?" That is, the caller can ask the staff member to provide a reason or account for asking for the name. Sacks (1995: 4) notes that "what one does with 'Why?' is to propose about some action that it is an 'accountable action'. That is to say, 'Why?' is a way of asking for an account." Sacks goes on to suggest that accounts "control activities." The important point here is that "This is Mr. Smith, may I help you?" may be a way of getting the other person to provide her name, but it is not an accountable action in that respect; one cannot say in response "Why do you want my name?" because the name was never asked for.

FISHING FOR INFORMATION BY TELLING "MY SIDE"

A second example is provided by what Pomerantz (1980, following Sacks 1995) described as a "my-side telling" in which one participant merely tells of her limited access to some state of affairs thereby eliciting information about it again without having to ask explicitly. So in the following well-known case, all Emma has to do is report "Yer line's been busy," and thereby convey her "limited access" to some state of affairs that the recipient knows about. This prompts Nancy to provide information about how it was that her phone was busy, who she was talking to, and why she was talking for such an extended period.

(1) NB:II:2:R

```
01  Nancy:     Hel-lo:,
02  Emma:      .hh HI::.
03             (.)
04  Nancy:     Oh:.'I::: 'ow a:re you Emmah:
05  Emma:      FI:NE yer LINE'S BEEN BUSY.
06  Nancy:     Yea:h (.) my u.-fuhh h-.hhhh my fa:ther's wife ca:lled me,h
07             .hhh So when she ca:lls me::,h .hh I always talk fer a lo:ng
08             ti:me cz she c'n afford it'n I ca:n't.hhh[hhh]°huh°]
09  Emma:                                              [OH:] :::::]:=
10             =my [go:sh ah th ]aht my phone wz outta order:
11  Nancy:         [--Ah ::::::, ]
```

Emma is able to elicit information without having to ask for it and thus without having to do something that might be characterizable as "nosey" and so on. Where the telling of limited access does not elicit the information wanted, a participant may follow up with an on-record, explicit question, as in the following case:

(2)   Geri-Shirley

01   Geri: Oka:y d'dju just hear me pull up?=
02   Shirley: =.hhhh -NO:. I wz -TRYing you all day.'n the LINE wz busy
03   fer like hours.
04   Geri: Ohh:::::::, ohh:::::. .hhhhhh We::ll, hhh ah'm g'nna c'm
05   over 'n a li'l while help yer brother ou:t,
06   Shirley: Goo[:d.
07   Geri: [.hh Cz I know he needs some he::lp, ((mournfully))
08   Shirley: .khh Ye:ah. Yeh he'd mention' that t'day.=
09   Geri: =M-hm,=
10   Shirley: =.hhh Uh:m, .tch.hhhh Who w'yih -ta:lking to:
11   (0.6)
12   Geri: Jis no:w?
13   Shirley: .hhhh No I called be-like between ele[ven en
14   Geri: [I: wasn'talkeen tuh
15   a:nybuddy. (b) Bo-oth Marla'n I slept 'ntil about noo:n,=
16   Shirley: =O[h.
17   Geri: [.hhhh en w'n I woke up, I wannid tih call my mother.
18   Shirley: Mm-[hm,
19   Geri: [.hhhh en I picked up the pho:ne, e:n I couldn't dial
20   out.'n[I thought ar phone wz out'v order.['n I- .hhh
21   Shirley: [Oh: (   ),   [Yeh,
22   Geri: said w'l oyll I: bet I know w't happened,=
23   =[(so) I walked-]
24   Shirley: =[Marla left th']phone o[ff the hook,]=

Here, when Shirley's initial conveyance of limited access does not elicit information about Geri's use of the phone, she eventually formulates a direct inquiry, asking, at line 10, "Who w'yih -ta:lking to:." Sticking with examples in which one participant reports trouble in reaching or finding another, we can see that not only is this utterly pervasive, it is also quite tightly structured. And so when, in example (3), Penny reports, "I triedju all morning long'n it wz really busy," prompting Pat's "Yeh I wz sleeping my mother wz answering," Penny then goes on to elaborate her "side."

(3)   Houseburning

```
01   Penny:      =.hh I said tih myself I triedju all morning long'n it
02               wz really busy. .hhhh[hhh]=
03   Pat:                     [Yea][h,
04   Penny:                        [=en: : :[d,
05   Pat:                                   [Yeh I wz sleeping my
06               mother wz answering, hh[hh
07   Penny:                            [.hh So- Uhri:ght.
08               Then, right, that's good.That's good. .hh
09               But so I've been trying all along en I thought maybe thet
10               chih took the phone off the hook.
```

My-side tellings serve as a technique for eliciting information without having to ask a direct (indeed, any) question. Given that actions are accountable, a person asking a question should be entitled to ask it and moreover
have a good reason for doing so. Responses to questions that take such
forms as "why do you want to know?," "why do you ask?," or even "it's none
of your business" hint at this accountability of actions as do reports about
a person being a "gossip," "nosey parker," "busy-body," and so on. With
this is mind we can see how the practice Pomerantz describes might have
important interactional uses since with it a person may elicit information
about some specific state of affairs without being accountable for having
asked a question.

ELICITING AN OFFER BY DESCRIBING A TROUBLE

Finally, we can see a similar kind of pattern across quite different examples
in which rather than make a request, a speaker merely describes a trouble, thereby inviting the other to offer what is wanted (see, for discussion,
Pomerantz and Heritage 2012). Routinely, description of a trouble leads
the recipient to offer a remedy, but again, if the offer is not made or is not
sufficient, the speaker can then "go on record" and make the request, as in
the following case in which a landlady initially establishes the presence of
a laundry machine in her basement apartment before going on to report
the problem of having "no water" to the tenant. When the tenant offers a
solution that would merely fix the immediate problem, Alice ends up going
on record with the request saying, "Well I don't want you to shut it off mid-
load, just don't run it anymore."

(4) YYZ-Shawn & Alice

```
01  Alice:    [˙hh Do you guys have a washer en dry:er er somethi:ng?
02            (0.6)
03  Shawn:    ah::=yeah,
04            we got a little washer down here. (.) °goin°.
05  Alice:    ↓oh::.
06            ok. [I didn']- I didn't know thet you guys ha:d tha:t
07  Shawn:        [water]
08            (0.4)
09  Shawn:    kay=
10  Alice:    =an u::m and I've got no water in my house. now.
11  Alice:    I-see-I  [jus]
12  Shawn:             [ ok]
13  Alice:    I don't have a big enough water heater for that.
14            [˙hh]
15  Shawn:    [ ok]
16  Alice:    in the house o(h)k(hh)?,
17            (0.4)
18  Shawn:    °noproblem.°=
19  Alice:    [=than-]                            [Tha:nks]
20  Shawn:    [=I' ll] ge Carrie to shut it off [°(som e] water)°
21            (.)
22  Alice:    well, I mean, don't-I don't want you to shut it off mid-load
23            bu:t (.) just don't run it anymore
24            (0.1)
25            after this one.
26  Shawn:    (.) °Ari:ght°
27  Alice:    Ok thanks
28  Shawn:    mbye
29  Alice:    Bye.
```

And in the following well-known case, Donny sets up his telling of a trouble with the pre-announcement "Guess what" in line 6. The problem is then described in incremental fashion (lines 8 and 10), but this does not elicit more of a response than the information receipt in line 11. At line 15 Donny seems to be on the way to formulating a request but leaves this unfinished in order to continue with the telling of the trouble. It is at this point that Marcia interjects, indicating that she has understood what Donny wants and that, if possible, she would comply.

(5)   Donnie & Marcia

```
01   Marcia:   Hello?
02   Donny:    'lo Marcia,=
03   Marcia:   Yea[:h
04   Donny:        [=('t's) Donny.
05   Marcia:   Hi Donny.
06   Donny:    Guess what.hh
07   Marcia:   What.
08   Donny:    °hh My ca:r is sta::lled.
09             (0.2)
10             ('n) I'm up here in the Glen>
11   Marcia:   Oh::.
12             [(0.4)]
13   Donny:    [°hhh] a:nd.hh
14             (0.2)
15             I don't know if it's possible, but [°hhh] see
16             I haveta open up the ba:nk.hh
17             (0.3)
18             a:t uh: (.) Brentwood?hh=
19   Marcia:   =Yeah: en I know you want- (.) en I
20             would, but- except I've gotta in aybout five
21             min(h)utes[(hheh)
22   Donny:              [Okay then I gotta call somebody
23             else.right away.
24             (.)
25   Donny:    Okay?=
26             =Okay  [Don    ]
27   Donny:           [Thanks] a lot.=Bye-.
28   Marcia:   Bye:.
```

And finally, in example (6) Ann is talking to Janet, whose daughter is at Ann's house for a visit. Here, all Ann has to do is remark that she is "running a bit late" to elicit from Janet the offer to "come and get her."

(6) xtr. 1

```
01  Ann:      =Hello::
02  Janet:    Oh=hi:_=it's Janet_  [Shelby's mo]m
03  Ann:                          [hi:    Janet]
04            How eryou(h) .h hh
05  Janet:    I'm goo:d,how are y [ou
06  Ann:                         [I'm fi:ne.h[we're actually: uhm
07  Janet:                                    [°good°
08            (0.2)
09  Ann:      we're running bit late=but we're
10            (.)
11            on our wa(h)y:
12  Janet:    Do you want me to come an' get her?
13  Ann:      Uhm:, it doesn't matte:r, like(hh)
14            (0.4)
15            .hhhhh
16  Janet:    I- I could.it's very easy.
17            so rather than you h:av(h)e(h)
18            (.)
19            you know (.) tuh get everybody ou[t
20                                             [.hhh
21            I'll justa
22            (0.2)
23            come dow:n.=
```

Across these examples then we see that the telling of a trouble or even the mere hint of one (as in the last example) can prompt from the recipient an offer of assistance or at least an account for not producing such an offer.

CONCLUSION

Examples such as these show us then that participants are acutely aware of the accountability that attaches to the actions they are recognized as doing and, in certain circumstances at least, seek to avoid that accountability by achieving their interactional goals by alternate means. Across all the cases discussed here there seems to be an interactional short-circuit whereby speakers are able to bypass the action/recognition node of the [practice] -> [action/recognition] -> [interactional goal] chain such that they are able to recruit the agency of another without being accountable for having done so. Recruited others provide their own names, provide information, or provide offers of assistance and thereby commit themselves as agents to some joint venture.

I have suggested that much of what gets done in interaction is accomplished by the use of practices of speaking that, when deployed in some specific sequential context, are recognized as implementing a particular action. So when Janet says, "Do you want me to come and get her?" this is understood to implement an offer rather than as merely asking about what Anne wants or desires. When speakers implement actions in this way, using practices that are designed to be recognizably implementing them, they "go on record" and are thus accountable for having done the action in question. Recipients, or nonrecipient participants, can thus ask why this action is being done ("why do you ask?," "why do you say that?," "why do you want to know?," etc.), or they can report that the action has been done ("she asked if I was going," "she complained that it was too hot," etc.). Obviously, formulations of prior actions can be challenged or contested (see Sidnell and Enfield 2014) but that does not change the underlying fact that participants become accountable for the actions that they are recognized as having done. Now of course there are various circumstances in which a participant might want to "fly under the radar of accountability"—that is, achieve some interactional outcome or goal without doing the action that would effect this and thus without being accountable for having done it. In this chapter I have briefly considered some cases in which we see how participants are able to do this.

ACKNOWLEDGMENT

I am indebted to Paul Kockelman for very helpful comments on a previous version of this chapter.

NOTES

1. By "communicative" I mean to distinguish what I am talking about here from various kinds of purposive social action that do not depend on intention recognition (e.g., Weber's woodcutter [1978:8–9]). By "purposive" I mean to distinguish what I am talking about from various kinds of communicative (typically, indexical) "effects" that are a consequence of acting (for more discussion of this distinction see Sidnell and Enfield 2014).
2. And there are many other ways in which the accountability may be made manifest. A report may be made about what happened for instance ("She

offered me ... ," "She asked if I wanted her to do it ... , " and so on). This sense of accountability is more expansive than one that emphasizes sanctions (e.g., Radcliffe-Brown 1954). Rather, on this view, an accountable action is one that can be the object of inquiry—"Why did you do that?" (see Sacks 1995) and that can be the subject of report (see Garfinkel [1967:1], "When I speak of accountable ... I mean observable-and-reportable, *i.e.* available to members as situated practices of looking-and-telling").

3. Some of the issues I develop here were originally raised by Pomerantz (1980) and, of course, by Sacks (1995). Rosenblum's (1987) discussion of "When is a question an accusation?" also bears on many of these issues although she does not herself thematize them.

REFERENCES

Garfinkel, H. 1967. *Studies in Ethnomethodology.* Englewood Cliffs, NJ: Prentice-Hall.

Pomerantz, A. M. 1980. "Telling My Side: 'Limited Access' as a 'Fishing Device.'" *Sociological Inquiry* 50: 186–198.

Pomerantz. A. M., and J. Heritage. 2012. "Preference." In *The Handbook of Conversation Analysis,* ed. J. Sidnell and T. Stivers, 210–228. Oxford, UK: Wiley-Blackwell.

Radcliffe-Brown, Alfred R. 1954. "Social Sanctions." In *Structure and Function in Primitive Society,* 205–211. New York: Free Press.

Rosenblum, K. 1987. "When Is a Question an Accusation?" *Semiotica* 65(1–2): 143–156.

Sacks, H. 1995. *Lectures on Conversation.* 2 vols. Edited by Gail Jefferson. Oxford: Blackwell.

Sidnell, J., and N. J. Enfield. 2014. "The Ontology of Action in Interaction." In *The Cambridge Handbook of Linguistic Anthropology,* 423–446. Cambridge: Cambridge University Press.

Weber, M. 1978. *Economy and Society: An Outline of Interpretive Sociology.* Berkeley/Los Angeles: University of California Press.

PART FOUR

Economy and Agency

CHAPTER 11

Distributed Agency and Debt in the Durational Ethics of Responsibility

JANE I. GUYER

INTRODUCTION: MODERN TIME

Walter Benjamin's concept of "modern time" as "homogeneous" and "empty" (Benjamin 1968:261) depicts the creation of time as a continuous variable, which can then open up to marking and coordination in terms of chosen punctuations and the dated time of a universal calendar (Guyer 2007). It provides the template for the temporal framing of contracts, which can then enter into formal model-building and projections, especially for formalizations that can be measured and calculated as rates: of interest, of depletion/erosion, of growth, and so on. The actual temporal durations relevant to a particular instance can then be inserted. Calculation and projection are fundamental to the intricate synchronization of a mechanically and bureaucratically mediated society and economy. What anthropologist Marc Augé (1995) calls the "non-places" of supermodernity, such as airports, would screech to a halt without modeled projections of temporal coordination for a vast variety of material variables, that also marshal people, seen as solitary, homogeneous individuals, into temporary crowds.

In social sciences such as economics, where quantification and projection are fundamental, the temporal variable can be conceptualized initially in terms of abstract time, which then renders it open to eventual marking, for particular purposes, in terms of specifically chosen punctuations (Guyer 2007). An abstract model depicts the punctuations in terms of a sequential series: time 1, time 2, time 3, and so on (written as T1, T2, T3 . . .). The simplest example for our purposes here would be the conclusion of a financial commitment (at T2), under conditions of compound interest, where the temporal space between T1 and T2 is then inserted to calculate the principal-plus-interest by the termination date. So two years, or five years, or any other temporal range is inserted into the abstract model for situational prediction for particular cases, and for their combination into systemic prediction. Some possible contingent interventions may also be turned into calculable probabilities and fed into the model. In some contracts, for example, there are stated conditions for inflation adjustment, if the currency value changes between T1 and T2. Or certain substantive possibilities can be made explicit. For example, kinship is central to the devolution of responsibility in case of the death of a party to a contract between T1 and T2. All these models, however, are aimed at exact calculability and predictability, through the assumption of abstract time, which then makes them amenable to combination into the regimes that are fundamental to "modernity." Large numbers of temporal commitments can be brought into tight consonance with each other when a debt that is incurred now, at T1, is to be repaid at a defined interest rate, at a defined T2, since this creates the conditions of the contract and the predictability of the encompassing regime. The individual is responsible only in the moments of the contract enactment: T1 and T2. The interim is left to his or her own management.

All possible contingencies, however, may not necessarily be calculable or legally definable with respect to all parties, all commitments, and all time frames. The "till death do us part" of the traditional marriage vows invokes two moments in a lifelong commitment, but time 2 is not predictable, nor is the temporal duration amenable to modeling the contract, and nor are these contingencies happening in "empty, homogenous" time. They can simply emerge from dynamics for which "modern," "empty, homogeneous" time hardly corresponds to the experiential time of relationships and of life. And yet people do still make such commitments, mediate such contingencies, and increasingly find that debt management—incurred in "modern time"—is deeply interwoven into the durational ethics of life (Guyer 2014). With respect to modernity, Augé has argued that the "anthropological"—that is, human and social—qualities of memory, relationship, and identity, which are grounded in "places," do remain. The question is then, in what form, with what implications, and for whom? "Modernity does not obliterate them but pushes them into the background": they "survive like the words that express them," "intertwined and tangled" together (Augé

1995: 77, 107). Of the awkward incompatibilities that can arise from such entanglement, the most obvious is between the homogeneous empty time of modernity, and the temporal micro-rhythms and indeterminacies of life in biological and social mode. People gain and lose employment and income, fall ill, age, organize and disorganize their social relationships, and live with sudden shifts in general conditions (war, disease, disaster, windfalls). And they may come together in existentially challenging ways. None of them—alone or in combination—can easily be calculated as "risk" and entered into debt contracts as such. It is in life, rather than debt law, that causation, intention, assessment, responsibility, blame, the source of ongoing momentum and the implications of failure to sustain it, work out. Whereas in life, they all refer, in ways that vary with philosophical principles, to a supple grid of ongoing interactions in textured time, to which people commit themselves, without knowing what contingencies may arise in life, and intersect with each other, in barely manageable ways. The attempt to recalculate, and to live, these as calculable probabilities may remain intractable to the abstract model, either by authorities, by experts, or by people themselves. In many philosophies of life, it is ritual, of both collective and intimate kinds, that mediates such temporalities and may well distribute agency within the life processes between the abstract T1 and T2 of modern time.

The recent expansion of debt regimes, framed in empty homogeneous time, meets these philosophies and exigencies in zones of tension. Debt management is at least 5,000 years old, according to Graeber (2011), and is fundamental to the financial regimes of present-day capitalism. It can therefore serve as an example of the modern effort to make the world of T1 and T2, and the intractable human realities and philosophical legacies, consonant with each other in an ever-expanding range of debt relationships. For example, under American law, personal bankruptcy can be declared, subject to the person's submission to a "reorganization plan" mediated by experts (United States Code, Chapter 13, Title 11). Such a law defines agency and responsibility in exact, individuated, modeled terms; the concept of "default" puts the individual at "fault," even if life became contingently intractable for them. My chapter suggests that this is one deeply consequential aspect of the individuation of modernity proposed by Max Weber in *The Protestant Ethic and the Spirit of Capitalism*: an important, although under-examined, entailment of the entrepreneurial proposition that Weber developed most strongly. Within debt practices, the older, intuitive, and culturally varied traditions of distributed agency face those of the present formalized world.

The social historical and anthropological records show that all temporal regimes are comprised of multiple durations of varying length, running concurrently. Most obviously, there are diurnal, lunar, seasonal/annual, and life cycles, nested within each other, with key moments of convergence, whose ritual marking is often managed and celebrated in complex calendrics that presume that people's trajectories intersect, and often apprehend and anticipate the possibility—day to day, or eventually at the end of time—intervention by non–human beings, whether spiritual entities or an all-present God. Probably only a fundamentalist faith in sovereignty of some kind—either "everything happens for a (divine) reason," or "the individual is master of his fate"—could remove all cultural and political framing of T1 and T2. Prospective imagination, in both cases, may invoke fate: "what will be, will be," and individuated responsibility. The passage of time itself, then, is so imbued with propositions of agency that its study can show the full range of the beings that are accorded, or deprived of, agency, and their mutuality of accompaniment, interruption, support. and failure.

The anthropological study of how T1 and T2 are mutually entailed is implicit in the ethnography of moments of convergence, such as the ritualized performances of the life cycle through which a person, him/herself, is transformed. Certain entailments of personhood in a past stage of life are abrogated, and new capacities are crafted into the enactment of social and ethical life for the next phase. In western law, by contrast, a person is defined as a child, a juvenile, or an adult on abstract calendrical time rather than social and biological time. For the ethnographic examination of agency, we first establish the parameters for personhood, and then turn to their implications for the T1/T2 mutual entailments among people. General ethical precepts may be explicitly evoked to make things work and to sanction people's failures, but for us to examine the distributed agency question closely, full immersion in the temporal process itself is required, with respect to what I have termed "durational ethics" (Guyer 2014). Commitment. Promise. Responsibility. Perseverance, that is, Fortitude, in classic Christian thought. Fortitude is one of the four cardinal virtues, alongside Prudence, Justice, and Temperance, without which these other three are impossible to realize.

By requiring a person to take on durational ethics, he/she creates an entailment between the T1 in which he or she is now living and the T2 when the agency will be fulfilled. A promise usually refers only to the two moments that are explicitly named, whereas a commitment or responsibility may be in play all the time, *between* any two moments. Parental responsibility for a child's safety is continual, not intermittent. In popular practice, both necessarily assume processes that continue alongside, and contribute to, realization: the durational cycles of life, the knowledge that others have taken on comparable commitments, under known material circumstances, and that the gods are still in the heavens. I may be accountable individually, but the place of others in "aiding and abetting," or "confounding" is always in the picture, in ways that vary by culture and philosophy. In a sense, distributed agency is the common-sense philosophy of most, if not all, durational ethics. That I can repay my debts depends on you fulfilling your promises to me, which you may neglect due to moral lapse or you may simply be unable, due to illness or other unforeseen demands. Do I make generous allowances for your difficulties? Do I explain them to my own creditor? Where does the responsibility rest: on those who seek for a narrow definition of contractual justice, or on those whose behavior most affects social harmony at large? By being aware of philosophies of distributed agency with respect to the temporality of debts, we may then focus on the history of the modern measures to *shear off* popular legacies of distributed agency, in order to produce a sparse definition and legal precision: individuals make choices, in neutral time, for which they are solely responsible.

DEBT AS RELATIONSHIP AND REGIME

The topic in which philosophies of agency with respect to temporality and agency, and to historical changes in such philosophies, can be most readily studied anthropologically in the present, and with the clearest implications for durational ethical and political regimes, is the topic of debt. A debt is an explicitly defined promise to repay something given, usually in a defined form and amount, at a defined date. In some systems, the initial giving gesture of extending credit is accorded a positive moral aura, whereas being in debt implies actual or potential culpability (Peebles 2010). The vast expansion of personal and national sovereign debt in the world economy of the past 30 years has created a system of mutual implication of debts among themselves that is often referred to as a debt regime, which then puts monetary debt and its moral underpinnings onto the intellectual radar screen for many disciplines. Lazzarato (2012) succinctly reviews large-scale political and philosophical approaches to debt, arguing that the agency question is an ideological one. The proposition that "the temporality of debt [is presented as one of] possibility, choice and decision" (2012:44) invokes completely individuated capacities, in modern time. As a regime, as distinct from a particular dyadic transaction, debt capacitates powerful centers of control, precisely because agency in neutral time frames makes initial conditions, and matters arising in the interim between T1 and T2, irrelevant to the implementation of the terms through which the debts, rather than the persons, are brought into substantive and temporal consonance. The individual debtor's agency is here shorn of the changing conditions that would otherwise distribute accountability across multiple intersecting durations and participants, accidents and life contingencies.

The new anthropological work on debt can be approached through two texts that work in ways that are classic to the discipline. David Graeber (2011) takes on the vast sweep of world social history over 5,000 years, largely from the vast library of documentary sources (with hundreds of footnotes and 37 pages of references). Clara Han (2012) studies a particular neighborhood of very poor people in Santiago, Chile, through classic ethnographic methods attending in detail to particularity, sometime after the fall of a dictatorship, so in the context of rapid change.

Graeber starts with the idea of "moral confusion" over debt. In theory a debt is always an obligation to repay. In practice, failure to pay, in the original terms and time frames, has been increasingly protected by state power, bankruptcy laws, and other instruments, which work highly selectively. Amato and Fantacci (2011) have made the same argument about the capacity of states and large corporations to delay repayment, repeatedly. The enactment of debt regimes at this macro level, they suggest, is engaged in T1 (including under duress) and then imbued with differential power in T2 when it comes to repayment. The preservation of any distributed concept of agency in the passage of time is then differentially distributed, in fact if not in explicit theory. The powerful can have recourse to the mitigating circumstances of sheer scale at T2, under the rubric of "too big to fail" and all the complex fallout that is projected if they would end up in failure. The powerless, by contrast—as we see later—have to submit to the debt regimen of debt regimes that impose a modernist temporal model. Both of these works, by both Graeber and by Amato and Fantacci, about the macro level of debt, point out the centrality of payment for war in the creation and validation of the commitments of the creditor (the taxpayer and financier in this case), while leaving the repayment by the state in non-monetary terms: eventual peace (a general reward), and favor in the postwar economy (specific benefits). In such a macro context, the small individuals may become "delinquent" on debt repayment in ways that would otherwise be wholly understandable in intimate contexts: they lost a job, someone died and they had to make up the gap somehow, the economy tanked, and so on. But they will be subject to a bankruptcy law that recuperates much of their assets and submits it to compulsory legal disciplines. Graeber's argument thus rests on the historical evidence for monetary debt having been the creation of states, along with markets and other monetary institutions. Meanwhile he notes (2011:116) the ongoing difficulty of people combining what they understand as sharing, implicitly in the distributed agency mode of their own long-term philosophies of life, with legally defined exchange relations predicated on debt and repayment, over precise time frames defined by the powerful.

Graeber's book ends with allusion to the biblical institution of the Jubilee, which is completely at variance with the modern-time debt regime. On a strict cycle of seven times seven years, all debts would be cancelled and all slaves freed. And social life would start over, rather than allowing indebtedness to become cumulative and to turn into a regime of ongoing life. In all the Abrahamic religions, the framing of lending on interest, which necessarily enlarges the amount to be repaid at T2, was morally prohibited among members of the same religious community (Leviticus 25:37), and failure to repay was not attributed to the singular agency of the borrower. The lender is not to press the borrower for repayment if the lender knows that the borrower does not have it (Exodus 22:24). There are 16 such framings for lending and borrowing among the classic mitzvot of Judaism, including the injunction to lend to the poor and the destitute (presumably beyond what is possible to supply through charity). The history and practice of "usury" is a long and vast one, but includes the implicit assumption of distributed agency, in the sense that a debtor may not be entirely responsible for his or her situation. The harvest failed; there was cattle disease; a woman became a widow. The conversion of time into a possible monetary valuation was achieved by the School of Salamanca in the late Middle Ages, and subsequently built on to create the mathematized debt projections underlying the current debt regime. In his final paragraph, Graeber takes in the import of this history and comparative anthropology, to return us from the sophisticated intricacy of modern debt regimes, created, he argues, through "math and violence," to the "promise," as a commitment, implicitly in the multiple temporal frames of life of socially and culturally based philosophies of distributed agency.

Clara Han's book *Life in Debt: Times of Care and Violence in Neoliberal Chile* (2012) takes up anthropology's other classic method, participant observation within particular times, places, and communities. Following the end of the Pinochet regime (1974–1990), the new government is embracing both a philosophy of moral indebtedness to the population for resilience and resistance, and promoting a neoliberal policy that introduces new modes of individuated credit and debt into the same people's ordinary lives. Han's closest focus is on the process of living in this debt regime. In nuanced and particular accounts, she shows how the temporality of debt increasingly fails to inter-digitate smoothly with the other temporalities of life. Indeed, its shaping power at T1, and its insistent threat of inflexibility at T2, actively disorganize relationships that unfold on another durational ethic. "The self is simultaneously enmeshed in different relations that entail different demands and desires" (Han 2012:20). "Monthly debt payments took up half of Rodrigo's income" (36), and bus fare to his job took up one-third of his income (38). And "this 'made time' rubbed against the temporality of monthly debt payments and the uncertainty of unstable wages that impinged on the home" (38). Regular commitments to children became disrupted: "You need to buy gifts for children" (49); the children don't understand debt. In our own terms here, this would imply that accountability for failure could be attributed by children to their parents, even when adults would see the fault elsewhere. Clearly the conditions of an inflexible debt version of T1 and T2 are incompatible with the temporalities of commitment in the current economy and in other domains of durational ethics, as understood by other participants in the nexus. The mutual implication of intimate lives is a key theme of this ethnography of debt in a world where different parties, different dimensions of life, different projections of what counts as T1 and T2, are examined in detail.

These two works show clearly how the specific distribution of agency is defined and shaped by different parties, living different temporalities and different durational ethics, in relation to regimes of "modern time." Both call attention to temporal phenomena as the ground on which agency and responsibility are built. As Augé argued for places, so also for temporalities: "Modernity does not obliterate them but pushes them into the background": they "survive like the words that express them" (1995:77), "intertwine[d] and tangle[d]" together (1995:107). With respect to debt regimes, the word "tangled" can be literally true rather than a metaphor: debts that are modeled in modernist time tie them in knots when it comes to living with their own conditions and the durational ethics of distributed agency and responsibility.

REFERENCES

Amato, Massimo, and Luca Fantacci. 2011. *The End of Finance*. Cambridge, UK: Polity Press.

Augé, Marc. 1995. *Non-Places: Introduction to an Anthropology of Supermodernity*. London: Verso.

Benjamin, Walter. 1968. *Illuminations*. New York: Schocken Books.

Graeber, David. 2011. *Debt: The First 5,000 Years*. Brooklyn, NY: Melville House.

Guyer, Jane I. 2007. "Prophecy and the Near Future: Thoughts on Macroeconomic, Evangelical and Punctuated Time." *American Ethnologist* 34(3): 409–421.

Guyer, Jane I. 2014. "Durational Ethics: Search, Finding, and Translation of Fauconnet's 'Essay on Responsibility and Liberty.'" *HAU: Journal of Ethnographic Theory* 4(1): 397–340.

Han, Clara. 2012. *Life in Debt: Times of Care and Violence in Neoliberal Chile*. Berkeley: University of California Press.

Lazzarato, Maurizio. 2012. *The Making of the Indebted Man: An Essay on the Neo-liberal Condition*. Amsterdam: Semiotext(e).

Peebles, Gustav. 2010. "The Anthropology of Credit and Debt." *Annual Review of Anthropology* 39: 225–240.

CHAPTER 12

Money as Token and Money as Record in Distributed Accounts

BILL MAURER

Money has always had agency, or, rather, has been an expression of agency, or even is agency itself, or . . . well, this is precisely the problem of money.

People have certainly imagined money objects to possess agency. Who among us has not thrown a coin into a fountain or picked one up imagining it would bring us luck, would change our destiny? Eighteenth-century English tracts on money, somewhere between didactic pamphlets and the early serialized novel, imbued both notes and coins with the ability to witness the affairs of humans around them, and to remark on questions of morality and social order as they were passed from hand to hand—unless, unfortunates, they ended up in someone's safe, or misplaced somewhere. Saved or lost money lost its powers of action and narration. Money in circulation, even counterfeit, chronicled the world of men and women, boys and girls, from every station of life and every corner of the world. And seemed to enjoy doing so, too.

In telling their tales, these coins and notes reflected upon the economies of which they were a part and which they were creating in their travels. They served as a distributed, collective memory bank, to use Keith Hart's (2000) phrase, each note or coin testifying to its transit during human exchange and, in the process, forming a collectivity having the potential to record all of human intercourse—or at least those aspects of it in which money was quite literally brought to bear. Money was not inert but nor was it completely fluid. It occupied a Goldilocks spot: just malleable enough to be impressed with others' stories, but not so malleable as to melt away. In that respect, the memory bank made by these money tokens imagined in these stories was not unlike the digital transaction records of contemporary means of payment, from credit cards to PayPal or Bitcoin, electronic means of recording transactions and human interrelation. They also bear a family resemblance to the databases inscribed on clay tablets in the ancient Sumerian temples and storehouses.

Like today, money in these narratives was brought to bear pretty much everywhere. There was no escaping it. Almost every interaction involved it. Money objects' distributed agency recorded the stories of humanity, mapping relations in time, space, and value, and memorializing—again, often for pedagogical purposes—the distributed action of humans, hapless or otherwise.

What do these stories teach us today? What do they teach us as our monetary relationships increasingly become an object of business concern—when Apple or Google wants to create and manage the record of all of our interchange, to create a new hoard of our interpersonal transactional data?

Insofar as they remain didactic for contemporary readers, it may be that these money narratives point up the fallacy that money is ever a mere token, just a thing that represents something else or else is valuable somehow in itself. It is about time we dispensed with this idea. The stuff of money is a lot of fun, and does indeed matter, as will become clear. But the stuff of money has also distracted monetary theorists and "money nutters" (Maurer 2011) alike: both those who would seek to understand money and those who would seek to solve any number of social, environmental, or political problems by making money anew err in their attention to its things absent its relations in time and space, the relations of debt and credit that the token helps mark. Commodity money theorists, sound money proponents, or survivalists preparing for the end of the world see a money object essentially the same way as in the tales of its origination in primitive barter (Graeber 2011). Money's qualities—rarity, portability, malleability, divisibility—and its qualities in themselves, not any agencies they might possess, are for such people what makes it an object of universal value.

Money's matter matters in a different way, however.

When people write IOUs, relations of credibility extend outward from person and paper, and can move across time and space often toward unplanned or unexpected ends, outside whatever original intention may have first animated them. When states issue currencies, they leverage their own credibility in a financial and moral sense, but then let money go to do what it will, whatever people will do with it, from underground to dark economies, to adornment and decoration and magic tricks. Private or public credit, money is regardless a record of all manner of relationships of credit and debt across time and space, and not just economic relationships of credit and debt.

In arguing that money is a "means of collective memory," a distributed record of all human intercourse, Hart (2005) implicitly poses the question of the relationship between those records and the infrastructures that produce and maintain them. It is not just cash circulating hand to hand that constitutes this great database; it is also all the systems for transferring money, recording those transfers, and creating great globally expansive ledgers into which human collectivity finds a kind of rhetorical and mathematical expression. *This* is the matter of money that matters, and the sense in which that matter matters: it affords a carriage across space-time and between other agents. Hart wondered whether the infrastructures—the internet, the electronic payment card networks like Visa and MasterCard—could be seized for "human," rather than simply corporate, purposes. Could they be decentralized rather than held in walled gardens, shared with the many whose everyday economic activity made them repositories of collective memory in the first place rather than enclosed for the profit of the few?

Early 21st-century experiments with digital currencies like Bitcoin respond to this challenge, despite the at times incoherent perspective on money they evince (Maurer, Nelms, and Swartz 2013). The center of the confusion is whether people understand, and then seek to create, money as "cash-based" or "ledger-based." For central banks, this is a primary preoccupation, since money in circulation and money on the books must be measured if the bank is to intervene in monetary affairs: cash money has to be ledgered. Eduard de Jong (2014), a pioneer in the development of digital currency systems—and the toll road payment network for the Netherlands!—uses these terms to distinguish between moneys that are emitted by a central source and then embedded in objects that leave no record of their passage from one agent to another, and moneys that by design record their passage in a database, the authority of which all accept. For a toll road, you might want what de Jong calls a cash-based system, if you are worried about the prying eyes of the state into your travels, or you just didn't care about the massive amounts of data generated at the toll booth about people's comings and goings every day, day after day, on their regular commutes. In such a system of value embedded in token, however, people can pour too much power into the money object. Some Bitcoin proponents thus evince a kind of digital metallism, imagining that the value of the bits in Bitcoin derives wholly from their scarcity, a scarcity built into the design. With the latter, the ledger-based system, people ponder whether the database must be centralized for it to have its authority. Must it be maintained and verified by a trusted, or simply overwhelmingly powerful, third party—a temple, a corporation, a notary, a government? Or can there be a democratically decentralized database, owned by none or owned by all, without the intercession of any scribes, bookkeepers, banks, or governments? Just how far can the distribution of agency go?

Bitcoin and other so-called cryptocurrency experiments rely on the existing network infrastructures of the internet and the electrical grid. On top of those systems—which are more or less centralized, depending on how you look at it— Bitcoin creates a database. This database has a specific structure. Imagine a great ledger book. Imagine further that everyone—everyone!—has a copy of that ledger. Anyone can make an entry of a debit or credit into that ledger. I credit you, while debiting myself. But then everyone has the opportunity to verify that entry (though not everyone does). Those who do the work of authenticating transactions are rewarded with a new credit line in the ledger. They can also levy a fee, in the form of an additional incremental credit, for their work of verification. A verified set of transactions—a complete ledger page—is called a block. The entire database is called the blockchain, a chain of groups of verified transactions. A great database, distributed among all participants, public yet pseudonymous, written by the collective, collaborative and competitive effort of the participants in the system. A Visa network without Visa, banks, or the government. Just computers and people (and electricity . . . and the internet). At least, this is the theory, anyway.

In one of the 18th-century money narratives, money objects possess distinct agencies, and multiple agencies within themselves, too, which the money objects can send out of their bodies and into the world, and into other bodies. In one story, a coin, an Indian gold rupee, describes itself as having multiple spirits, though it names only three. They are Ductility, Malleability, and Fusibility. "Men have foolishly called them qualities," he says (Scott 1782, in Bellamy 2012:36). But they are not qualities, in the conventional sense of the term. They are different aspects or externalizations of its core self: agents. They are also among the properties of precious metal that Enlightenment philosophers and, earlier, the Greeks had imagined to be perfectly suited to serve as money. But the story suggests that what matters is not their matter in itself but the agency the qualia afford, to carry value across time and space and between persons. They are also infrastructure, then—something that transports or transmits other things. Again, this is the sense in which the matter of money matters—it bestows the ability to act over distances, but it does not possess by virtue of those qualities any intrinsic value in itself.

The rupee is able to dispatch its spirits and send them into people's minds, or, more precisely, into their brains. There, the spirits can peer into a person's history by reading the literal inscriptions on a specific region of the brain where memories are recorded. Or, not memories exactly: the word our rupee uses is *transactions*:

> One of my subordinate spirits immediately mounted his cella turcica [the structure in the skull holding the pituitary gland] by my command, from which spot the brain above may be seen marked with impressions, like figures on a celestial globe. These impressions are nothing but the scratches made by objects which have been presented to the senses, and of which memory makes use in her operations. By reading these, we can discover all the transactions of any consequence in which a man has been engaged. (Scott 1782, in Bellamy 2012:51)

We have qualities—ductility, malleability, fusibility—that are agents that can read individual humans' memories. Those memories are literally written on the brain, like tally marks, at the seat of the human person's own agency, which is revealed by the money object to be itself a great database of transactional records. This is a wondrous hall of mirrors: money objects, distributed throughout all humanity, replicate at a higher level of scale the transactional database in each person's brain. Money's agencies, embodied in money's qualities, intermediate between the great transactional database of all human interaction and the personal archive of every individual's memories. This places money—all of money, that is, all the money in the world—in the position of serving as the record of all of human history. A memory bank, indeed!

It is difficult to think of a coin as a record-keeping instrument. But this is precisely what the rupee's tale reveals.

The earliest coins were themselves a kind of receipt, the insignia on their faces a constant reminder of the sovereign from which they were issued and to which, through tribute or tax, they would return. Users of the first coins sometimes stamped their own marks on them, announcing their presence to the wider community of people among whom the coins circulated. It is as if people still lived with a cuneiform mentality, the urge to record one's own symbol on coins so great that one numismatist, examining a collection in the British Museum, noted that some examples were so covered with these countermarks as to be losing their material integrity (Hill 1919).

In Sumer, ancient bureaucrats kept cuneiform tablets in central temples and palaces (Hudson 2000). Later, in Anatolia, coins were issued from mints and allowed to circulate. Agency centralized; agency dispersed. Yet the latter was no less a giant record book than the former. Similarly, coin and cash are no less a system of credits and debts and no less an infrastructure or an archive for being materialized in what comes to our hands as individual objects, individual tokens. Just a distributed archive. All the money in circulation is a distributed database of all our credits and debts, if we take the point of view of our Indian rupee.

If money's qualities could extend outward from money objects to look into personal trajectories, today electronic payment systems disaggregate and distribute the agency of the person across spatial and temporal scales, while opening up the person's prior—and, predictively, future!—transactions. If transactions in the 18th century were recorded as traces on the brain, many of today's transactions are recorded in other memory banks: the computer servers that store the transactional data of these electronic systems.

With Bitcoin or with new electronic payment systems—ApplePay, PayPal—what falls outside of this archive are precisely the relations our rupee was able to witness: the hand-to-hand transfers of cash and coin. From a digital computational point of view, these transactions are virtually invisible, especially if there is no electronic receipt-producing device like a cash register or point-of-sale terminal linked to computers processing and storing other data that may enter into the system. Corporate entities at the time of this writing are actively seeking to enclose this "commons"—a term used by more than one payments industry professional in conversations with me.

Experts have predicted the obsolescence of physical instantiations of money almost as soon as 19th- and early 20th-century governments standardized their issue. They have a point but miss their mark. Before there was coin, there were centralized ledgers, records of transactions warranting other transactions and literally inscribing (in clay, stone, papyrus) the distributed agencies of human interaction. Financial crisis and "disruption" in the payments industry—the business of transferring value—in the early 21st century again raise the question of money-as-ledger, making the era of cash and coin seem like a brief interregnum in the deep history of value transfer. Asking after the infrastructures facilitating that transfer leads to the role of accounting not as a record of monetary interaction, but as that interaction itself. It is precisely a question of the distribution of agency: who shall make entries into the great ledger of human transaction and exchange? As the ledger pluralizes, who controls the cross-referencing, the gateways between newly dispersed accounts? Will it be the new corporate masters of multiple, independent or interdependent temples, each holding its own record of our interactions (a twist on Peebles's (2008) story: instead of the hoards migrating to the banks, they migrate to the great server farms of our era)?

Or, as a joint commitment par excellence—something we do together, with it, over it, through it, because of those Goldilocks qualities—can money be made to redistribute agency, away from the Apples and Googles and Facebooks, and toward another economy? Ledgers, after all, are vulnerable: to fraud, to damage, to fire. Their intentional destruction can have world-changing consequences, from the burning of the Inkan khipu by Spanish colonials to the burning of the tally sticks—and the fire's spread through the House of Commons—in early 19th-century England. If money's agencies are increasingly being locked up now in corporate ledgers, hoarded like a rupee in a safe, removed from the human interaction that once delighted it, can we help set them free so they can tell their—our—stories?

Or shall they burn?

ACKNOWLEDGMENTS

I would like to thank Geoffrey Bowker for bringing the Indian rupee tale to my attention. I would also like to thank Lana Swartz, Taylor C. Nelms, and Scott Mainwaring for many productive hours and days of fieldwork, conversation, writing, and thinking together. Mrinalini Tankha, Ursula Dalinghaus, and Nathan Coben offered helpful criticism and advice, as did Paul Kockelman. Research in the payments industry has been supported by the US National Science Foundation (SES 0960423 and SES 1455859). The opinions presented here are the author's own and do not reflect those of the National Science Foundation or any other organization.

REFERENCES

de Jong, Eduard. 2014. "Towards an Open E-currency System." Lecture given at MoneyLab, Amsterdam, March, 23, 2014. Available at http://networkcultures. org/moneylab/2014/03/23/edward-de-jong-towards-an-open-e-currency-system/, last accessed November 15, 2014.

Graeber, David. 2011. *Debt: The First 5,000 Years*. Brooklyn, NY: Melville House.

Hart, Keith. 2000. *The Memory Bank: Money in an Unequal World*. London: Profile.

Hart, Keith. 2005. "Notes toward an Anthropology of Money." *Kritikos: An International and Interdisciplinary Journal of Postmodern Cultural Sound, Text and*

Image 2, available at http://intertheory.org/hart.htm, last accessed November 15, 2014.

Hill, G. F. 1919. "Notes on the Imperial Persian Coinage." *The Journal of Hellenic Studies* 39 116–129.

Hudson, Michael. 2000. "Introduction: The Role of Accounting in Civilization's Economic Takeoff." In *Creating Economic Order: Record-keeping, Standardization, and the Development of Accounting in the Ancient Near East, Volume IV*, edited by Michael Hudson and Cornelia Wunsch, 1–22. Bethesda, MD: CDL.

Maurer, Bill. July 2011. "Money Nutters: *Economic Sociology_The European Electronic Newsletter* 12(3): 5–21.

Maurer, Bill, Taylor C. Nelms, and Lana Swartz. 2013. "When Perhaps the Real Problem Is Money Itself!": The Practical Materiality of Bitcoin." *Social Semiotics* 23(2): 261–277.

Peebles, Gustav. 2008. "Inverting the Panopticon: Money and the Nationalization of the Future." *Public Culture* 20(2): 233–265.

Scott, Helenus. 2012. *The Adventures of a Rupee*. London: J. Murray, 1792. In *The British It-Narratives, 1750–1830, Volume 1: Money*, edited by Liz Bellamy, 31–71. London: Pickering and Chatto.

PART FIVE

Distributing Agency within Selves and Species

CHAPTER 13

Distribution of Agency across Body and Self

RUTH H. PARRY

Many chapters in this book examine distribution and attribution of agency across multiples of people, or people and artifacts. Here though, I look at attribution of agency *within* persons: how agency, and thus flexibility and accountability, can be distributed across body—or body parts—and self. To do so, I draw on a corpus of video recordings of physical therapy treatment sessions, supplemented with brief examples from recordings made in other settings—so as to illustrate that the phenomena I examine are not peculiar to physical therapy.

I demonstrate that people can construct three broad configurations:

1. The body (or body part) and the self are constructed as agents separate to one another, disaggregated, capable of "independently": acting one upon the other.
2. The self and body (or body part) are constructed as connected: with the self possessing the body or body part and having an associated control, flexibility, and accountability for bodily actions.
3. The self and body are constructed as one and the same entity and agent: an integrated, accountable, flexible individual.

I describe the seemingly innocuous and subtle interactional practices we use to construct these quite radically different embodiments/identities

(Kockelman 2007a). I will show that we can do so in reference to our own self, or to other persons. The practices I describe and illustrate comprise the following:

- Ways that body parts get referred to: whether, for example, we refer to *the* thumb, or to *your* or *my* thumb.
- What we put in the subject and object position of our utterances: for example, whether I say that *I* do something, or that my leg does something.
- Eye gaze—through which we can show ourselves to be talking to a part of our interlocutor's body—and thus separating it out from a larger whole. Conversely, we can show that we are talking to the "inner" or whole person by looking him or her in the eye.
- Meanings (i.e., semantics) and metaphors that provide for different configurations of the person, body, and self.

It's worth briefly mentioning that the first practice is available in English but not in all languages—although it seems likely that in different languages, other practices are available to do the same kind of work. It is also worth noticing that these configurations have a dualist character, something I will consider as I go along.

As well as describing *how* people manage to construct different body/self configurations, I examine *when* and *why* they do so. In the context of this book, it should come as no surprise that this has to do with how humans attribute and convey capacity and responsibility for their actions, failings, and endeavors. In a final section, I outline some implications for how we understand and conceptualize distributed agency, and consider how the dualist character of personhood so prevalent in our talk makes sense in social terms. That is, whatever the material discoveries of neuropsychology, and their echoes in linguistic understandings of inalienable possession (Kockelman 2007b), I am going to show you that when we talk and interact with one another, we *do* and we *can* make self and body more, less, or completely—for all practical purposes—separate.

First though, I need to attend to two terminology issues. Frustratingly for me, English does not currently provide a word that signifies, exclusively, the particular part or aspect of a person that is other than the person's body. *Soul* might once have been used, but has lost some of its value in the context of current understandings that brain, consciousness, and body are utterly intertwined in physical terms. In this piece though, I need to refer to this non-body aspect of a person, and to do so I use *self*. Also, rather than *the body or body part(s)*, hereon I use the shorthand *body/part*.

CONFIGURING BODY AND SELF AS UNIFIED, OR AS MORE OR LESS SEPARATE

To put flesh on the bones of the three broad configurations, I examine a series of cases drawn from a much larger set. What I say about the practices and their patterning and functioning in these individual cases reflects analysis of 70 sequences of interaction, nearly all of which involved more than one, often many more than one reference to body/part. Forty-five cases were drawn from a dataset of 86 hours of video-recorded physiotherapy treatment sessions, and 25 were collected from other recordings and transcripts of everyday conversations and also other healthcare interactions. All transcripts presented here are simplified versions of the more detailed transcripts created during analysis.

CASE 1: "KEEPING YOU IN THAT POSITION"
In this example, a therapist (T) and a patient (P) who is receiving rehabilitation for a stroke are talking about a particular goal of his therapy: getting his back and pelvis area more flexible. In the course of this, the therapist describes the physical problem:

Parry PD DT1_2.35

1	T:	And what's <u>happening</u> is your pelvis is tilting
2		forwards. So it's keeping you in th<u>a</u>t position.
3		and then you're quite rounded h[ere a]t the shoulders
4	P:	[Mmm]

Using everyday, mundane language resources, the therapist moves rapidly and seamlessly (lines 1–2) from (a) referring to *your pelvis* with its implication of a possessive connection between patient's self and body, to (b) formulating the pelvis as a separate agent that is keeping the self of the patient in a particular posture. The second formulation entails referring to the pelvis with the impersonal pronoun *it*, and doing so in the subject position, with *you*—the self/patient, in the object position. This subject/object arrangement works to convey the pelvis as an agent, and the self/patient as being acted upon by it. In other words, the therapist constructs a part of the patient's body as a discrete, separate agent that acts upon the self of the patient.

As she continues her description (line 3), the therapist uses another means to separate or distance the self of the patient and his pelvis. The subject/object arrangement is different, the patient—*you*—is now the subject and thus agent over *the shoulders*. The distancing here is done through the pronoun *the*. In extracts to follow, I will demonstrate and examine how people recurrently use impersonals such as *the*, *this*, or *a* when naming a body part, and the way that this distances the body part from the self.

Why do people talk in ways that distance, disaggregate a self and their body (or body parts)? Recurrently, as above, they do so when referring to something that is a problem—an undesirable physical state or movement. By talking in a way that makes the body part a separate agent acting on the self, or in a way that avoids using possessives such as *my* or *your*, one can camouflage the connection—sometimes referred to as "inalienable possession"—between the person whose physical state is referred to and his or her body/part. One thereby implies that the person neither controls, nor bears accountability, fault, and responsibility for the undesirable bodily state or action. One can sever, so to speak, the connection—physically as much as psychologically.

The next case once again illustrates use of *the* rather than *your*, and also introduces another way people can do this disaggregation: through their gaze patterning.

CASE 2: "ALWAYS THE SLOW ONE"

A patient and therapist have been working together on a balance exercise in which the patient kneels up on a mat, trying to keep herself upright with straight hips and bottom tucked in. The patient repeatedly sinks back and down because of hip weakness. The therapist is kneeling behind the patient and encouraging her to squeeze her buttock muscles to keep upright (as in line 1). As the patient begins to sink downward once again (line 3), the therapist says *"Go on an' again this one especially. There"* while touching and tapping on the patient's right hip and buttock—urging the patient to straighten up, and in particular to do so by using her right buttock and hip.

Parry PD GT1_26.49

1	T:	That's better. Go on <u>squeeze</u> sq<u>ue</u>eze lovely,
2		(4.4)
3	T:	<u>Good</u>. Go <u>on</u> an' ag<u>ai</u>n this one
4		especially. Th<u>e</u>re ((gazing to P's hips))

5		(1.5) ((T taps on P's right hip, P continues to attempt to keep upright, then shifts body position leaning towards front of P))
6	T:	This right one's always the- ((gazing to P's face))
7	P:	This [one yes the sl]ow one
8	T:	[the slow one.]
9	T:	Yea[h]
10	P:	[This one is] (like) the slow one
11	T:	Now see whether you can find your balance.

When giving instructions (lines 1, 3, 4), the therapist looks to the back of the patient's hips. She moves on to give a reason for her "this one especially" instruction (lines 6, 8). By the time she starts this talk about a reason, she has shifted her body enough to allow her to direct her gaze to the patient's face and make eye contact. Through this conduct, the therapist treats the patient's body and self as separate agents: the body as agent of the physical action, and the self—or consciousness—as agent with regard to hearing and understanding a reason for the action. This gaze patterning is recurrent in the physical therapy data (Parry 2013), with therapists using their gaze and associated body positioning in a way that disaggregates patients' body parts from their reasoning minds—their selves. As noted, this case also features use of an impersonal pronoun: the therapist talks of *this right one*, not *your right one* (line 6). This brings us neatly to case 3, in which an impersonal pronoun *the*, and the personal pronoun *your*, are used in rapid succession.

CASE 3: THE THUMB YOUR THUMB
This patient's traumatic brain injury has left him with difficulties controlling his left side. The therapist here has been moving and stretching his affected left hand and thumb. As we join the session, the therapist asks the patient to try to shake her hand with his left hand.

Parry PD KT3_9.15

1	T:	C'you shake my hand?
2		(3.7)
3	T:	Pleased to meet you ((jokey tone))
4		= uh huh huh heh huh
5		(0.9) ((P lets go of T hand))

6	T:	Now
7		(0.4)
8	T:	'S not bad
9		(0.6)
10	T:	'Part from, part from the thumb it's fine Andrew
11		(0.2)
12	T:	And can you take your hand away from my hand?
13		(1.9)
14	T:	See if you can try again but making more
15		of a space for your thumb.
16		(2.4)
17	T:	Yeah. That's- that feels- that feels better to me.
18	P:	I got the thumb splint.
19		(0.7)
20	T:	Yeah, and whe- how long are you wearing that for.

The therapist says *the* thumb (line 10) when *your* thumb would be equally grammatical, and in a context where it is perfectly clear which of his two thumbs she is referring to. As in the other cases, she does this when referring to a physical shortcoming. The thumb is, for all practical purposes, conveyed as a separate entity at this point: the patient's self and thumb are disaggregated, and this reduces the implication that he is responsible or accountable for the physical failure being talked of. This case also illustrates a counterpart: when she moves into instructions the therapist says, *can you take your hand away* and [*make*] *more of a space for your thumb*. By using *your* at this juncture, she foregrounds the patient's connection with—in other words, his control over—his hand and thumb. So now, the thumb is portrayed as under the patient's control.

In the physical therapy recordings, both therapists and patients frequently use possessives in situations where controlled, purposeful action is talked about and/or encouraged. Using *your* or *my* (when alternatives are possible) treats self and body as connected, and people do so when there is good reason to emphasize someone's control, responsibility, and physical agency in relation to their body.

The rapidity with which one can move between different configurations of the body/self/person relationship is particularly evident in this case, as is the fact that in doing so, a speaker does not need to do anything extra as it were—one does not need to provide talk that, for instance, cancels out an earlier meaning or gives some reason for the change.

CASE 4: IT COLLAPSED; YOU WERE CONTROLLED

The final case from physical therapy illustrates particularly clearly how people use different body/self configurations to convey just who or what is responsible for a physical success or a physical failure. The patient, whose stroke has resulted in left-sided weakness, is standing with feet slightly apart. The therapist is encouraging her to shift her weight from one foot to the other. A key point of the exercise is for the patient to try to keep her weaker left leg and knee straight as she shifts her weight to this weaker left side.

Parry PD QT2_20.17

```
1   T:    Okay that's- that was better that time
2         because the first time it just kind
3         of collapsed ((smiley, gentle tone))
4         (0.9)
5   T:    That time you were more controlled.
6         (0.2)
7   T:    Now, as you come back over towards me I want you to . . .
```

At line 2, the therapist's *it* refers to the patient's left knee and leg. Her talk ascribes this as the entity that *collapsed*. When she describes the recent successful *controlled* performance of the exercise, the patient and her body are construed as a single unified agent: *you*. The therapist is thereby able to praise the patient and treat her as responsible for the success.

A series of shorter cases now supplement the detailed analysis above by demonstrating that not just therapists but also patients construct different body/self configurations via the same resources; also that the same kind of phenomena arise in other healthcare settings and in informal conversations between friends.

CASE 5: MY BRAIN DOESN'T TRUST THE LEFT SIDE

Near the start of a treatment session, a patient who suffered a stroke two weeks previously talks to a therapist about his difficulty in standing up from a sitting position:

Parry Doc HT3_17.03

```
1   P:    Still my brain doesn't trust? the- the er
2         t[he le]ft er [tha]t's why- that's why
3   T:    [yeah]      [yeah]
```

4	P:	every time I stand up? I-I put most of
5		the- my weight on my le-=on my right.
6		(0.2)
7	P:	Because my brain doesn't trust the left side

Here the patient makes *my brain* the subject of his talk, and his *left side* the object. This subject/object arrangement has parallels to case 1, in which the therapist's talk constructed the patient's *pelvis* as an agent that was making the patient *rounded*. There are differences though: rather than self and body part, the patient disaggregates two body parts: *brain* and *left side*. Nevertheless, it is reasonable to hear him treating *my brain* as in some sense his controlling self, and *the left side* as separate to this brain/self.

CASE 6: I'VE GOT A FOOT
This case is from a different healthcare setting: a consultation with a primary care doctor. The extract comes from the start of a consultation.

Robinson and Heritage 2005 page 487: Extract 11: lines 1-5 (simplified)

1	D:	What you up to?
2		(.)
3	P:	I've gotta bad foot that I can't- get well.
4		(0.2) ((Doc moves his chair close to foot))
5	D:	Which part.

Here, the patient uses both an impersonal pronoun, *a,* and a verb phrase *that I can't get well.* These work to disaggregate her self, as an agent, from her foot—upon which she has been attempting to act.

CASE 7: THOSE BIG TOENAILS
With this case, we move to everyday conversations. Two friends, Emma (E) and Lottie are talking on the telephone. We join the conversation as Emma describes, in dramatic terms, a fungal infection affecting her toenails.

NB IV:10R (original transcript line 1472-6) (simplified)

1	E:	Oh God it's terrible Lottie my toenails
2		they're jis look so sick those big toenails it jis
3		u-makes me sick. Yihknow they're diss (.) u-dead.
4		Everything's dead I d- I sat out (.) tihday en
5		I said my God em I jis (.) DYING it's (.) like
6		I'm ossified.

Emma switches from the personal *my* toenails (line 1), to the impersonal *those* (line 2) in the context of escalating from "terrible" to nauseating. She also moves from describing a situation—*it's terrible*—to conveying what she sees as she looks at *those big toenails*. The impersonal pronoun *those* adds to the conveyed sense of an external view. By line 6, she reaches a further configuration: her whole self is conveyed as *ossified*.

CASE 8: PHYSICALLY, NOT MENTALLY

Another everyday conversation case comes from a telephone call between friends. Ava (A) has called Bee (B), and at the point we enter the call, Bee has been checking with Ava where she is calling from.

TG Ava and Bee, page 15 Line 09 (simplified)

```
1    B:    I finally said something right. (0.2)
2          You are home. Hmm
3    A:    Yeh- I believe so.  [Physically anyway
4    B:                        [mmh
5    A:    Yea –a-h Not mentally though ((smiley, slightly laughing
           voice))
```

Within a jokey exchange, Ava makes a dualist claim—spatially separating her *mental* and *physical* self via semantic resources (the meanings of her words) as opposed to the grammatical or gaze resources we saw above.

CASE 9: MY BODY DIDN'T NEED IT

Similarly, in this next case, in an everyday conversation between Sherry (S), Carol (C) and Ruth (R), we see semantics in use to configure the physical body and self as separate.

SN-4_05_lines 01-06 (simplified)

```
1    S:    Hi Carol
2    C:    H[i]
3    R:      [Caro]l, Hi
4    S:    You didn't get an icecream sandwich
5    C:    I know, I decided that my body didn't need it
6    S:    Yes but ours did heh-heh-heh
```

CASE 10: SOMETHING BEHIND HER

This final case comes from a telephone conversation between friends Marsha and Erma. Erma (E) is describing her son's girlfriend Ilene:

MDE:MTRAC:60-1:5 (simplified)

1	E:	Cause she's gotta <u>very</u> pretty face she ez gorgeous
2		blue eyes, and she really pays very little at<u>t</u>ention
3		to it and I kind'v am not supri<u>z</u>ed when Joey says
4		that she wants to go into Social <u>Ser</u>vices, she
5		seems like that kind. Y'know w't I m<u>e</u>an she seems
6		like she has a lot (.) there's something be<u>h</u>ind her.

Erma builds a sense of connection but also a distinction between the inner, private Ilene (*behind her*—line 6) and Ilene's physical aspect—*gorgeous eyes*, and *a pretty face*. This sense is built both through the design of her description—Ilene *has* physical attributes, and the semantic and metaphoric use of prepositions to indicate this character of selfhood.

CONCLUSIONS

People can allocate to the body, or parts thereof, agency that is more or less separate from the agency of the self. In our social lives at least, while the body and self can be a unified and fused entity, the body and self can also be disaggregated, fissioned, divided. That is, in our interactions, we commit to a form of dualism. This is not a strict "here is body, there is mind" type of dualism, but rather a continuum that can be cut in a variety of places. We commit to this form of dualism as a way of understanding ourselves, our personhood. This enables us to manipulate—to shape—the meaning of our own, and other people's, physical successes, failures, and features.

As I have shown above, these kinds of allocation of agency are accomplished via rather basic design features of body movement and talk, including gaze, and grammatical and semantic resources. Through the meanings we thereby build, we can encourage others to hear matters of fault, responsibility, endeavor, and achievement with regard the physical as more or less attributable to the body or body part, or to the "true," "inner" self (the soul, or even the brain). It is noticeable that the more distancing configurations are noticeably charitable—we might even say compassionate; the person talking can absolve the person/self being talked about. Being able to allocate responsibility and even blame for physical problems to the body (and therefore as less—or even not at all—the actual person's fault) helps us to limit negative emotional and relationship consequences of criticizing or blaming another's physical state or behavior. Conversely, being able to convey that positive performances and attributes are integral to the person him- or herself allows us to emphasize that person's personal competence, and thus praise, motivate, and encourage him or her, facilitating alignment in terms of both local actions and the ongoing sense of relationship between the people involved.

My analysis has shown that people locally constitute agency and relations between selves and bodies in a moment to moment way that is fitted to social circumstances and also highly flexible. Previous research that has shown that the way one refers to another person is not random; rather, it does work—it performs social actions—such as conveying another person as more or less close to the speaker (Enfield and Stivers 2007; Stivers 2007). My analysis shows that the way we refer to our bodies and our selves is also not a random or haphazard matter, but a socially shaped means of working up distinct embodied identities fitted to interpersonal circumstances and relationships. Finally, the evidence I have presented shows that in order to understand fully the distribution of agency, we need not only to recognize the ways and means through which it can be distributed, fissioned, and fused "across and among individuals" (Enfield 2013:104), but also to add the recognition that people also distribute agency within individuals.

REFERENCES

Enfield, N. J. 2013. *Relationship Thinking: Enchrony, Agency, and Human Sociality*. New York: Oxford University Press.

Enfield, N. J., and T. Stivers. 2007. *Person Reference in Interaction: Linguistic, Cultural, and Social Perspectives*. Cambridge: Cambridge University Press.

Kockelman, P., 2007a. "Agency." *Current Anthropology* 48(3): 375–401.

Kockelman, P. 2007b. "Inalienable Possession and Personhood in a Q'eqchi'-Mayan Community." *Language in Society* 36(3): 343–369.

Parry, Ruth H. 2013. "Giving Reasons for Doing Something Now or at Some Other Time." *Research on Language & Social Interaction* 46(2): 105–124.

Stivers, T. 2007. "Alternative Recognitionals in Person Reference." In *Person Reference in Interaction—Linguistic, Cultural and Social Perspectives*, edited by N. J. Enfield and T. Stivers, 73–96. Cambridge: Cambridge University Press.

CHAPTER 14

Distributed Agency in Ants

PATRIZIA D'ETTORRE

Agency in humans is characterized by a distributed nature; we have an extraordinary capacity to share agency via multilevel cooperation but also via coercion and different forms of social exploitation. Agency as experienced in human societies is unique—or is it?

I argue that distributed agency is an inherent consequence of social life and it is proportional to the degree of social complexity. Many animals live in groups that may be structured at different levels, ranging from simple aggregations to small family groups, up to cooperative breeding societies, such as those of meerkats with clearly defined helper roles (Clutton-Brock et al. 2001). However, some invertebrates, the social insects, have reached the apex of social organization: eusociality, characterized by reproductive division of labor, cooperative care of young, and overlapping generations (for a clear and complete definition of eusociality, see Boomsma 2013).

With this social structure, social insects (all ants and termites; some species of bees and wasps) have become tremendously successful in colonizing almost all terrestrial habitats. In tropical forests, social insects represent around 30% of the total animal biomass and 80% of the insect biomass.

Ants, with more than 14,000 described species, have evolved a multitude of life histories and adaptations to a variety of environments. Ant societies show several similarities with human societies (Wilson 2012). Ants build cities, maintain infant nurseries and cemeteries, and construct elaborate nests, which can contain hundreds of rooms connected by a complex network of galleries, such as those of harvester ants (Tschinkel 2004).

Ants and other social insects have evolved sophisticated techniques of waste management (e.g., in leaf-cutting ants; Bot et al. 2001) and practice social prophylaxis by acquiring immunity via social contact with infected individuals (e.g., in the garden ant; Ugelvig and Cremer 2007). Ants, like humans, store food: for instance, harvester ants collect seed in the warm season and put them in long-term stores to be consumed later (Johnson 2001). Ants practice agriculture and animal husbandry. Some species of ants cultivate fungi for food. These fungus-growing ants have evolved an obligatory association with fungal symbionts, which they provide with growing substrate and protection from pathogens and parasites (Poulsen and Boomsma 2005). Many ant species keep aphids as we keep cows and regularly "milk" them for their honeydew secretion (Ivens et al. 2012). In exchange, ants protect the aphids against predators, such as ladybird beetles, and give them shelter. Ants conduct wars and slave-raiding. They are aggressive against same-species competitors and engage in prolonged battles and tournaments (Hölldobler and Wilson 1990). Some ant species are specialized social parasites: they raid other ant colonies, pillage their brood, and bring it to their own colony. Upon reaching adulthood, these "slaves" will work for the parasitic colony as if they were in their original mother colony (d'Ettorre and Heinze 2001).

The highly specialized division of labor among individual ants, with the evolution of morphological differentiations (queen and worker caste, and in some cases different types of workers), has given rise to the analogy between the ant colony and the body of a Metazoan animal. The ant colony is considered as an individual of a higher order, a "superorganism" with unique emergent properties (Hölldobler and Wilson 2008). Recently, the term *superorganism* has been questioned based on the observation that many other organisms originated as groups of genetically distinct members, including eukaryotes, and are not called *superorganisms*. A broad definition of *social organism* has been proposed: "a unit of high cooperation and very low conflict among its parts" (Strassmann and Queller 2010), which includes eusocial insects. The central concept remains that of an entity made of different specialized components and characterized by the cooperative partitioning of work. Like prokaryotic cells joined together in a symbiotic union, giving rise to eukaryotes, solitary individuals started working together into social units (colonies), which then evolved nonreproductive castes, resulting in advanced division of labor.

Unlike most human societies, ants are perfectly able to live in a condition of anarchistic socialism without the need of a leader (Wheeler 1910). In the absence of any centralized order, the individual ant workers behave collectively, following self-organized processes to solve, for instance, a foraging task. Therefore, the behavior of the ant colony is an emergent property resulting from the dynamics of feedback loops between interacting ant workers, each following simple decision rules. A typical example is the selection of the shortest route to a food source. Ants are central-place foragers and they come back to the nest once they have found a suitable food source. In many ant species, nestmates are recruited to recently discovered food sources by a trail pheromone, the Ariadne's chemical thread between the nest and the food. Small ants no longer than one or two centimeters can cover considerable distance (a hundred meters) during their foraging trips in an environment that is heterogeneous and full of obstacles. Indeed, they have evolved strategies to select the shortest and most efficient path from the nest to the food. Laboratory experiments with the Argentine ant, *Linepithema humile* (formerly *Iridomyrmex humilis*), have been among the first to elucidate the mechanisms underlying this collective strategy and to model the ant foraging behavior (Gross et al. 1989). In one of these experiments, the nest and the foraging arena are linked by a bridge with two branches of different lengths in a way that each ant must choose between the shorter or the longer branch two times when going from the nest to the food, and back (Figure 14.1). Argentine ants mark the substrate with their

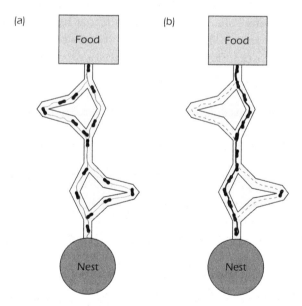

Figure 14.1 A colony of Argentine ants selecting the branches of a bridge between the nest and the food area: (a) four minutes after the placement of the bridge ants choose branches randomly; (b) eight minutes after the placement of the bridge ants choose the shortest route between the nest and the food.
(Modified from Gross et al. 1989)

trail pheromone both when leaving and when returning to the nest. At the beginning of the experiment, explorer ants use both branches randomly (Figure 14.1a); however, after a few minutes, additional ants are recruited to the food source and the shortest route is suddenly selected by the vast majority of ants (Figure 14.1b).

How is this possible? Each ant leaves a pheromone mark both ways (from and to the nest); ants that take the shortest route arrive earlier to the food and come back earlier to the nest, compared to ants that take the longest route. Therefore, it takes less time to the shortest branch to be marked by an increasing amount of pheromone left by the ants. The chemical signal on the shortest route will be amplified quicker and, as a consequence, more and more ants will be recruited on this shortest route. It is a simple positive feedback mechanism based on an indirect communication between nest-mate ants (via the trail pheromone), which results in an *intelligent* collective decision. This is a relatively flexible, context-dependent, adaptive solution.

In such cooperative tasks based on self-organized processes, the agency is totally distributed and gives rise to an emergent phenomenon: the sudden collective choice of the shortest path from the nest to the food. In this process, each individual ant has very little flexibility, particularly because the response to pheromones is typically "hardwired" (so-called *innate*). An ant has no other choice than responding to the highest concentration of pheromone, and therefore she will follow the path that has been marked more heavily by her nestmates. This lack of flexibility results in little accountability. It might well be that there is individual variation among the various ants, with some individuals being, for instance, less sensitive to the trail pheromone and thus not able to perceive the difference in concentration between the two trails when this difference is still small. These individuals may choose the long path when the majority of ants go for the short path. Nevertheless, the ants on the short path will continue being faster in coming back to the nest, and soon the pheromone trail will reach a concentration that will be attractive to every ant. In a cooperative collective task, it does not matter if few individuals do not participate: the system is automatically buffered. Indeed, there are usually more ants coming to a food source than the number required to bring that particular amount of food back to the nest.

In a social group characterized by extreme cooperation, agency is distributed beyond the individuals (the single units forming the group) and there is a very low individual level of flexibility and accountability. Ants, and other social insects, are a paramount example of distributed agency because they pushed the division of labor to its extreme form: the partitioning of reproduction. In many ant species, such as the Argentine ant, workers are totally sterile and the only way they can pass on their genes to the next generation (new colonies) is by assisting their mother queen to reproduce. Therefore, it is in the workers' best interest to work for the good of the colony (even when this involves committing suicide: e.g., a honey bee worker stinging a vertebrate); workers do not have any other option.

Yet, ant societies are not always behaving as harmonious cooperative units. In some species, workers—which are all females—retained the ability to produce eggs. As in other hymenoptera, ants have a haplodiploid sex-determination system: males develop from unfertilized eggs and are haploid, while females develop from fertilized eggs and are diploid. This means that even if workers cannot mate, they can lay male eggs and thus achieve direct reproduction. A worker is always more related to her own sons than to the sons of her mother (the worker's brothers); therefore a worker should prefer laying eggs instead of caring for her brothers. Indeed, some ant workers do so. Worker reproduction reduces overall colony efficiency because workers that reproduce do not work efficiently. This conflict over male production is resolved by a collective mechanism named "worker policing": workers preventing each other from reproducing by eating worker-laid eggs or by aggressively suppressing reproductive workers. Worker policing by egg eating was first observed in the honey bee (Ratnieks 1988) and then in several species of bees, ants, and wasps. We showed that in colonies of the ant *Pachycondyla inversa* some workers specialize in policing behavior (van Zweden et al. 2007). Workers in this species present the typical ant polyethism, with specialization in tasks such as foraging, nest defense, and brood care, but these societies evolved also a worker role specialized in tackling social corruption: the policing force (Figure 14.2). These

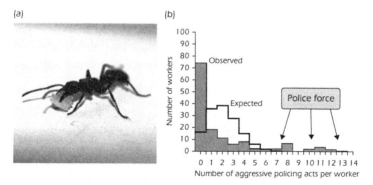

Figure 14.2 (a) A worker of the ant species *Pachycondyla inversa* holding eggs.
(Photo: Mauro Patricelli)
(b) Frequency distribution of aggressive policing acts among workers. The observed sharing of policing tasks is significantly more skewed than would be expected from random chance.
(Modified from van Zweden et al. 2007)

policing workers act for the collective interest of the workers as a whole (the colony) and they are not moved by selfish benefits since none of the policing workers showed developed ovaries, suggesting that they do not kill other workers' eggs or attack reproductive workers (so that they cannot reproduce) to be able to reproduce themselves.

This ant example shows that when individual units are allowed some degree of flexibility (e.g., the possibility to develop ovaries), they might attempt to act in their best selfish interest (e.g., by reproducing), but they are held accountable for their behavior and therefore punished by other members of the community. When the risk of destabilization is high—if many workers reproduce, the colony as a whole would collapse—societies should evolve specialized units (e.g., the ant policing force) to restore and maintain social cooperation. Coercion, defined as a social pressure in the form of punishment of group members to prevent them from acting selfishly and thereby harming the group as a whole, has been described in a variety of species, including humans (review in Ratnieks and Wenseelers 2008). Indeed, levels of cooperation across human societies are correlated with the degree to which uncooperative individuals are punished (Henrich et al. 2006), suggesting that coercion plays a key role in the evolution and maintenance of cooperative systems.

In conclusion, I argue that when individual units of a social group are prevented from acting selfishly by drastically reducing their flexibility, agency becomes better distributed and individual units cannot be considered accountable for their behavior. On the other hand, when some flexibility is retained in a cooperative system, individual units may pursue their direct benefits and cause a "tragedy of the commons." Cooperative systems that have survived natural selection are likely those that have found effective strategies to make individuals accountable for their behavior, thus enforcing cooperation. The more sophisticated the social organization, the higher the level of cooperation, the wealthier the common good, and the more specialized the retaliation system against free riders should be. Some ant species have solved the problem by evolving individual units that are totally sterile and act as cells in a body. As a consequence, flexibility was obliterated, giving rise to completely distributed agency.

ACKNOWLEDGMENTS

Many thanks to the editors N. J. Enfield and P. Kockelman for having invited me to join this project and for their insightful comments on a previous version of the manuscript.

REFERENCES

Bot, A. N. M., C. R. Currie, A. G. Hart, and J. J. Boomsma. 2001. "Waste Management in Leaf-Cutting Ants." *Ethology Ecology & Evolution* 13: 225–237.

Boomsma, J. J. 2013. "Beyond promiscuity: mate-choice commitments in social breeding." *Philosophical Transactions of the Royal Society B: Biological Sciences* 368 (1613): 20120050.

Clutton-Brock, T. H., A. F. Russell, L. L. Sharpe, P. N. M. Brotherton, G. M. McIlrath, S. White, and E. Z. Cameron. 2001. "Effects of Helpers on Juvenile Development and Survival in Meerkats." *Science* 293: 2446–2449.

d'Ettorre, P., and J. Heinze. 2001. "Sociobiology of Slave-Making Ant." *Acta Ethologica* 3: 67–82.

Gross, S., S. Aron, J. L. Deneubourd, and J. M. Pasteels. 1989. "Self-Organized Shortcuts in the Argentine Ant." *Naturwissenschaften* 76: 579–581.

Henrich, J., R. McElreath, A. Barr, J. Ensimger, C. Barrett, A. Bolyanatz, J. C. Cardenas, M. Gurven, E. Gwako, N. Henrich, C. Lesorogol, F. Marlowe, D. Tracer, and J. Ziker. 2006. "Costly Punishment across Human Societies." *Science* 312: 1767–1770.

Hölldobler, B., and E. O. Wilson. 1990. *The Ants.* Cambridge, MA: Harvard University Press.

Hölldobler, B., and E. O. Wilson. 2008. *The Superorganism: The Beauty, Elegance, and Strangeness of Insect Societies.* New York: W. W. Norton.

Ivens, A. B. F., D. J. C. Kronauer, I. Pen, F. J. Weissing, and J. J. Boomsma. 2012. "Ants Farm Subterranean Aphids Mostly in Clone Groups—An Example of Prudent Husbandry for Carbohydrates and Proteins?" *BMC Evolutionary Biology* 12: 106.

Johnson, R. A. 2001. "Biogeography and Community Structure of North American Seed Harvester Ants." *Annual Review of Entomology* 46: 1–29.

Poulsen, M., and J. J. Boomsma. 2005. "Mutualistic Fungi Control Crop Diversity in Fungus Growing Ants." *Science* 307: 741–744.

Ratnieks, F. L. W. 1988. "Reproductive Harmony via Mutual Policing by Workers in Eusocial Hymenoptera." *American Naturalist* 132: 217–236.

Ratnieks, F. L. W., and T. Wenseleers. 2008. "Altruism in Insect Societies and Beyond: Voluntary or Enforced?" *Trends in Ecology and Evolution* 23: 45–52.

Strassmann, J. E., and D. C. Queller. 2010. "The Social Organism: Congresses, Parties, Committees." *Evolution* 64: 605–616.

Tschinkel, W. R. 2004. "The Nest Architecture of the Florida Harvester Ant, *Pogonomyrmex badius.*" *Journal of Insect Science* 4: 21.

Ugelvig, L. V., and S. Cremer. 2007. "Social Prophylaxis: Group Interaction Promotes Collective Immunity in Ant Colonies." *Current Biology* 17: 1967–1971.

van Zweden, J. S., M. A. Fürst, J. Heinze, and P. d'Ettorre. 2007. "Specialization in Policing Behaviour among Workers of the Ant *Pachycondyla inversa.*" *Proceedings of the Royal Society of London B* 274: 1421–1428.

Wheeler, W. M. 1910. *Ants: Their Structure, Development and Behavior.* New York: Columbia University Press.

Wilson, E. O. 2012. *The Social Conquest of Earth.* New York: Liveright.

PART SIX

Social Bonding Through Embodied Agency

CHAPTER 15

Group Exercise and Social Bonding

EMMA COHEN

INTRODUCTION

Group exercise, broadly construed, is a cultural universal. From the ceremonial rituals and persistence hunting of foraging bands to the beach festivals, team sports, and urban marathons of large-scale communities around the world, people everywhere get together to move together. The ubiquity of coordinated, physical, exertive movement in everyday social activity points to its significance not only for individual physical and mental health, but for social well-being also (Davis, Taylor and Cohen, 2015). Anecdote, theory, and evidence indicate that when people coordinate in group movement and exercise, powerful and unique psychological and physiological effects are generated over and above those that occur when individuals perform the same activities alone. For the theologian Michael Novak, team *spirit* is no misnomer: "For those who have participated on a team that has known the click of communality, the experience is unforgettable, like that of having attained, for a while at least, a higher level of existence" (in Murphy and White 2011:15–16). Such tightly coordinated teamwork, characteristic of many sports, dissolves boundaries between individual and social agency: "In rowing . . . it feels like you have at your command the power of everybody else in the boat. You are exponentially magnified. What was a strain before becomes easier. It is absolutely the ultimate team sport."[1] What is this "click of communality"? Are there special psychological and physiological effects of exercising with others as compared to doing it alone? Is individual agency magnified in group exercise?

This chapter draws on research in evolutionary anthropology, sports and exercise physiology, clinical neuroscience, and social psychology to begin to address these broad questions and to develop an account of the reciprocal causal links between group movement and social bonding. The account comprises two interconnected claims: group movement and exercise forges social bonds between participants; social bonds, in turn, alter, and potentially heighten, participants' motivations and performance abilities. The claim that exercise increases bondedness among participants is developed in the first two sections, which focus specifically on the social effects of exercise highs ("social high") and coordinated behaviour ("social sync"). The third and final sections explore how social context influences exercise participation and performance. Specifically, we consider uniquely human motivations to collaborate in joint activities ("social drive") and capacities to benefit from social support in physically and psychologically challenging conditions ("social boost").

SOCIAL HIGH

Although prolonged aerobic exertive movement is typically associated with high levels of physical stress and pain, people also frequently report responses to exercise that include improved affect, sense of well-being, anxiety reduction, and post-exercise calm. Extremes of these exercise-related changes are popularly known as "runner's high." The effect is not limited to running or sports, however; anthropologists' descriptions of ceremonial rituals frequently describe dancers achieving similar euphoric states (e.g., Radcliffe-Brown 1948).

The neuropharmacological mechanisms that make these activities pleasurable appear to involve two core neurobiological systems—the opioidergic system and the endocannabinoid system. The first is our body's natural morphine; the second is its natural cannabis. In addition to their role in pain modulation, these systems produce feelings of euphoria, transcendence, and pleasure. Boecker et. al. (2008) first tested the exercise-opioid link on endurance runners via a measure of endorphin levels in the brain and a self-report mood measure. They found positive and correlated effects for post-exercise endorphin activity and self-reported euphoria. Similarly, recent tests of the endocannabinoid hypothesis in runners and cyclists found significantly increased concentrations of anandamide, an endocannabinoid previously associated with aerobic activity in other cursorial species, in participants' blood after moderately intense exercise (e.g., Raichlen et. al. 2013).

Our endogenous pain relief and reward systems, although ancient and involved in many different bodily functions, were likely recruited in human evolution to reduce pain associated with the physical exertion of running and to enhance motivation. Endurance running may have played an important role in human evolution, facilitating the exploitation of protein-rich resources via hunting, chasing, and scavenging. Consistent with this hypothesis, evidence suggests that endocannabinoid-based pleasure induced by exercise is an ancient trait that evolved to encourage aerobic activity (e.g., Bramble and Lieberman 2004; Raichlen et. al. 2012). Insofar as persistence hunting typically occurred within and benefited from a cooperative and cohesive group context, a tight association between endurance aerobic exercise, analgesic and euphoric mental states induced by endocannabinoid and endorphin activity, and social bonding may be hypothesized.

Evidence supporting these claims includes findings that, compared with solo exercise, group exercise enhances activity in pain and reward systems. A series of studies with rowers and runners using side-by-side ergometers and treadmills found that participants tolerate significantly greater pain following group synchronous workouts than after solo or group non-synchronous workouts of the same basic form, intensity, and duration (e.g., Cohen et. al. 2010; Sullivan et. al. 2014). This suggests that there is greater endorphin and endocannabinoid activity among participants who train together in synchrony than among those who train alone. A separate body of research has implicated endorphins and endocannabinoids in social interaction and bonding across a range of contexts (e.g., primate grooming, social play, drug-taking activity). Taken together, these findings support the claim that forms of group exercise that effectively activate opioidergic and endocannabinoid rewards may have particularly powerful effects on individual mood, well-being, and group camaraderie and cohesion via what might be called an exercise-induced "social high."

SOCIAL SYNC

Sports and exercise in group settings typically entail the tight coordination of bodies and minds in time in space, both intra- and interpersonally. Coordinated, synchronous behavior with others in ritual, dance, singing, and drill has long been thought to enhance social solidarity (e.g., Durkheim 2012), and similar effects may be integral to the most intimate human activities (e.g., in mother-infant interaction, lovemaking). Experimental evidence shows that synchronous marching, singing, and even simple finger tapping significantly increase cohesion, liking, affiliation, perceived similarity, and generosity among participants. In a seminal study on synchrony and cooperation, Wiltermuth and Heath (2009) found that people who marched and sang with one another under controlled experimental conditions cooperated more in subsequent economic exercises than those who participated in similar, non-synchronous activities.

This interpersonal synchrony effect is thought to derive in part from the tight attentional union that occurs between individuals when they match the content and timing of their actions. By performing the same action at the same time, interpersonal similarity is enhanced and self-other boundaries become blurred in action processing and recall. In a recent study by Miles et al. (2010), pairs of participants were instructed to sit opposite one another and perform arm-curling movements while alternately pronouncing aloud a series of country names that were played through personal headphones. They were then individually asked to identify who had said which country names. When participants had performed the same arm-curl movements in synchrony with one another, their recall accuracy for who had said what was significantly poorer than when they had performed the same movements in anti-phase synchrony (i.e., when participants raised and lowered arms in opposite alternating order). The self-memory advantage that strangers normally exhibit in such tasks was eliminated via a simple and subtle behavioral synchrony intervention that appears to have shifted participants' attentional focus from self to other. This effect on memory was similar to that commonly observed among people who have long-standing interpersonal connections.

Self-other blurring may be central to the "magnifying" effect described by the team rower in the anecdote at the beginning of this chapter. In experienced crews, all oars touch and exit the water at the same precise instant. Multiple bodies—legs, backs, arms, and wrists—bend in perfect unison to generate a singular force propelling the boat forward. In this moment, crew members' relative efforts and effects on the boat they all occupy are individually indistinguishable. The resultant blurring of self-other boundaries potentially generates a physical-proprioceptive illusion that one's own effort and output are exponentially magnified. This sensation, in turn, appears to give rise to unique psychological states variously described by those who have experienced them as "pure pleasure" and "exultation" (Brown 2013: 161, 269).

It is unlikely that all group exercise activities achieve these psychological effects to the same degree, or that they are associated with such intense psychological reward. Indeed, long and hard hours of training are often required to perfect a team's capacity for coordination. Across many group movement contexts, however, the combination of attentional union and self-other blurring among participants, together with the magnifying effects of jointly coordinated physical effort, may account in part for the "click of communality" experienced by participants. Culture exploits this basic package of features across many different social interaction contexts. Dance, song, music, play, sports, and ritual have been the focus of considerable social scientific speculation about the possible role that synchronous movement has in promoting social solidarity and cooperation. Mounting evidence from the behavioral and psychological sciences now indicates a powerful causal association between synchronous group activity and social cohesion.

SOCIAL DRIVE

Motivations that underpin participation in sports and group exercise are highly variable across activities, individuals, ages, and cultures. Evidence reviewed below suggests that, irrespective of the many differences, the common social context of group exercise activities is a compelling factor in participants' motivation and pleasure.

From an evolutionary perspective, selection favored those of our ancestors who were best able to coordinate with others—that is, those who had the skills and motivations to coordinate with others and to identify and recruit other suitable coordinators. Evidence from developmental, social, and comparative psychology suggests that species-specific forms of human sociality depend upon a complex set of social-cognitive mechanisms and processes. These include joint attention abilities as well as abilities to infer others' intentions and goals, share common knowledge, detect cheaters, evaluate fairness, make decisions about punishment, and prefer in-group over out-group members. Successful social interaction permits a wide range of fitness-enhancing behaviors such as group hunting, collective child-rearing, warfare, and exchange.

Our unique sociality is not all down to cognitive skill, however. Humans have unique social motivations also. We are motivated to collaborate, cooperate, and coordinate together across many different interaction contexts. The possibility that collaborative forms of sociality, including group exercise, music, religious ritual, and sports, are intrinsically rewarding is consistent with a selectionist account of human social and cognitive evolution. Intrinsic motivations to collaborate and cooperate together may originate in evolutionary advantages reaped not only in the material domain, such as subsistence and defense, but from successful reputation management and strong social attachments in increasingly complex and interdependent group settings. Observational and experimental studies have shown that young children engage in coordinated, collaborative activity with others even when this offers no immediate material advantage over acting alone. In contrast, chimpanzees engage others in collaborative activities only when there are obvious advantages to doing so (e.g., obtaining more food than would otherwise be possible). This suggests that interspecific differences in sociality may to some extent reflect differences in social motivations rather than divergent social-cognitive skills (Melis and Tomasello 2013). These social motivations are exhibited at a basic level in a general and pervasive attraction to connectedness and aversion to loneliness. For humans, doing things together offers intrinsic psychological rewards—in other words, the winning, or pleasure, is in the taking part.

The importance of social motivations and pleasure for sustaining exercise motivation and performance is well established in sports psychology research. Despite the cross-cultural ubiquity of exercise and its many known benefits, physical inactivity is an important contributor to ill health across the developed world. Many people take up exercise for health reasons, but the bulk of evidence suggests that, when it comes to motivating and sustaining participation, education and informed decision-making are no match to intrinsic affective pleasure (Ekkekakis et al. 2011). Further, in a meta-analysis that included 87 studies and almost 50,000 participants, Carron and colleagues found that, from an adherence perspective, exercising with others was superior to exercising alone. More specifically, motivation and pleasure in exercise settings is significantly predicted by group cohesion and intragroup similarity (Burke et al. 2008). Uniquely human social motivations potentially link these two findings—exercise in cohesive social settings sustains pleasure and, therefore, participation. Cohen et. al.'s (2010) study with rowers further suggests that social context can also positively impact performance, reducing perceptions of pain and giving a higher high. In the following section, we consider in more detail how the support of a cohesive group might come to have such powerful effects on perceived effort and pain.

SOCIAL BOOST

Participants in sports and exercise often experience pain, stress, and physical discomfort in the pursuit of their goals. In many competitive sports, the person or team who can go harder, faster, and longer, conquering fatigue and intense pain, ultimately wins the prize. Groundbreaking neuroscientific and psychological research is currently illuminating our understanding of the ways in which social context influences pain perception and activity in pain-related neural circuitry. This work has potential relevance for understanding how and why social context influences the stamina, endurance, and performance outcomes of individuals and teams.

Studies on placebo analgesia—pain relief through treatment that has no active ingredient—have revealed significant effects of belief alone on reported intensity of pain and on neural processes that mediate pain. Placebo analgesic effects are known to operate through expectations based on, for example, beliefs about efficacy or previous experience of the treatment. There is increasing evidence that these beliefs may be influenced via both implicit and explicit cognitive processes. Humphrey and Skoyles (2012) have suggested that evolved mechanisms governing conscious and unconscious calculations about the costs and benefits of recovery under variable environmental conditions may be responsible for the placebo response in analgesia and in immune system defense more broadly.

Cognitive neuroscientific research into placebo analgesia has mostly taken place within clinical contexts in which, for example, experts explicitly inform patients of the efficacy of a particular medical intervention, thereby influencing patients' expectations about the possibility of relief. Bingel et. al. (2011) investigated responses of 22 participants to pain stimuli (using controlled heat) and pain relief (Remifentanil administered via controlled infusion pump). At baseline, participants' average reported pain intensity was 66 out of 100 (where 0 means "no pain" and 100 means "unbearable pain"). Ratings dropped to 55 when a controlled dose of Remifentanil was administered without participants' knowledge. Participants were then informed that they would receive a dose of powerful pain reliever; the average pain rating fell further to 39. They were then told that the pain relief was being withdrawn, though in reality it was not; scores returned to baseline levels (64). Positive expectations therefore effectively doubled the effect of Remifentanil, while negative expectations abolished it. These differences in self-reported pain ratings were reflected in changes in unpleasantness and anxiety ratings and activation in core areas of the cerebral pain network. Recent social neuroscience research outside of a strictly clinical context has shown that merely holding a photo of an attachment figure (e.g., romantic partner, as compared with photo of a stranger) can have similar effects on pain perception and associated neural activity (Eisenberger et al. 2011).

In conditions of distress and pain, the relief, comfort, and feelings of security that the presence of loved ones can bring is well known. The studies described above have established that social context influences not just the perception of pain, but its underlying neurochemistry and neurophysiology, including opioidergic and endocannabinoid activity. This indicates a possible role for such "social placebo" effects in group exercise. According to the social placebo account, the presence of close others, or possibly even mere cues to their presence (e.g., photographic images, team colors) or to social cohesion (e.g., behavioral synchrony), can significantly influence these factors for success, reducing pain and pain perception, fatigue, unpleasantness and anxiety, thereby enhancing performance and reward. Future research on the role of implicit and explicit social placebo holds great promise for understanding the links between social cohesion and pain, performance, and motivation in group exercise. More generally, there is enormous scope to investigate the range of social triggers for placebo analgesia.

CONCLUSION

Humans' combined physical, cognitive, and social capacities for coordinated and exertive movement are unique. They are thought to have served important survival functions in human evolution, for example, in hunting, travel and communication, and defense. For most people today, however, the substantive rewards of group exercise are less obvious and immediate. Modern technologies have largely dissociated coordinated group exercise from everyday subsistence and communications. Yet, despite the huge emotional and energetic costs that group exercise often incurs, it remains a pervasive feature of human culture. Why is sustained, coordinated aerobic activity such a recurrent feature of everyday life, cross-cutting cultural domains as varied as religion, sport, music, and play?

The independent lines of research reviewed above suggest a powerful role for physical exercise in individual well-being and social cohesion and, in turn, a powerful role for social context in exercise psychology and performance. Together, they substantiate sporting anecdote and social theory alike, elucidating how physical exercise can promote camaraderie among participants, how the perceived boundaries between the physical actions of self and other can become blurred in perception and memory, how the self's power to act can be (and be perceived to be) thrillingly magnified by social collaborators, context, and cues, and how the efforts and output of a cohesive group of individuals can be significantly greater than the sum of their parts. In "the ultimate team sport"—in other words, euphoric, in sync, cooperative, and supportive—the normal physical, biological, and psychological limits of individual agency are dramatically lifted. This, per-haps, is the agency of the team's spirit.

NOTE

1. http://usatoday30.usatoday.com/educate/college/careers/hottopic7.htm, accessed October 11, 2014.

REFERENCES

Bingel, U., V. Wanigasekera, K. Wiech, R. N. Mhuircheartaigh, M. C. Lee, M. Ploner, and I. Tracey. 2011. "The Effect of Treatment Expectation on Drug Efficacy: Imaging the Analgesic Benefit of the Opioid Remifentanil." *Science Translational Medicine* 3(70): 70ra14.

Boecker, H., T. Sprenger, M. E. Spilker, G. Henriksen, M. Koppenhoefer, K. J. Wagner, M. Valet, A. Berthele, & T. R. Toll. 2008. "The Runner's High: Opioidergic Mechanisms in the Human Brain." *Cerebral Cortex* 18(11): 2523–2531.

Bramble, D. M., and D. E. Lieberman. 2004. "Endurance Running and the Evolution of Homo." *Nature* 432(7015): 345–352.

Brown, D. J. 2013. *The Boys in the Boat*. London: Pan MacMillan.

Burke, S. M., A. V. Carron, and K. M. Shapcott. 2008. "Cohesion in Exercise Groups: An Overview." *International Review of Sport and Exercise Psychology* 1(2): 107–123.

Cohen, E. E. A., R. Ejsmond-Frey, N. Knight, and R. Dunbar. 2010. "Rowers' High: Behavioural Synchrony Is Correlated with Elevated Pain Thresholds." *Biology Letters* 6(1): 106–108. doi: 10.1098/rsbl.2009.0670.

Davis, A., J. Taylor, and E. Cohen. 2015. "Social Bonds and Exercise: Evidence for a Reciprocal Relationship." *PLoS ONE* 10(8): e0136705. http://doi.org/10.1371/journal.pone.0136705.s012.

Durkheim, E. (1912) 2012. *The Elementary Forms of the Religious Life*. Mineola, NY: Courier Dover Publications.

Eisenberger, N. I., S. L. Master, T. K. Inagaki, S. E. Taylor, D. Shirinyan, M. D. Lieberman, and B. D. Naliboff. 2011. "Attachment Figures Activate a Safety Signal-Related Neural Region and Reduce Pain Experience." *PNAS* 108(28): 11721–11726.

Ekkekakis, P., G. Parfitt, and S. Petruzzello, S. J. 2011. "The Pleasure and Displeasure People Feel When They Exercise at Different Intensities." *Sports Medicine* 41(8): 641–671.

Humphrey, N., and J. Skoyles. 2012. "The Evolutionary Psychology of Healing: A Human Success Story." *Current Biology* 22(17): R695–R698.

Melis, A. P., and M. Tomasello. 2013. "Chimpanzees' (*Pan troglodytes*) Strategic Helping in a Collaborative Task." *Biology Letters* 9(2): 20130009.

Miles, L. K., L. K. Nind, Z. Henderson, and C. N. Macrae. 2010. "Moving Memories: Behavioral Synchrony and Memory for Self and Others." *Journal of Experimental Social Psychology* 46(2): 457–460.

Murphy, M., and R. A. White. 2011. *In the Zone: Transcendent Experience in Sports*. New York: Open Road Media.

Radcliffe-Brown, A. R. 1948. *The Andaman Islanders*. Glencoe, IL: Free Press.

Raichlen, D. A., A. D. Foster, G. L. Gerdeman, A. Seillier, and A. Giuffrida. 2012. "Wired to Run: Exercise-Induced Endocannabinoid Signaling in Humans and Cursorial Mammals with Implications for the 'Runner's High.'" *The Journal of Experimental Biology* 215(8): 1331–1336.

Raichlen, D. A., A. D. Foster, A. Seillier, A. Giuffrida, and G. L. Gerdeman. 2013. "Exercise-Induced Endocannabinoid Signaling Is Modulated by Intensity." *European Journal of Applied Physiology* 113(4): 869–875.

Sullivan, P. J., K. Rickers, and K. L. Gammage. 2014. "The Effect of Different Phases of Synchrony on Pain Threshold." *Group Dynamics: Theory, Research, and Practice* 18(2): 122–128.

Wiltermuth, S., and C. Heath. 2009. "Synchrony and Cooperation." *Psychological Science* 20(1): 1–5.

CHAPTER 16

Social Bonding Through Dance and 'Musiking'

BRONWYN TARR

INTRODUCTION: SOCIAL GROUPS

From a biological perspective, successful interpersonal interactions are critical in the establishment and maintenance of social groups. As a gregarious species, much of our survival depends upon these social groups; more cohesive and tightly bonded networks are well coordinated, and group-level selection predicts that members of these groups are more likely to survive than those acting alone or in less bonded units (Dunbar and Shultz 2010). In humans, experimentally manipulated social support influences a range of physiological measures such as blood pressure, cortisol levels, and heart rate, and social isolation is correlated with reduced life expectancy (for a review see Thorsteinsson and James 1999).

Primate social groups (particularly those of anthropoid primates) are characterized by a large number of interpersonal relationships between non-kin and non-sexual partners. These "social bonds" (feelings of, and behaviors signaling, closeness and affiliation) are frequently termed "friendships," and form the backbone of our social networks. Large, complex, and cohesive social groups place a high cognitive load on interacting members; each agent needs to establish interpersonal connections and keep track of ongoing interactive histories with other agents in their social network (Dunbar 1998). These cognitive constraints associated with sociality contribute toward a species-specific upper limit to group size, a relationship that is reflected by covariance between mean group size and neocortical volume (relative to the remaining volume of the brain; Dunbar 1998).

We have particularly large social networks (approximately 150 individuals) compared to our primate cousins, who establish and maintain their smaller networks predominantly via reciprocal allo-grooming (reviewed in Dunbar 1998). Grooming is subject to time constraints: it is typically a dyadic activity, and the number of individuals one can groom in a day is limited by the amount of time that can be spared from other activities, such as foraging and sleeping (Dunbar 1998). In the case of large human groups, this time investment is unfeasible. Our extensive networks require bonding behaviors that can involve multiple agents building affiliation simultaneously, or "grooming at a distance" (Dunbar 2012).

DANCE AS A MEANS OF "GROOMING AT A DISTANCE"

A number of different behaviors are likely to have helped humans establish social bonds with multiple individuals simultaneously, and to maintain those bonds with relatively little time investment. One hypothesis is that rhythmic bodily movement and synchronization may have played (and continue to play) an important role in contributing to group cohesion and social bonding. This has been termed the "social bonding hypothesis" of dance, although it is generalizable to other activities involving music (e.g., Koelsch 2014).

To our knowledge, there is no human culture that does not possess some form of group music-making and dance. Clearly the stylistic and socio-contextual details of these activities are by no means homogenous across cultures, making definitions of these activities challenging. Nevertheless, underpinning this diversity is the curious fact that the production of organized, expressive sound (broadly "music") and the coordination of our movement to music of some form and with others (broadly "dance"), are prominent features in ritual, religion, and human expression generally (Ehrenreich 2008; Tomlinson 2015). Arguably, these activities are fundamentally cooperative in nature; not only do they demand complex sensorimotor coordination, but we tend to do these activities with others. Music-based group activities demand some degree of coordination of actions and cooperation in terms of establishing a joint goal and shared intention (Koelsch 2014). The social bonding hypothesis suggests that ritualized group dance and music activities foster social contact, social cognition, homogenous emotions, communication, coordination, cooperation, and group cohesion (Koelsch 2014). Furthermore, as we can engage in these activities simultaneously with many individuals, music-based activities could provide an effective means of bonding on a large scale.

Evidence that social bonding arises from, and also is signaled by, various music-based activities has been provided by, inter alia, ethnographers, historians, ethnomusicologists, biomusicologists, and experimental researchers. Empirical studies have focused on the fact that music-based activities generally involve participants synchronizing their movements to a rhythmic beat (usually provided by music), and to one another.

SYNCHRONY AND SOCIAL BONDING

Experiments involving simple finger tapping, walking, and rocking in chairs have demonstrated that engaging in coordinated, specifically synchronized, activities increases interpersonal closeness. Compared to asynchronous or solo conditions, performing movements in synchrony leads to increased trust between co-actors, liking each other more, being more willing to help each other, and feeling similar in personality (literature reviewed in more detail in Tarr et al. 2014). These positive effects on social bonding are evident when individuals perform synchronized movements in small groups of three or four and when the synchronized action involves singing and/or moving (Wiltermuth and Heath 2009) and dancing with others to music (Tarr et al. 2015). Furthermore, the capacity for synchronized tasks to increase interpersonal social bonding is evident from a young age: children are more likely to display helping behavior after moving and singing in synchrony than those in a non-musical control condition (Kirschner and Tomasello 2010).

These studies demonstrate that performing similar movements in a predictable, rhythmic fashion leads to individuals feeling socially bonded. This phenomenon is thought to be based on action-perception networks facilitating a blurring of the sense of "self" and "other" during synchronized action (e.g., Demos et al. 2012), which leads to a social bond between actors. Additionally, there is growing evidence that synchronized action is associated with various neuropharmacological mechanisms (see chapter 15 by Cohen in this volume). For example, synchronized rowing (see chapter 15) and dancing in synchrony (Tarr et al. 2015) elevates pain threshold, a common proxy measure for endorphins due to the close relationship between opioids and perception of pain. Given the role of endorphins in social bonding across a range of other mammals, it is plausible that opioids play a role in underpinning the social closeness that arises during synchronized bonding activities such as dance (Tarr et al. 2014).

In addition to synchrony, a number of other important factors contribute toward increased interpersonal affiliation when dancing together. For example, shared attention with co-actors, working toward a joint goal and improved mood after successful co-engagement, all contribute to increasing feelings of closeness. These elements do not arise exclusively in music-based activities, and are clearly evident in a range of human behaviors such as team sports (see chapter 15). What sets dance apart from other similarly complex, coordinative, and exertive human activities is the fact that it involves responding directly and purposefully to music.

HOW MUSIC MOVES AND BONDS US

Music adds to the social bonding effects that can arise in situations of group coordination in various ways. First, people spontaneously synchronize to music (Janata et al. 2012), and as a consequence music encourages and facilitates occurrences of synchrony. People naturally entrain to a rhythmic beat embedded in music, and are capable of doing so from a very young age (discussed in more detail in Koelsch 2014). Music can therefore establish a shared and predictable, rhythmic scaffolding, thereby facilitating synchronization of timing between multiple individuals. In large groups, it is difficult to coordinate synchrony and observe the movements of all the other participants simultaneously, arguably making "self-other" merging a less likely prospect. Rhythmic music can facilitate synchrony for large numbers of people, perhaps by providing a central "other" to which each participant can direct their attention (e.g., drill marching), thereby leading to the social closeness described above.

Indeed, synchrony with music *itself* appears to improve interpersonal affiliation. Demos et al. (2012) found that participants who performed a chair-rocking task to music reported feeling more connected to each other than those who performed the task without background music. This interpersonal connectedness was predicted by synchrony with the music, and not by synchrony with one another. Accordingly this study suggests that synchrony to music is sufficient to cause bonding effects, and synchrony *between* people may be irrelevant when they are engaging with a shared external source of rhythm as provided by the music.

But the effects of music go beyond its capacity for facilitating synchronous movement. In addition to the predictability provided by a rhythmic beat, listening to music induces strong emotional and pleasurable effects. These arise via core brain regions generally involved in processing affect (including areas that are responsible for releasing endorphins), and those associated with reward and motivation (Koelsch 2014). When we engage with shared music alongside others, this can homogenize participants' emotional states (Koelsch 2014), which could theoretically play an important role in increasing interpersonal cohesion and decreasing social conflict.

Aside from moving us emotionally, music literally moves us. According to PET scans, intense pleasurable responses experienced when merely listening to music (and not moving physically) are associated with activation in areas of the brain involved in movement control (Blood and Zatorre, 2001). More often than not, listening to music *does* induce some form of actual physical movement, be it simple head bobbing, foot tapping, or finger tapping in time with the rhythmic beat. At a neurological level, certain elements of music are particularly good at inducing a motor response, for example certain tempos. At a higher level, the ability of music to induce body movement and dance has been described as "groove" (e.g., Janata et al. 2012), and certain musical styles with particular musical elements appear better at inducing groove. The close relationship between music and our often spontaneous and unconscious urge to move is likely a consequence of a tightly coupled and ancient relationship between movement and music, originating from a time when our engagement with music was directly linked to a performance of agency.

"MUSIKING": AN EXPRESSION OF AGENCY

Our immense aptitude and appreciation for sound and movement as a means to express, communicate, and connect has probably been part of humanity for a very long time. The oldest identified instruments (bone "flutes") are dated to approximately 50,000–35,000 years ago (for references see Kirschner and Tomasello 2010), but arguably our first instruments were our voice and body. When music first originated, our bodies likely acted as a moving, percussive instrument (Cummins 2009). Indeed, at the most fundamental level, it is not possible to create sound without vibration, and, by extension, the production of music requires movement. Consequently, movement is involved when we use any instrument to produce sound, but also when we attach bells, shakers, heels, and so on to the body to accentuate the production of sound associated with each step or movement. When our bodily movements contribute to musical stimulus (for example when we have bells attached to our stomping feet) we are exercising agency over the production of the music. Clapping, snapping, and stomping while dancing is evident in many cultures today, with both audiences and performers using their bodies to create, or at least add to, the musical stimuli. Indeed, in many cultures, music and dance are considered indistinguishable and some languages do not have separate words to describe them (Blacking 1995).

This close link between movement and music fits with Christopher Small's term "musiking," defined as "[taking] part, in any capacity, in a musical performance, whether by performing, by listening, by rehearsing or practicing, by providing material for performance (what is called composing), or by dancing" (Small 1998:9). Given that dance most likely co-evolved with music as a means of generating rhythm and sound (Cummins, 2009), it is understandable that music tends to make us want to move, and specifically *synchronize*, with the musical beat. In matching our movements in time to a musical rhythm, we are simulating the timing of movements that could have conceivably contributed toward the production of that rhythmic beat.

The ability to have agency over the production of musical sounds through movement has been shown to have significant physiological and psychological effects. For example, varying the degree of musical agency for people exercising in a group can influence their ability to perform strenuous exercise and their mood. In a high agency condition, exercise machines were linked to musical output software such that a musical sound resulted from each movement, and consequently individuals "created" music as they exerted themselves (Fritz et al. 2013). This experiment (and others by the same authors) demonstrated that when movement (during group exercise) results in musical feedback, participants perceived exertion to be lower, reported enhanced mood, and felt a greater desire to exert themselves further, in comparison to when they were exercising while listening (passively) to independently provided music not connected to their movements (Fritz et al. 2013). According to these results, musical agency (i.e., executing purposeful movement that results in musical sounds) feels good and improves the capacity to withstand strenuous exercise.

Although the exercise scenario described above is clearly a contrived case of musical agency, the findings likely reflect the fact that we are wired to engage with music in a context in which we do in fact have agency over the production of sound. In reality, unless we are a member of a band or play a musical instrument, we more frequently engage passively with music, which rarely involves a context in which our movements directly contribute to the music. We frequently enjoy prerecorded music, which involves a decoupling of our engagement with that music from the social context and movement evident at its source. Under these modern circumstances, and in the absence of having any of our music-induced movements actually result in some direct contribution to the music, perhaps when we move to music we are attempting to *pretend* we possess some agency over the production of that music. The more tightly we couple our movement with the music, for example, the better we synchronize our movement with the beats, the more convincing is this simulated agency. In this manner, even if we are not actually making the music to which we dance, our synchronization with the musical beat simulates movement required to explain, or physically justify, that musical beat.

CONCLUSION

Humans' social agency occurs in the context of large, interconnected social networks that are established and maintained by a variety of group activities, such as dance. Our tendency to move in time to music, and the ubiquity of music-based activities such as dance are important aspects of what makes us human. Dance and synchronizing to music facilitates interpersonal closeness, providing a means to build and maintain large social groups. Furthermore, the way we engage with music is likely embedded in an ancient history, in which movement, sound, and agency were intertwined. Based on this account, music-making and dance, which are conceptualized here as a single, coupled concept—"musiking"—provides an invaluable, naturalistic empirical and theoretical platform for understanding foundations of our social agency.

REFERENCES

Blacking, J. 1995. *Music, Culture, & Experience: Selected Papers of John Blacking.* Chicago/London: University of Chicago Press.

Blood, A. J., and R. J. Zatorre. 2001. "Intensely Pleasurable Responses to Music Correlate with Activity in Brain Regions Implicated in Reward and Emotion." *Proceedings of the National Academy of Sciences of the United States of America* 98: 11818–11823. doi:10.1073/pnas.191355898.

Cummins, F. 2009. "Rhythm as an Affordance for the Entrainment of Movement." *Phonetica* 66: 15–28. doi:10.1159/000208928.

Demos, A. P., R. Chaffin, K. T. Begosh, J. R. Daniels, and K. L. Marsh. 2012. "Rocking to the Beat: Effects of Music and Partner's Movements on Spontaneous Interpersonal Coordination." *Journal of Experimental Psychology: General* 141: 49–53. doi:10.1037/a0023843.

Dunbar, R. I. M. 1998. "The Social Brain Hypothesis." *Evolutionary Anthropology* 6: 178–190. doi:10.1080/03014460902960289.

Dunbar, R. I. M. 2012. "On the Evolutionary Function of Song and Dance." In *Music, Language and Human Evolution*, edited by N. Bannan. 201–214. Oxford: Oxford University Press.

Dunbar, R. I. M., and S. Shultz. 2010. "Bondedness and Sociality." *Behaviour* 147: 775–803. doi:10.1163/000579510X501151.

Ehrenreich, B. 2008. *Dancing in the Streets: A History of Collective Joy.* New York: Metropolitan.

Fritz, T. H., J. Halfpaap, S. Grahl, A. Kirkland, and A. Villringer. 2013. "Musical Feedback during Exercise Machine Workout Enhances Mood." *Frontiers in Psychology* 4: 921. doi:10.3389/fpsyg.2013.00921.

Janata, P., S. T. Tomic, and J. M. Haberman. 2012. "Sensorimotor Coupling in Music and the Psychology of the Groove." *Journal of Experimental Psychology* 141: 54–75. doi:10.1037/a0024208.

Kirschner, S., and M. Tomasello. 2010. "Joint Music Making Promotes Prosocial Behavior in 4-Year-Old Children." *Evolution and Human Behavior* 31: 354–364. doi:10.1016/j.evolhumbehav.2010.04.004.

Koelsch, S. 2014. "Brain Correlates of Music-Evoked Emotions." *Nature Reviews Neuroscience* 15: 170–180. doi:10.1038/nrn3666.

Small, C. 1998. *Musicking: The Meaning of Performing and Listening.* Hanover, NH: Wesleyan/University Press of New England.

Tarr, B., J. Launay, and R. I. M. Dunbar. 2014. "Music and Social Bonding: 'Self-Other' Merging and Neurohormonal Mechanisms." *Frontiers in Psychology: Auditory Cognitive Neuroscience* 5: 1–10. doi:10.3389/fpsyg.2014.01096.

Tarr, B., J. Launay, E. Cohen, and R. I. M. Dunbar. 2015. "Synchrony and Exertion during Dance Independently Raise Pain Threshold and Encourage Social Bonding." *Biology Letters* 11: 1–3. doi:10.1098/rsbl.2015.0767.

Thorsteinsson, E. B., and J. E. James. 1999. "A Meta-analysis of the Effects of Experimental Manipulations of Social Support during Laboratory Stress." *Psychology & Health* 14: 869–886. doi:10.1080/08870449908407353.

Tomlinson, Gary. 2015. *A Million Years of Music: The Emergence of Human Modernity.* Cambridge, MA: MIT Press.

Wiltermuth, S. S., and C. Heath. 2009. "Synchrony and Cooperation." *Psychological Science* 20: 1–5.

PART SEVEN

Agency and Infancy

CHAPTER 17

Timescales for Understanding the Agency of Infants and Caregivers

JOANNA RĄCZASZEK-LEONARDI

THE PROBLEM

Consider an everyday event: an infant looks at an object, his mother follows the gaze and, if the object is movable, picks it up and moves closer, wiggles it in front of the baby, or, if it is safe, and the child can already grasp, hands the object to the baby. The question is, who moved the object? One intuitively obvious answer is, the mother. From the gaze of the baby she has read the direction, selected an object, assessed its movability and safety and then, on the basis of some assumptions about the infant's needs and intentions, decided to give it to the baby.

But perhaps this slice-in-time explanation packs too much into the head of the mother, losing many aspects of the sense of this episode. Much in a cognitive psychological way, it focuses on (a very important) "how" question, neglecting "why" the whole episode is structured in this way. I will argue that such events do not happen only here and now, but rather are instantiations of processes operating on several timescales, and involving several different systems. If we take this into account, the story (what happens, who is the main protagonist) becomes more complex but perhaps more sensible.

In what follows, I will try to show this with a microanalysis of an interaction between a baby and his caregiver, which is an instance of an everyday, mundane activity. The goal is to identify the sources of forces behind current, online behaviors by looking at them as points on several trajectories at the same time. Some causes for behavior will indeed, as cognitive psychology wants, lie in the heads of individuals at a given moment. Yet for others we will have to look at systemic levels, for example, dyadic, group, or population, and toward slower timescales at which relevant processes unfold.

TIMESCALES IN THE EXPLANATION OF HUMAN BEHAVIOR

The importance of timescales and multi-systemic nature of human cognitive and behavioral phenomena is increasingly often acknowledged. It helps to identify important factors to be included in the explanations of current behaviors (Rączaszek-Leonardi 2003, 2010; MacWhinney 2005; Enfield 2014), and to tackle questions about the origins of cognitive skills (Dumas, Kelso, and Nadel 2014) and about outcomes of individual and collective behaviors (MacWhinney 2005; Smith, Brighton, and Kirby 2003; Rączaszek-Leonardi 2009).

To give just one example of how such explanations work and how they differ from the explanations by individual mental mechanisms, let's look at Smith et al.'s (2003) study of the sources for language compositionality. Traditionally, the main explanation of this feature of language was based on the individual's universal grammatical device, which accounted for structuring of language in the face of the "poverty of stimulus" argument (e.g., Chomsky 1980). Smith and his colleagues used elegant computer simulations to show that, given the iterative processes of communication and the nature of intergenerational learning (a "bottleneck in transmission"), which is necessarily based only on a subset of possible language expressions, the compositional systems are simply the only systems that are stable. Thus, while acknowledging the main constraint on the system (the poverty of stimulus), the authors do not see the necessity for building explanation for compositionality by referring to individual mental constructs. Instead, the vital elements of the explanatory framework consist of events happening on two different timescales: ontogenetic processes and cultural evolution of a linguistic system. In later studies (e.g., Kirby, Cornish, and Smith 2008) the importance of those slower timescale processes were confirmed in experiments with real participants in the lab.

One of the main messages from such a systemic approach is that moving a level up, or down, focusing and refocusing on faster or slower processes gives access to qualitatively new explanatory variables and shows that the concepts of emergence, self-organization, and the relation of reciprocal causality between the levels and timescales can be very helpful in constructing viable theories of complex phenomena. This, of course, is important not only for understanding, but also for finding points of leverage through which it is possible to change a given dynamic system. By adapting tools for the analysis of dynamic systems to social and behavioral sciences, we have ways to study and to quantify the effects of action and interaction of those different forces, and to relate processes on different timescales (Kelso 1995).

However, since scientific explanations strive for simplicity, the multi-systemic and multi-timescale approach may seem to blur the picture rather than provide a useful analysis. The strategy is thus to focus only on certain timescales and subsystems, chosen for their relevance on the basis of previous work and theoretical hunches, while remembering that they are only a subset of what might become relevant. For the question of agency examined in this chapter we focus mainly on four timescales (with a fifth, that of biological adaptation, lurking behind): cultural, ontogenetic, history of interaction between particular individuals ("social"), and the online time scale of current behavior.

TIMESCALES FOR AGENCY

So let us look at an episode like the one mentioned above more closely. Here I describe in detail an interaction from the corpus of video data gathered by Iris Nomikou and Katharina Rohlfing in Bielefeld (Nomikou and Rohlfing 2011). This useful data set consists of a defined event (changing the diaper) videotaped in 17 mother-infant pairs in natural settings (home) longitudinally, at five time points between the third and eighth months of the baby's life (for more detailed analysis of these data from the point of view of tuning attention for coaction and development of routines, see Rączaszek-Leonardi, Nomikou, and Rohlfing 2013).

The interaction chosen for illustration involves a three-month-old baby and his mother. The baby is lying on his back and the mother is going to change his diaper. At one point the baby turns the head to the right, where, approximately 7 centimeters from the baby's face (probably much too close for him to focus on), there is a colorful soft toy cube. The mother immediately (within 1 second)[1] shifts her gaze to the cube, at the same time asking, "What is there?" Then, within the next second, she looks into the baby's eyes, repeating the question, but this time leaning over the baby. In the meantime she is taking the diaper off, which eventually requires her to move back to see what she is doing. However, with her words, in a steady rhythm, she keeps the "topic" of the cube in focus, addressing the baby

"Little mouse?" (1 second) "Hmm?" (1 second) "What is there" (1 second) "is this a cube?" At this point, the cube is very close beside the head of the baby and the baby seems to be looking slightly above it. After the mother has disposed of the diaper, she asks again "Is this a cube?" and this time picks up the cube and moves it away from the baby and higher, on the border of the changing table, saying "Look!" (1 second) "Yes, Look!"

There is nothing special about this interaction. There are thousands just like this one between caretakers and babies every day. And here is the point: an infant after thousands such interactions is just not the same as before. Rich cultural structuring of coaction with a conspecific, enacted by a caretaker, affects the perception and movement dispositions of a baby by "coercing" him into taking a part in a holistic event. In other words, the baby is being tuned for a meaningful, situated interaction. This requires that the baby start to perceive own actions as enabling others' behavior and start perceiving others' actions as affordances for own actions (for more detailed analysis of the social aspect of affordances, see Costall 1995; Rączaszek-Leonardi et al., 2013). The tuning happens in a "movement first" way: the movement performed by the baby is embedded in coaction and—by this very coaction—is given meaning as a part of a social event.

Let's examine "frame by frame" how and why it happens and determine the mechanisms and causes behind the subsequent moves in this interaction. A look to the side (most probably accidental) is reacted to by the mother by a shift of her gaze to the nearest salient object. The same behavior would be expected as a response to any look to the side by a conspecific: the biological propensity to focus on eyes (e.g., Johnson et al. 1991) shaped by interactions within culture is responsible for it. It does not require any conscious reflection on the mother's side. Due to biological and cultural constraints, this is what she does automatically when seeing the gaze of others. In a sense the baby's look to the side *makes* the mother look in the same direction.

A normal, in other words, culturally stabilized, course of events would be to read the intention from the gaze of a conspecific and act accordingly (or on the contrary, depending on the situation) toward the object. Since the mother is in interaction with a baby who probably cannot be credited at this age with intending to indicate something with his gaze, she shows the baby, in an exaggerated way, how such an episode usually works. The focus here is on the ontogenetic timescale: if you see, a thousand times, what other people do after you look at the object, you will learn the power of your gaze. The embedding of the infant's behavior within the caretaker's own actions *makes* the infant's behavior acquire meaning in the course of development.

Thus this interactive event is a re-enactment (exaggerated, designed for the audience this young) of a cultural script that has been stabilized in cultural evolution. By drawing the baby's behavior into the meaningful event, as a vital part of it, the mother is letting the baby experience the causal power of his gaze. Hence "What is there?"—communicates her interest in what he is looking at. A second later, she leans over the baby, bringing her own face and eyes within his visual field—this might be to show the importance of his gaze, or to check what the baby is really looking at. Since she cannot immediately act on the object (having both hands busy with taking the diaper off), she keeps up the topic of gaze with rhythmically spaced utterances (that the baby, at this moment, presumably has no understanding of, but with time will), and, finally, performs the eventual action toward the object of the gaze, involving the baby (putting the cube directly on the gaze line).

Here, in this single interaction, three timescales meet: the behavior *here and now* is an enactment of a *culturally* shaped event, which—enacted repetitively—has its *developmental* effect. Due to the lack of space we have neglected a fourth timescale: that of shaping and regulation of a particular relationship between this mother and this infant. Apart from enacting cultural scripts for making the movements of the baby meaningful, the mother is also regulating a *social* relationship with her own baby, by giving her own, systematic, variation to the enactments. Thus the effect is not only a biologically and culturally adequate ontogeny (learning to interact like my conspecifics within my culture) but also a socially adequate one (learning to interact like my mother's son).

The above analysis may sound like a just-so story. However, it seems to be helpful in organizing data and posing testable hypotheses. In Rączaszek-Leonardi, Nomikou, and Rohlfing (2013) we document numerous instances in which a baby's movements are made to be part of culturally structured events, tailored appropriately to the age of the baby. In an attempt to distinguish categories of behaviors, we noticed frequent attempts of "catching the eye" of a baby, making a mother's own movements as though elicited by the infant's moves, making pauses for eliciting infant's behaviors relevant for an event, treating random behaviors as planned to fulfill the infant's part, or even actually physically moving a baby to perform a desired move. Very little, in this process, has to be attributed to mental operations on representations, depending on elaborate theories of mind, planning and/or conscious education: the baby and the mother are physically there to serve as their "best models" (Brooks 1990) in interaction.

CONCLUSION: SO WHO DID MOVE THAT?

In this small example I wanted to convey the intricacy of the mesh of individual, social, and cultural factors and forces bearing on a simple movement in an interaction. Let us return to the original question: Who moved the object? The infant? The mother? An infant-mother interactive system? An encultured and socialized infant-mother interactive system? The mother did perform the decisive move, but her actions were evoked by a gaze of a child and constrained by the ontogenetic process of tuning for coaction, which, in turn, involves re-enacting cultural scripts. The re-enactment of the cultural scripts does not necessitate planning and conscious action on her part. Constrained by living in a particular culture, slowly and appropriately for the infant's age she brings up the child, through co-movement, basing on biological adaptations, into a culturally established coaction.

Connected to the question of agency and equally important for this volume is the question of accountability. The dynamic shifts in accountability for behavior as developmental and socialization processes progress is a particularly interesting issue. It requires philosophical, moral, and cultural level analyses that are far beyond the scope of this short contribution. Yet the identification of the threads of agency, unfolding within multiple systems and on multiple timescales, which help recognize the sources of agency in a particular action, seem to be an important step in the analysis of accountability.

Even though most cognitive psychology in the last five decades has tended to neglect the slower scales, and systems larger than an individual, obviously sciences such as sociology or anthropology never did. For them, the points raised here may be rather banal: it is obvious that in every deed we are constrained by our culture, shaped in development, and driven by our social relations. Yet the notion of timescales and the methods of dynamic systems give us tools and a framework within which studying mutual dependencies among the systems and reciprocal causality between levels can become easier.

NOTE

1. The times given here are approximate. It is sufficient for the illustrative purposes of this paper. However in the investigations of the emergence of coaction patterns within dynamical framework, recording the exact timing is crucial.

REFERENCES

Brooks, R., 1990. *Elephants don't play chess. Robotics and Autonomous Systems* 6, 3–15.

Chomsky, N. 1980. *Rules and Representations*. Oxford, UK: Basil Blackwell.

Costall, A. 1995. "Socializing Affordances." *Theory and Psychology* 5: 467–481.

Dumas, G., J. A. S. Kelso, and J. Nadel. 2014. "Tackling the Social Cognition Paradox Through Multi-scale Approaches. *Frontiers in Psychology* 5: 882. doi: 10.3389/fpsyg.2014.00882.

Enfield, N. J. 2014. *Natural Causes of Language: Frames, Biases, and Cultural Transmission*. Berlin: Language Science Press.

Johnson, M. H., S. Dziurawiec, H. Ellis, H. and J. Morton. 1991. "Newborns' Preferential Tracking of Face-like Stimuli and Its Subsequent Decline." *Cognition* 40: 1–19.

Kelso, J. A. S. 1995. *Dynamic Patterns: The Self-Organization of Brain and Behavior*. Cambridge, MA: MIT Press.

Kirby, S., H. Cornish, and K. Smith. 2008. "Cumulative Cultural Evolution in the Laboratory: An Experimental Approach to the Origins of Structure in Human Language." *Proceedings of the National Academy of Sciences* 105(31):10681–10686.

MacWhinney, B. 2005. "The Emergence of Linguistic Form in Time." *Connection Science* 17(3–4): 191–211.

Nomikou, I., and K. J. Rohlfing. 2011. "Language Does Something. Body Action and Language in Maternal Input to Three-Month-Olds." *IEEE Transactions on Autonomous Mental Development* 3(2): 113–128.

Rączaszek-Leonardi, J. 2003. "The Interrelation of Time Scales in a Description of Language." *Views & Voices* 1(2): 93–108.

Rączaszek-Leonardi, J. 2009. "Symbols as Constraints: The Structuring Role of Dynamics and Self-Organization in Natural Language." *Pragmatics and Cognition* 17(3), 653–676.

Rączaszek-Leonardi, J. 2010. "Multiple Time-scales of Language Dynamics: An Example from Psycholinguistics." *Ecological Psychology* 22(4): 269–285.

Rączaszek-Leonardi, J., I. Nomikou, K. J. Rohlfing. 2013. "Young Children's Dialogical Actions: The Beginnings of Purposeful Intersubjectivity." *IEEE Transactions in Autonomous Mental Development* 5(3): 210–221.

Smith, K., H. Brighton, and S. Kirby. 2003. "Complex Systems in Language Evolution: The Cultural Emergence of Compositional Structure." *Advances in Complex Systems* 6(4): 537–558.

CHAPTER 18

Movement Synchrony, Joint Actions, and Collective Agency in Infancy

BAHAR TUNÇGENÇ

INTRODUCTION

Social encounters begin with infants' interactions with their caretakers in give-and-take relationships and continue all throughout toddlerhood and beyond, as children explore and learn from their environment and play with their peers. Much of this social interaction involves infants getting together with others in various ways to achieve common goals. As natural as they may seem, the ubiquity and human specificity of such joint actions, as well as the early development of social, cognitive, and motor skills required to carry them out are quite remarkable from a broader, evolutionary perspective.

One important feature of joint actions is their implications for agency. For instance, when a child kicks a ball, it is clearly the child who is the "agent" of this kicking action and it is the ball that is the "recipient" of the action. Yet, the distinction between an agent and a recipient starts to get blurred in, for example, a football game. Although agents can still be identified for individual kicking actions, there emerges an overarching collective agency, where individuals can be counted as agents even for the actions that they have not fully executed. Now, it is *us* who play the football game, rather than *me* kicking the ball and *you* kicking it back at me. In other words, by joining actions, we also join agency.

The emergence of this "we-ness" relies initially on infants' understanding of others' goals and intentions, which then contributes to engaging in joint actions as infants start sharing attention with others. A key element of both goal understanding and attention sharing is physical coordination of movements among the interactants. Moving in well-coordinated ways with others may have significant long-term effects on social development. Thus, the development of each one of these aspects—goal understanding, attention sharing, and performing synchronous, coordinated movements in joint actions—is crucial for understanding the emergence of collective agency.

GOAL UNDERSTANDING AND AGENCY ATTRIBUTIONS IN INFANCY

Imagine a person reaching for a water bottle; as an observer, you might automatically make the inference that the person wants to drink some water. Viewing actions as goal-directed and attributing agency to actors is a prominent feature of human cognition. Categorizing the world in terms of "actors with goals" and "things acted upon" assumes two different roles in an interaction: agents and recipients. What kinds of cues do infants make use of while identifying the agents and recipients in an interaction?

A number of behavioral cues can guide infants' attribution of goal-directedness and agency. To assess this, in one seminal study, nine-month-old infants were shown a small circle making contact with a large circle by jumping over an obstacle that separated them (Csibra, Gergely, Biro, Koos, and Brockbank 1999). Next, infants were shown the same objects moving in irrational ways, namely "jumping over" even when the obstacle was no longer there. The infants' surprise reactions to this irrational action were taken as evidence that they perceive the objects' previous actions as goal-directed. Importantly, however, the small circle's movements had certain properties: the circle initiated its own movements (self-propulsion), got bigger/smaller in response to the large circle's size changes (contingency), pursued contact with the large circle even when their positions were different (equifinal variation), and followed alternative paths in order to reach its goal (flexibility in actions). Under these conditions, nine-month-olds showed surprise, suggesting that they interpreted this evidently inanimate and non-agentive small circle's actions as goal-directed. Evidently, infants have a tendency to over-attribute goal-directedness and agency even to inanimate objects, provided the objects' motions meet certain criteria. Yet, they are not alone: adults also over-attribute agency frequently, for instance, when they see faces in the clouds or exclaim their frustrations at a malfunctioning computer or car engine.

In addition to behavioral cues, infants also make use of social cues while attributing agency to animate and inanimate objects. The social cues may be certain physical properties such as the presence of eyes and a face or communicative behaviors that the actors perform. Arguably, these social cues become particularly relevant when there is uncertainty about the actors or the conditions under which an event takes place. For instance, when an inanimate object engages in a brief "small talk" with an adult prior to performing some actions, 12-month-olds who observe this inanimate object are more likely to attribute agency to the object than if the object did not provide communicative cues (Johnson, Shimizu, and Ok 2007). Another example is when infants observe only the end-state of an action (an object appearing on the scene) without observing the initial state (an actor bringing the object into the scene). When asked to guess the actor for such actions whose initial states are not available to the infants, 10-month-olds assume that an animate (i.e., human hand) rather than an inanimate (i.e., toy train) actor must have been the agent that brought the object into the scene (Saxe, Tzelnic, and Carey 2007). Similar to the previously mentioned studies, infants' agency attribution in these studies is evident by increased surprise reactions that they show upon viewing the inanimate rather than the animate actor perform the action. Indeed, infants are quite good at picking up sociality even from minimal cues; they readily attribute agency to toy puppets that have facial features, for example (Saxe et al. 2007). This indicates the importance of social cues as well as how flexibly infants integrate information from various sources as they consider agency.

Understanding the goals behind others' actions and identifying the agents and recipients of an action are important first steps on the way to collective agency. Infants seem to develop an understanding of goal-directedness within the second half of the first year of life. Gradually, they start including more intricate features of the actors to evaluate agency in more complex circumstances. Following on from there, another milestone on the way to collective agency is the ability to understand what others intend to do and to align one's own intentions with those of others. The next section will deal with how understanding the intentions of others facilitates attention sharing.

INTENTION UNDERSTANDING AND ATTENTION SHARING
IN INFANCY

Recall the example of a person reaching for the water bottle and the common inference that the person would be reaching for the bottle to drink some water. There are, indeed, many other sub-goals involved in that action: holding the water bottle, bringing it closer to one's mouth, pouring water into the mouth, so on and so forth. It seems, however, that the human mind often ignores these middle steps in reading the behavior. Depending on what that particular circumstance brings, we identify an ultimate *intention* behind the action being performed—for example, quenching thirst—and focus on that instead. How, then, do infants understand the intentions of agents? When and how does this understanding transform into infants' sharing attention and engaging in joint actions with others?

Reading the intentions of others might be tricky, partly because different intentions might motivate similar action-outcome sequences. Still, an adult would hardly ever miss the difference between a person purposefully throwing a water bottle on the floor and a person dropping it accidentally. Similar comparisons were made to investigate infants' understanding of intentional and accidental actions. In one study, nine-month-old infants interacted with an adult who was not giving them the toy that they wanted (Behne, Carpenter, Call, and Tomasello 2005). Crucially, the adult was either teasing the infants and was unwilling to give them the toy (intentional action) or actually wanted to give them the toy but was unable to do so due to clumsiness or other physical obstacles (accidental action). Although the adult's actions looked very similar in both conditions, infants reacted with more frustration and impatience when the adult was unwilling as opposed to unable to give them the toy. This indicates that at nine months, infants understand the intentions of agents, even if the observed actions and outcomes may look similar. This understanding influences the infants' emotional state and how they respond to the actor of the intentional/accidental actions. Understanding others' intentions is a crucial step in starting to share intentions with others. Sharing intentions on objects of mutual interest is what makes joint actions possible. Hence, a closer look at infants' developing abilities to share intention with others is important.

A well-studied method for sharing attention and intention with others is using the pointing gesture. As soon as someone points to an object with an index finger, most people automatically turn their heads and look at the object being pointed out to. Although young infants may use the pointing gesture merely to attract attention, a more advanced use of it is communicative and involves the intention to share attention with others. At least from 12 months of age, infants can use the pointing gesture for the latter purpose, for example, to inform adults of the locations of objects that they have been looking for (Liszkowski, Carpenter, and Tomasello 2008). A more detailed analysis further reveals a bidirectional developmental pattern between infants' comprehension and production of the pointing gesture. From 8.5 months of age onward, those infants who comprehend others' pointing gestures as directed at objects also point themselves to direct others' attention to objects they find interesting (Woodward and Guajardo 2002). This indicates that infants already start sharing attention before the age of one. This can be considered as a preliminary form of joint action, where the infant and the adult act jointly, by looking in the same direction and sharing the intention to attend to this object of mutual interest.

More elaborate forms of joint actions are also observed within the first year. They usually take place in infants' interactions with their mothers as they play together or engage in give-and-take type relations, such as when a mother feeds her baby. One notable feature of these joint actions is the high coordination observed among the interactants. Coordinating the timing of actions can ease attention sharing, action prediction, and thereby expand the scope of joint actions the infants can perform (Reddy, Markova, and Wallot 2013). In the following section, we will examine this issue more closely to highlight the role of highly coordinated, synchronous movements in infants' joint actions.

MOVEMENT COORDINATION AND JOINT ACTIONS IN INFANCY

Adding some more detail to our water bottle scenario, let us assume that there is another individual, a baby, in the storyline, and that the person reaching for the bottle is a mother who wanted to feed her baby. In this case, the baby's behaviors would suddenly be pivotal as well. It would be crucial that the mother's and the baby's movements are well coordinated: the baby should open his mouth as the mother reaches toward him, and the mother should start the pouring action at the right time to avoid any accidents. Although such precise coordination in movements might require highly developed skills, infants and mothers do nevertheless coordinate their behaviors with each other in various forms from very early on. Coordinated interactions feed into children's later abilities to work together with others on a shared goal, communicate in socially acceptable ways, and develop a sense of what is entailed in collective actions. Due to these significant consequences on social development, coordinated interactions offer a promising context in which to explain the development of abilities underlying collective agency.

From as early as at six weeks of age, infants begin to display instances of coordinated movements in their interactions with others. For instance, infants time their eye movements with their mothers' vocalizations by shifting the direction of their gaze toward and away from the mother's face according to the time when the mothers start and stop talking (Crown, Feldstein, Jasnow, Beebe, and Jaffe 2002). By nine months, infants start comprehending the structure of adultlike communication and take turns in their vocalizations as they interact with their mothers (Jasnow and Feldstein, 1986). Notably, this is also the time when infants initiate attempts to re-engage their play partners in a joint game, by using communicative tools such as frowning, pointing to the toys, or vocalizing to express their frustration when their play partners disengage from the game (Ross and Lollis 1987). Through coordinating the timing of their actions, then, infants learn the appropriate means to communicate with others. Such coordinated interactions also have important implications for other aspects of social development. For instance, the frequency of bidirectional coordination observed between mother-infant pairs at four months has been shown to predict infants' secure attachment to their mothers and unfamiliar others, as well as infants' cognitive skills, communicative competency, and socio-emotional adaptation, at 12 months of age (Jaffe et al. 2001). These findings point to the importance of coordinated movements in infants' social lives. Thus, a simple aspect of development—namely, matching the timing of one's actions to those of others— may have important implications for the development of joint actions and collective agency.

Recently, researchers have started to investigate the specific role of highly coordinated, synchronous movements in infants' social cognition. Despite being in an infancy of its own, this line of research has begun to show quite promising results. One study has shown that 12-month-old infants, but not nine-month-old infants, distinguish between synchronous movements that take place in social and non-social settings, and have a preference for synchronously moving partners only in the former case (Tunçgenç, Cohen, and Fawcett 2015). Taken within the broader framework of coordinated interactions in early infancy, these results indicate that precisely timing actions to one another might facilitate social bonds among interaction partners. Furthermore, rather than being innate, these facilitatory effects emerge toward the end of the first year of life, possibly as a factor of infants' increasing exposure to synchronous, coordinated movements in joint action settings with their caretakers. This social meaning embedded in coordinated movements might similarly imply "we-ness" in more elaborate joint action settings. One study has revealed that following a face-to-face bouncing phase with an adult, 14-month-old infants helped the adult more if they had bounced to the same rhythm (synchronously) than if they had bounced to different rhythms (asynchronously) with the adult (Cirelli, Einarson, and Trainor 2014). Importantly, moving synchronously with others does not induce a general state of helpfulness. Instead, infants were shown to help only those individuals who have moved synchronously with them and those who were close affiliates of their synchronizing partners (Cirelli, Wan, and Trainor, 2016), but not to neutral observers (Cirelli, Wan, and Trainor 2014). This suggests that performing synchronous movements might serve as a cue for social bonding and cooperative behavior among interactants.

To date, how synchronous, coordinated movements produce these social outcomes is largely unknown. It might be that moving in similar ways with another person gives rise to the inference that the interactants are similar to one another in other respects as well. The contingency involved in coordinated movements might ease predicting the future actions of others. This, in return, may imply a potential for being good cooperation partners in future joint action settings. Overall, increase in perceived similarity and closeness toward one's interaction partner might blur the boundaries between self and other, ultimately reinforcing the emergence and maintenance of collective agency.

CONCLUSION

Adapting to a world filled with agents who continuously share goals and perform collective actions is not trivial. Accurate interpretation of a simple action, such as reaching for a water bottle, requires the development of a suite of social, cognitive, and motor skills. Still, infants in the first year of life already demonstrate an understanding of others' goals and intentions and point to objects to share attention with other people. Elaborate forms of joint actions can also be observed in infants' interactions with their mothers from birth onward. One prominent feature of these actions is the high coordination of movements performed by the interactants.

The effects of performing synchronous, coordinated movements on children's social development have recently attracted attention from researchers. Evidence is accumulating on the importance of action timing for social cognition and joint action development. Although far from being conclusive, these new findings suggest that the similarity and contingency of movements involved in synchronous, coordinated interactions might create an enhanced feeling of "we-ness" among the interactants. This way, synchronous, coordinated movements can facilitate social bonding starting from early years of life and pave the way from individual to collective agency.

REFERENCES

Behne, T., M. Carpenter, J. Call, and M. Tomasello. 2005. "Unwilling versus Unable: Infants' Understanding of Intentional Action. *Developmental Psychology* 41(2): 328–337. doi:10.1037/0012-1649.41.2.328.

Cirelli, L. K., K. M. Einarson, and L. J. Trainor. 2014. "Interpersonal Synchrony Increases Prosocial Behavior in Infants." *Developmental Science* 17(6): 1003–1011. doi:10.1111/desc.12193.

Cirelli, L. K., S. J. Wan, and L. J. Trainor. 2014. "Fourteen-Month-Old Infants Use Interpersonal Synchrony as a Cue to Direct Helpfulness." *Philosophical Transactions of the Royal Society of London. Series B, Biological Sciences* 369(1658). doi:10.1098/rstb.2013.0400.

Cirelli, L. K., S. J. Wan, and L. J. Trainor. 2016. "Social Effects of Movement Synchrony: Increased Infant Helpfulness only Transfers to Affiliates of Synchronously Moving Partners." *Infancy*. doi:10.1111/infa.12140.

Crown, C. L., S. Feldstein, M. D. Jasnow, B. Beebe, and J. Jaffe. 2002. "The Cross-Modal Coordination of Interpersonal Timing: Six-Week-Olds Infants' Gaze with Adults' Vocal Behavior." *Journal of Psycholinguistic Research* 31(1): 1–23. doi:10.1023/A:1014301303616.

Csibra, G., G. Gergely, S. Biro, O. Koos, and M. Brockbank. 1999. "Goal Attribution Without Agency Cues: The Perception of 'Pure Reason' in Infancy." *Cognition* 72: 237–267.

Jaffe, J., B. Beebe, S. Feldstein, C. L. Crown, M. D. Jasnow, P. Rochat, and D. N. Stern. 2001. "Rhythms of Dialogue in Infancy: Coordinated Timing in Development." *Monographs of the Society for Research in Child Development* 66(2): 1–132. doi:10.1111/1540-5834.00137.

Jasnow, M., and S. Feldstein. 1986. "Adult-like Temporal Characteristics of Mother-Infant Vocal Interactions." *Child Development* 57(3): 754–761.

Johnson, S. C., Y. A. Shimizu, and S-J. Ok. 2007. "Actors and Actions: The Role of Agent Behavior in Infants' Attribution of Goals." *Cognitive Development* 22(3): 310–322. doi:10.1016/j.cogdev.2007.01.002.

Liszkowski, U., M. Carpenter, and M. Tomasello. 2008. "Twelve-Month-Olds Communicate Helpfully and Appropriately for Knowledgeable and Ignorant Partners." *Cognition* 108(3): 732–739. doi:10.1016/j.cognition.2008.06.013.

Luo, Y. 2011. "Three-Month-Old Infants Attribute Goals to a Non-human Agent." *Developmental Science* 14(2): 453–460. doi:10.1111/j.1467-7687.2010.00995.x.

Reddy, V., G. Markova, and S. Wallot. 2013. "Anticipatory Adjustments to Being Picked Up in Infancy." *PLoS One* 8(6): e65289. doi:10.1371/journal.pone.0065289.

Ross, H. S., and S. P. Lollis. 1987. "Communication Within Infant Social Games." *Developmental Psychology* 23(2): 241–248.

Saxe, R., T. Tzelnic, and S. Carey. 2007. "Knowing Who Dunnit: Infants Identify the Causal Agent in an Unseen Causal Interaction." *Developmental Psychology* 43: 149–158. doi:10.1037/0012-1649.43.1.149.

Tunçgenç, B., E. Cohen, and C. Fawcett. 2015. "Rock with Me: The Role of Movement Synchrony in Infants' Social and Non-social Preferences." *Child Development* 86(3): 976–984. doi:10.1111/cdev.12354.

Woodward, A. L., and J. J. Guajardo. 2002. "Infants' Understanding of the Point Gesture as an Object-Directed Action." *Cognitive Development* 17(1): 1061–1084. doi:10.1016/S0885-2014(02)00074-6.

PART EIGHT

The Agency of Materiality

CHAPTER 19

The Agency of the Dead

ZOË CROSSLAND

In this chapter I consider how human remains are thematized as agentive within the field of forensic anthropology. The flourishing popular literature on forensic science commonly summons the image of the corpse that speaks or testifies. Here I explore how the corpse's agency is imagined in these texts, and how the forensic anthropologist's agency is positioned relative to the corpse. How might these common claims of corpse agency prompt us to think more critically about the agentive aspects of the dead? As an ontologically ambiguous entity that appears simultaneously as an object and as a person, the dead body provides a productive site for thinking about how agency works in relation to people and things. Particularly in moments when the corpse is found outside of its proper place in the tomb, it seems to harbor some kind of problematic animacy that may be expressed as hauntings, dreams, or, as I show here, in ways that are channeled through a language of science and evidence.

Mass-market texts about osteoarchaeology, forensic anthropology, and forensic pathology are insistent in their use of the figure of the speaking corpse. "Dead Men Do Tell Tales" assert the front covers of memoirs by forensic anthropologists William Maples (Maples and Browning 1994) and William Bass (Bass and Jefferson 2003). Peggy Thomas's book *Talking Bones: The Science of Forensic Anthropology* (Thomas 1995) locates the speaking corpse within a rhetoric of science, while *Witnesses from the Grave: The Stories Bones Tell* by Christopher Joyce and Eric Stover (1991), situates the words of the dead within the performance of testimony, gesturing toward the important forensic dimensions of the image. The corpse's testifying role is reiterated in *Silent Witness* by Roxana Ferllini (2002), which also points to the paradoxical dimensions of the figure: these are dead bodies that speak while manifestly remaining silent. The speaking corpse is a complex image that reveals a folk theory of agency at the heart of the assertively scientific fields of forensics. Clearly, these statements are meant metaphorically, yet it is productive to explore the modes through which the corpse speaks, and to ask what this might reveal about where the corpse's apparent agency lies. To think through the corpse's treatment as agent, and to explore its entailments, I take a semiotic approach that draws on the work of Charles S. Peirce (1931–1935, 1958), and on Paul Kockelman's recent theorization of agency in semiotic terms (2007).

How do the forensic dead speak? When we look at what the dead say within forensic texts, it becomes clear that they always speak truthfully, challenging lies and misinformation about their lives and deaths. Forensic anthropologist Clyde Snow remarks that "bones make good witnesses. Although they speak softly, they never lie and they never forget" (Joyce and Stover 1991:144). These are personal, autobiographical narratives, specific to the individuals in question. "Bones tell stories of identity, trauma, and postmortem mutilation," explains forensic anthropologist Kathy Reichs (Owen 2000:8). The forensic corpse tells of childhood accidents, visits to the dentist, and, most importantly, of how it died. Anything that has left a visible trace upon the body can be expressed, but the vast range of lived experience is left unspoken. The forensic dead may never lie, but theirs is a constrained and descriptive field of speech that does not deal with feelings, wishes, or desires. This restricted speech channels the apparent animacy of the dead into a medico-legal language of science and of evidence, in which only certain kinds of statement are recognizable.

The speaking corpse shares in the broader empiricist image of facts that speak for themselves, offering a kind of poetics of empiricism, a way of imagining the status and efficacy of fact or evidence. Dead bodies act as a metaphor for fact, and the investigative work that takes place around the corpse provides a field for imagining the relationship of fact to interpretation. The empiricist view of the dead body as self-evident fact is complicated however by the imagery of testimony that is commonly attached to the figure of the speaking corpse. Dead bodies are said to act as "witnesses" and "testify" in the service of truth. Yet witnesses are notoriously unreliable, their testimony fraught with uncertainty, whether from the frailties of memory or from deliberate obfuscation. In bringing the language of witnessing into the realm of fact and observation, the subjectivity of the witness is inserted into the apparently uncontestable realm of fact. This is a hazardous move, potentially throwing the special truth-telling abilities of the corpse into doubt, and putting claims to objectivity at risk. The willingness to take such metaphorical risks suggests that the image of the witness offers something important that the notion of fact on its own does not. To suggest that facts are witnesses is another way of stating that facts act as evidence. Indeed these two terms—fact and evidence—are often conflated in the popular literature on forensics.

In the context of law courts, evidence has traditionally been solicited from the speech or documents of human witnesses. Yet, within the realm of medical fact, evidence is usually conceptualized in terms of the visual. Indeed, the very term *evidence* encompasses a claim for the primacy of sight, grounded in the Latin verb "to see," *videre*, and echoed in the emergence of the modern practice of autopsy (to see with one's own eyes). Here the emphasis is primarily on the researcher as active agent, as someone who interprets the passive body that lies ready to be dissected (as discussed by Sawday 1995). In contrast, the testifying corpse seems to offer the recognition of a relationship between those who speak and those who listen. The dual transitive and intransitive nature of the verb *to speak* seems to be important here: I may speak regardless of who is present, or I may speak directly *to* someone. This allows for an image of fact as something that simultaneously stands alone, and acts as evidence for or to someone. The corpse's speech exists on its own terms, whether witnessed or not, but it is also directed to a potential or anticipated audience: the expert who is able to hear and decode this speech.

The figure of the expert adds another complication to the corpse's speech, for the speech of the dead needs to be heard and interpreted. The forensic specialist must move between the facts of the case and the argument that he or she composes from such facts. This is a troublesome relationship. In the context of forensic evidence, it is problematic to lay too much emphasis on the work of interpretation, and this is because the theory that underlies forensic work is one that asserts a straightforward separation between fact and value. On the one hand are the data, on the other the necessary but fraught work of their interpretation and presentation by the forensic witness. Within this frame it is understood that those witnesses who are most expert will not pollute the facts with their own values, but instead act as intermediaries, decrypting rather than translating the language of the corpse. This points to another effect of the figure of the speaking corpse. It not only constrains the agency of the dead but also denies some agency to the analyst: the expert does not speak, the evidence does. This is to transfer agency to the dead, and along the way to acknowledge some of the conflicted emotions that work with the dead entails—emotions that are foreclosed to scientists working within a legal context.

The image of the speaking corpse folds together different evidential fields, including law, science, medicine, history, and biography. Each field has its own determinants of what counts as evidence, and how it should be assessed. Evidence is here situated within different regimes that govern what is allowed to enter in as material fact and how it is evaluated. Drawing on Peirce, we can conceptualize evidence not as something that stands alone, but as a semiotic relation. So in this sense evidence is always for something—for prosecution, for historical narrative, for medical training. Yet at the same time, it is also evidence of something. Evidence for prosecution might be evidence of violent events in the past. Evidence for medical training might be of pathological changes in bodily tissues. In thinking about the ways in which the dead are presented as evidence, we need to attend both to how the different relationships between these elements are composed and to the evidential regimes that govern how, when, and for whom or what something acts as evidence. These may be more or less explicitly formulated. Moving away from the problematic fact-value distinction, Peirce's triadic sign relation offers a means to unpack the evidential relation as specified under different regimes, and hence to explore the axes along which the corpse might be understood to act. Below I briefly sketch out three different evidential configurations, before returning to consider the image of the speaking corpse. To do this I map the material evidence of the dead onto the Sign that stands at the heart of Peirce's sign relation. The sign of the body stands for a number of different possibilities, events and processes ("Objects" in Peirce's terms). So bodily traces may be narrowly construed within a forensic sphere as signs of injury or harm, or understood in ways that are less closely specified. The body may act as a sign of possibility, of things that may have happened, or indeed as a sign of things that should have happened, as I explore below. What is this relationship for, however? For whom or for what does the body stand as a forensic trace of violence, or as a sign of potential? What is evidence if it is not marshaled in the service of a truth-finding project? Peirce directs us to the insight that evidence is ineluctably triadic. A third term (Peirce's "Interpretant") is necessary to complete the evidential relation, so that material traces can be understood as both signs of something and signs for different possibilities, goals, and projects.

For relatives of the dead, the corpse presents ambivalently as their family member, but also as the necessary evidence of death. It is common in the popular literature on forensic exhumation to hear reported claims that friends and families cannot find a measure of peace without the presence of the body. The recovery of the dead shifts the status of those who are missing from possibility to actuality. The here-and-now-ness (or haecceity) of the body acts as a concrete sign of death. What is important for families in this context is recognition. Are these remains recognizable? Is this the sought-for family member? This recognition is often based on a relation of similitude or iconicity that might not stand up in a law court. For example, in the search for those killed from Srebrenica, in the former Yugoslavia, photographs of clothing and possessions found with the dead were compiled by human rights organizations. These were meant for display to relatives in order to mediate their experience with the traces of the dead, and to aid identification. However, DNA analysis showed that some identifications carried out this way were mistaken (Huffine et al. 2001:274; Wagner 2008: 99–100). Here we see the weaknesses of a purely iconic relation for forensic inquiry. Ewa Klonowski (2007:167) describes how, in early exhumations before DNA testing was introduced, she observed traumatic situations "in which two different families claimed the same remains because of recognition of familiar clothing or shoes." For a legal case, much hinges on the ability to demonstrate a specific causal relationship between past events and present traces. Certainly, iconic elements are important in these claims. For example, if a jacket can be shown to resemble one worn by a missing individual, this iconicity has a powerful visual force, useful in a law court for evoking a feeling of recognition and convincing a jury. However, to be accepted as evidence within science and law, an indexical relationship has to be demonstrated; it is not enough that the traces are the same. Even when the relation of resemblance is idiosyncratic and specific to the individual—the torn pocket that was never fixed; the button sewn back on with mismatched thread—the connection with the missing must be demonstrated. Clothing acts as a powerful potential marker of identity because of its indexical relation with the person who wore it. Clothes take on something of the person who inhabited them and in cases such as these can come to stand metonymically for the missing. Such indexical traces may link crime scene and perpetrator, or human remains and the missing, but the chain of evidence must always be preserved so that the nature of this indexical trace can be maintained and assessed. Sarah Wagner (2008:99) recounts how men who fled from the violence at Srebrenica swapped clothing or were given identity cards and photos by the wounded. These actions led to confusion over presumptive identifications made on the basis of clothing. Here the sequence of events was unclear and the nature of the indexical sign was misjudged: the clothes and personal items did indeed point to their owners, but they had become separated from them at some point. The particularities of a forensic sign relation are fundamental to its efficacy and authority. However, the specific indexical or causal link between the trace and the thing that made it has to be carefully documented and preserved. In the legal context this translates into a concern with the chain of evidence, which itself testifies to the indexicality of the trace, and to the claim that no tampering has taken place. It is only on the basis of an undisturbed and confirmable indexical trace, as interpreted as a fact, that a forensic argument can be made about what happened at a specific moment and locale. Family members may be relatively unconcerned with the evidential strictures of science and law. Rather, recognition often seems to take place in an affective and relatively unexamined way. Yet this form of immediate perceptual judgment certainly has its place and is operational within scientific and legal inference. The difference lies not so much in the feeling of recognition, as the way in which these semiotic domains assess such judgments and specify the nature of the relation of material evidence to its referent (or Object).

Finally, moving to wider historical narratives, another evidential dimension comes into view. Whether constructing stories of nationalism and reconstruction, or narrating anthropologists' work around the dead body, corpses come to stand for a range of meanings established through convention. The dead are often used to evoke larger entities: a group, an event, the body politic, or indeed facts themselves. These conventions are often embedded in perceived similarities and connections between the corpse and the kind of narrative being told. For example, the work of exhumation, of revelation, offers a powerful and commonly used metaphor for the recovery of history in situations of political repression, a symbolic relation that also draws upon iconic and indexical elements for its potency. In such narratives the individual often drops out of view, subsumed within a broader accounting. The conventional or symbolic relation between the sign of the dead and the thing that it stands for brings me back to the speaking corpse as a complex metaphor for fact. Although, before returning to this theme, I should note that the above discussion presents a highly schematized sketch of the field of shifting evidential relationships in forensic work. Claims that center on the signs of the dead draw on all of these dimensions, but may at different moments privilege one element of the sign relation more than another.

Turning back to the speaking corpse, we can see that it provides a useful way of imagining the different dimensions of forensic inquiry, and of thinking about forensic evidence. In its restricted speech the image acknowledges the way in which the dead body can constrain particular readings within certain evidential regimes. The figure of the speaking corpse also recognizes the disturbing animacy of the dead in a context where it cannot normally be recognized. Finally, the image allows the analyst to act as mediator while effacing his or her agency. And this is at the heart of the question of where evidence sits in the relationship between fact and value. The concept of evidence is fundamentally troubling for any attempt to separate the world into passive fact and agentive interpretation, precisely because of the way in which it is simultaneously motivated (evidence *for* something) and yet understood to stand apart from that motivation (as evidence *of* something else).

What does the figure of the corpse that speaks offer for thinking about the agentive dimensions of the corpse? It is clear that the indexical traces of violence can push back against narratives that assert that a person simply left home and was living elsewhere, or had died accidentally, or in battle. Those responsible for such traces may lie about what took place, but the signs of the dead can correct them, and so restrict their semiotic agency. Drawing upon Paul Kockelman's (2007) terminology, we could say that the semiotic flexibility or ability to control the expression of forensic signs is highly constrained. In the former Yugoslavia, the dead were even dug up and reburied in an attempt to hide what had taken place (Skinner et al. 2002). But as the French criminalist Edmond Locard famously noted at the start of the twentieth century "Every contact leaves a trace"—even in changing the location of the dead, new iconic-indexical traces were left that could be tracked and used as evidence. This illustrates too the limited degree of influence that one has over how the indexical relation is composed, speaking again to the constraints placed on the semiotic freedom of the guilty. Perhaps even more significant is the ability of the signs of the dead to elicit accountability—forensic traces can force the culpable to account against their wishes. This is not experienced as a purely passive kind of constraint. Although evidence is specified under particular regimes, and the indexical traces of forensic evidence seem to have the most agentive ability to intervene in the lives of others, it is also important to take account of how evidence itself works to constitute the context. When the sign of a corpse is revealed, action must be taken, and a certain kind of action is required. The discovery of human remains immediately points to something disturbing that happened in the past, and in so doing demands a particular response. The unexpected appearance of the dead petitions for investigation and for their status to be established. This starts with what Peirce called an *abduction*—at its most rudimentary, a feeling of unease when confronted with something out of place, and at its most developed, the hypothesis made by a forensic expert in seeing clues and, Sherlock Holmes-like, inferring the solution. There is something unfinished in this kind of evidence, but it is not simply waiting to be activated, it also shapes the ways in which it is acted upon.

This is to move away from a view of agency as inhering only in the living, and instead to view it as a collaborative semiotic project that is also shaped and constrained by the dead. The goals of prosecution and justice cannot be carried out without them. The image of the testifying corpse recognizes these agentive dimensions. But where does this leave the idea of fact as something that stands alone and speaks for itself? When facts speak for themselves they act as Signs that have been conflated with their Objects and prescinded from the Interpretant relation. This is to fetishize the power of the indexical relation and to underplay the different interpretive possibilities to which it gives rise. To move away from a folk understanding of the agency of the dead and to fully engage with the ability of the dead to intervene in the lives of the living needs a theory of agency that is fundamentally relational, while also able to recognize the ways in which that relationality can be hewn and circumscribed. Bruno Latour has approached this question by considering how facts are treated as stable "black boxes" when they are enrolled successfully into scientific work. At moments of breakdown or challenge such facts are revealed to be composed of relational networks in which many different actors are involved (Latour 1999). However, in considering the agency of the forensic dead, our attention is drawn not only to the relational constitution of the corpse as fact, but also to the different regimes under which certain evidential relations are brought into view or removed from the realm of possibility. Here it seems most helpful to think of agency as an adjective rather than a noun, reconceptualizing it in terms of agentive constellations that permit different forms of action (Crossland 2014:100–137). This opens the way to more fully decenter agency as well as to acknowledge that it is always a project that is grounded in particular material conditions, and which unfolds over time relative to certain goals.

REFERENCES

Bass, William, and Jon Jefferson. 2003. *Death's Acre: Inside the Legendary Forensic Lab the Body Farm, Where the Dead Do Tell Tales.* New York: Penguin.

Crossland, Zoë. 2014. *Ancestral Encounters in Highland Madagascar: Material Signs and Traces of the Dead.* Cambridge: Cambridge University Press.

Ferllini, Roxana. 2002. *Silent Witness: How Forensic Anthropology Is Used to Solve the World's Toughest Crimes.* Willowdale, Ontario: Firefly Books.

Huffine, Edwin, John Crews, Brenda Kennedy, Kathryn Bomberger, and Asta Zinbo. 2001. "Mass Identification of Persons Missing from the Break-up of the Former

Yugoslavia: Structure, Function, and the Role of the International Commission on Missing Persons." *Croatian Medical Journal* 42(3): 271–275.

Joyce, Christopher, and Eric Stover. 1991. *Witnesses from the Grave: The Stories Bones Tell.* Boston: Little, Brown and Company.

Klonowski, Eva-Elvira. 2007. "Forensic Anthropology in Bosnia and Herzegovina: Theory and Practice amidst Politics and Egos." In *Forensic Archaeology and Human Rights Violations*, edited by Roxana Ferllini, 148–169. Springfield: Charles C. Thomas.

Kockelman, Paul. 2007. "Agency: The Relation Between Meaning, Power and Knowledge." *Current Anthropology* 48(3): 375–401.

Latour, Bruno. 1999. *Pandora's Hope: Essays on the Reality of Science Studies.* Cambridge, MA: Harvard University Press.

Maples, William R., and Michael Browning. 1994. *Dead Men Do Tell Tales: The Strange and Fascinating Cases of a Forensic Anthropologist.* New York: Doubleday.

Owen, David. 2000. *Hidden Evidence. Forty True Crimes and How Forensic Science Helped Solve Them.* Buffalo, NY; Willdowdale, ON: Quintet Publishing; Firefly Books.

Peirce, C. S. 1931–1935. *Collected Papers.* Vols. 1–6. Cambridge, MA: Harvard University Press.

Peirce, C. S. 1958. *Collected Papers.* Vols. 7–8. Cambridge, MA: Harvard University Press

Sawday, Jonathan. 1995. *The Body Emblazoned: Dissection and the Human Body in Renaissance Culture.* London/New York: Routledge.

Skinner, Mark F., Heather P. York, and Melissa A. Connor. 2002. "Postburial Disturbance of Graves in Bosnia-Herzegovina." In *Advances in Forensic Taphonomy: Method, Theory, and Archaeological Perspectives*, edited by William D. Haglund and Marcella H. Sorg, 293–308. Boca Raton, FL: CRC Press.

Thomas, Peggy. 1995. *Talking Bones: The Science of Forensic Anthropology.* New York: Facts on File.

Wagner, Sarah E. 2008. *To Know Where He Lies: DNA Technology and the Search for Srebrenica's Missing.* Berkeley and Los Angeles: University of California Press.

CHAPTER 20

Distributed Agency in Play

BENJAMIN SMITH

INTRODUCTION

When Alberto and his brothers go out to play marbles, they can't help but do other things. In the Peruvian, Aymara-speaking Andes, they must take their family's alpacas and sheep out to far-flung grazing areas. And, once there, Alberto—the oldest brother—occasionally keeps an eye on the animals as they drift toward uneaten pastorage. The area where they play marbles, then, is part and parcel of a landscape that is quite unlike, for example, the radically transformed, angular spaces where games like basketball and football (ideally) get played. Although treeless and shrubless, it is a landscape that is dense with rocks small and large, thick clumps of grass, short twigs, holes, eroded gulleys, and inclines and declines. In such a case, marbles play must go where alpacas and sheep go, and virtue must be made of this necessity. And, frankly, it is. When Alberto and his brothers play marbles, they must shoot them through this thicket of things, aiming for a series of small holes dug into the ground. Much of the intrigue of the game consists, then, of whether and how these material things serve as agents in marbles, and whether and how boys contend with the way in which these things act. Does a rock divert a marble's path? Does it do so across several turns of play? What does a boy do in response? From the perspective of an Aymara boyhood imagination, the stakes here are quite high. Is a marbles player who cannot contend with a rock really a boy? How might rocks make and unmake men?

The Aymara game of marbles (*t'inka*) invites a concern with a form of agency that has rarely been object of sustained analytic attention: the agency of material things in childhood play and games. In his classic study of marbles, for example, Jean Piaget gives just a passing description of marbles and their material context before moving on to his account of the development of moral judgment in children (1965). The object of his concern are the rules of the game as well as the changing attitudes that children have with respect to those rules. Do children think of the rules of the game as inviolable and even sacred? Do they think of them as subject to negotiation and compromise? In posing these questions, Piaget privileges two dimensions of childhood games: the sense in which they are regulated by social norms (or rules) and the sense in which they are the object of psychological processes (in this case, morally valenced attitudes). The end result of such an analysis, inevitably, is to foreground children themselves as agents in play. They are the ones whose behavior gets evaluated relative to the rules of the game, and they are the ones who interpret rules in flexible ways. This is an account, then, that precludes a serious concern with the distribution of agency across children and material things in play and games. And, in doing so, it is a token of a type. With only a handful of notable exceptions,[1] the study of play and games takes the child as its hero.

In what follows, I give an account of the game of marbles among Aymara boys, showing especially how material things wield an agency within it. To do so, I focus on a specific moment in the regular sequence of marbles play: the task of engineering or designing the marbles playing field. This is a moment that will show how the marbles playing field gets made into a specifically semiotic agent, an agent that, genuinely, interprets its material context and is made to have regular consequences on its surrounding world (including, especially, its surrounding social and symbolic world). In other words, it is not just the case that children play with toys and the material contexts of those toys. Material things, also, play with children.

ENGINEERING A FIELD, EMBEDDING A WORLD

When boys head out to herd animals and play marbles, they must, at some point, transform some patch of ground into a playing field. This is a moment that, however brief, most clearly reveals the connection between the semiotic agency of material things and social categories like masculine, human, and nonhuman. When carving out a playing field, boys must first of all create a space that can accommodate the set of physical relations projected by the rules of the game. In this local variety of marbles, there must be four spots that serve as the goals or targets for a boy striking a marble. These are, typically, four holes that are created to have a diameter just a bit wider than the width of a marble. Three of these holes must conform to a line that is more or less straight, and the fourth sits off to one side of this line. In order to play, a boy must first advance a marble through these holes, ending in the fourth one off to the side. Advancing a marble means striking it with one's pointer finger and having it successfully land inside of the targeted hole. A boy has two marbles and may continue advancing them until he misses a target with each marble. Once a marble has reached the fourth hole, it attains a new status. It now has venom (or *wininu*). Once it has venom, it can, upon striking another marble, kill it (literally, *jiwayaña*, "to kill"). Once all of one's opponent's marbles are dead, this player—the one who has at least one marble still alive—wins, and the game is over. Although a game of marbles technically ends when all but one or two marbles are dead, games more frequently than not end before this moment arrives. This happens for a number of reasons: alpacas and sheep drift towards other places, it's time to bring everyone home, or it's time to eat, etc.

The act of creating an actual playing field happens quickly, and it is managed by the oldest boy in a group (in most cases, an oldest brother).[2] There is a balance that must be achieved. On the one hand, there are plenty of sites where it would be essentially impossible to play a game of marbles (e.g., steep hillsides, boulder-strewn areas, areas too thick with grass). On the other hand, there are at least a couple of areas where it would be too easy (e.g., the flat road that runs through the community). To put it in a semiotic idiom, finding and making an appropriate marbles playing field is an act of phatic labor, to use Elyachar's (2010) term.[3] It is a task of finding a field in which there are number of possible channels through which the sort of thing that is a marble can be struck towards a series of holes dug about four feet apart from one another. It must be a field in which not all possible channels are available, but certainly a majority of possible ones. More often than not, the challenge of creating a playing field—at least, for the first three of the holes—requires a marbles player to remove certain things that would gum up too many of the possible channels. In the moments before a game begins, for example, an oldest boy will direct a younger one to dig the four holes, and he himself will start to groom the playing field. If there is a rock too large, a twig too thick and long, a piece of trash too large (e.g., a two liter plastic bottle), then he will pick it up and throw it aside. There is an implicit logic to this kind of act: these are things that would likely enclose or surround a marble struck toward them (a large rock, a long, thick stick, etc.), and these are the things that must be removed. To the extent that some number of channels are made more fully available, then the communicative value of the flicking of the marble—i.e., its value as a strategic act within the game—is more likely to be legible to marbles players, onlookers, and anthropologist.

In these moments of designing a field, players are just as invested in making sure that at least some possible channels are closed off, made less fully available or, at least, made more challenging to traverse. Although this is true with respect to the entire playing field, it becomes a matter of special concern with respect to the fourth and final hole, the one that gives a marble its venom. In the moments before play, for example, an oldest boy—the engineer of the field, if you will—takes special care to locate this last hole in an area that is more fully dense with debris or higher or lower up on a slope, among other possibilities. If the already existing landscape does not provide such possibilities, he will toss some rocks, twigs or trash into the area of the fourth hole (sometimes drawing on things collected from the other areas of the playing field). These moments are ones in which it becomes especially clear that a playing field—in other words, this network of possible channels—is something that is at least partly engineered or designed. And, it is designed as a kind of sieve, in Kockelman's sense (2013). Depending on the specific area within the playing field, it is an artifact that is designed to more or less easily let certain things through (i.e., a marble) or to have those things either get stuck or be diverted. In other words, it has been engineered to select for a certain kind of sign (again, a marble),[4] and it has been made to bring about certain kinds of consequences—in other words, interpretants, in Peirce's (1955) sense— for that kind of thing (diverting marbles, getting them stuck, letting them pass through). It is in this sense that the playing field counts as a complex, internally differentiated semiotic agent, albeit one whose peculiar form of agency has been partly embedded in it through processes of engineering or design. In acting as such an agent, a skillfully designed marbles playing field helps to reveal marbles shots that are more or less skillful and more or less strategic.

The marbles field, then, is designed to act and to signify, but it also gets understood, symbolically or ideologically, as an agent. This is implicit, even, to the narrative arc that it instantiates. This is most fully apparent in the design of the field that surrounds the fourth hole. The region around the fourth hole, after all, is designed to make available fewer and more challenging channels for marbles to cross. It is strewn with debris or located on a slope. However, it is also serves, narratively, as a moment of culmination or, even, as a rite of institution (Bourdieu 2001). Once a marble lands in this fourth target, after all, it attains a new status: it acquires venom, and it can thereby kill other marbles. In this case, then, the semiotic agency of the playing field—that is, its design as a sieve—comes to be understood relative to a game sequence that is framed, narratively or symbolically, as a kind of quest. A boy and his marble encounter their greatest challenge (that is, the dense sieve that surrounds the fourth hole), and a marble is thereby rendered a more potent and indeed venomous instrument. There is, in other words, an analogy that is made across the kind of embedded semiotic agency that the playing field exerts and the symbolic, narrative-like rendering of that agency. In this area of the playing field, the sieve is dense and the challenge great. There are additional reasons for this interpretation. When boys add rocks, twigs, and trash to the area around the fourth hole, they often describe these things as *qhincha*, or "bad luck." These things are explicitly framed, in other words, as challenges for players:[5] *qhincha* is, after all, something that, according to Urton, is a "principal cause of the emergence of a state of imbalance and disequilibrium" (1997:147). These observations suggest a more sweeping analogy or relation of iconicity. The playing field is not just a sieve for marbles. It is a sieve for men who confront the challenge of *qhincha*. The interpretive (or, better: interpreting) world that is embedded in the marbles play field is fully "commensurable" with (Latour 2005:74)—or, more strongly, compatible with and necessary for—the sociocultural meaningfulness of the game. Or, to capture the insight in an aphorism: only the skillful marbles shot shall pass, and only the tough man shall win.

CONCLUSION

Marbles is one among many games that implicate material things as agents. A quick perusal of Avedon and Sutton-Smith's edited compendium on games (1971) reveals a bewildering number of examples. In Brewster's article on games in Shakespeare, for example, he describes games that involve seeds, dice, a leather belt, knives, an object "thrown onto the ground" (39), a "wooden image (usually of a Turk or a Saracen) mounted on a pivot" (42), cards, plates, a table, a shilling, marbles, and a game that consisted of "rolling small balls into holes at one end of the game-board" (47). In a more anthropological contribution, Erasmus describes forms of play that require shews, bowls, beans, and small sticks, a series of "twenty holes separated in the middle by a wider space called a river" (119), and, more familiarly, boards that provide a flat surface. Few of these material things exert an agency that is like the one described here: that is, as a field of material things that acts as a sievelike catcher of marbles and men. This does not contravene the analysis I've provided, but it does suggest that the problem at stake is a tremendously larger one. How can we theorize the full variety of ways in which material things (are designed to [Murphy 2013]) select and act in games and play?

How much do these "missing masses" (Latour 1992)—in other words, the material things that are not visible in many accounts of play—matter? This is a question that has as many answers as there are approaches to the study of play and games in childhood. In the case of Aymara marbles, for example, an analysis of these missing masses is necessary for the anthropological project of understanding the form of masculinity that is at stake for Aymara boys. A number of other, more general possibilities stand out. How do material things provide an anchor and model for forms of "make-believe" or "fantasy play" in childhood? To what extent are processes of "design" and "engineering" a part of play, and how might such processes mediate the kinds of sociocultural worlds and cognitive processes that are at stake in play? What kind of object is an object-for-play, and how might its artifactuality differ from other kinds of objects and technologies? What role do material things and other nonhuman agents play in producing the category "human"? Piaget might have also asked: how might the relative adaptability and design-ability of material things in play help to socialize the kind of negotiability that Piaget—and, increasingly, anthropologists— see as being central to our moral and social lives?

NOTES

1. I should mention here some of the work inspired by Vygotskyan or Latourian frameworks, especially authors like Goodwin (2006) and Brembeck (2011).
2. See Smith (2014) for an account of the caretaking relationships presupposed in this example.
3. Elyachar draws upon Jakobson's refinement of the concept of phatic function. These are acts that serve to "establish, prolong, or discontinue communication" (Jakobson 1960:350).
4. One complexity I have had to gloss over here are the "inter-material" relations between a marble and its playing field. For instance, the agency of the playing field makes sense only relative to the sort of thing that a marble is and the sort of action that a marble undertakes (i.e., after being struck).
5. See Smith (2010) for a longer account of bad luck in Aymara marbles play.

REFERENCES

Avedon, Elliott M., and Brian Sutton-Smith. 1971. *The Study of Games*. New York: Wiley.

Bourdieu, Pierre. 2001. *Masculine Domination*. Stanford, CA: Stanford University Press.

Brembeck, Helene. 2011. "Toys Matter. McDonald's Toys and Nordic Childhoods." *Revue D'Histoire Nordique* 12: 161–178.

Brewster, Paul. 1971. "Games and Sports in Shakespeare." In *The Study of Games*, edited by Elliott M. Avedon and Brian Sutton-Smith, 27–47. New York: Wiley.

Elyachar, Julia. 2010. "Phatic Labor, Infrastructure, and the Question of Empowerment in Cairo." *American Ethnologist* 37(3): 452–464.

Erasmus, Charles J. 1971. "Patolli, Pachisi, and the Limitations of Possibilities." In *The Study of Games*, edited by Elliott M. Avedon and Brian Sutton-Smith, 109–129. New York: Wiley.

Goodwin, Marjorie H. 2006. *The Hidden Life of Girls: Games of Stance, Status, and Exclusion*. Malden, MA: Blackwell.

Jakobson, Roman. 1960. "Closing Time: Linguistics and Poetics." In *Style in Language*, edited by Thomas Sebeok, 350–359. Cambridge, MA: MIT Press.

Kockelman, Paul. 2013. *Agent, Person, Subject, Self: A Theory of Ontology, Interaction, and Infrastructure*. Oxford: Oxford University Press.

Latour, Bruno. 1992. "Where Are the Missing Masses? Sociology of a Few Mundane Objects." In *Shaping Technology, Building Society: Studies in Sociotechnical Change*, edited by Wiebe Bijker and John Law, 225–258. Cambridge, MA: MIT Press.

Latour, Bruno. 2005. *Reassembling the Social: An Introduction to Actor-Network Theory*. Oxford: Oxford University Press.

Murphy, Keith M. 2013. "A Cultural Geometry: Designing Political Things in Sweden." *American Ethnologist* 40(1): 118–131.

Peirce, Charles S. 1955. "Logic as Semiotic: The Theory of Signs." In *Philosophical Writings of Peirce*, edited by Justus Buchler, 98–119. New York: Dover.

Piaget, Jean. (1932) 1965. *The Moral Judgement of the Child*. New York: Free Press.

Smith, Benjamin. 2010. "Of Marbles and (Little) Men: Bad Luck and Masculine Identification in Aymara Boyhood." *Journal of Linguistic Anthropology* 20(1): 225–239.

Smith, Benjamin. 2014. "Metacultural Positioning in Language Socialization: Inhabiting Authority in Informal Teaching among Peruvian Aymara Siblings." *Linguistics and Education* 25: 108–118.

Urton, Gary. 1997. *The Social Life of Numbers: A Quechua Ontology of Numbers and Philosophy of Arithmetic*. Austin: University of Texas Press.

CHAPTER 21

Contingency and the Semiotic Mediation of Distributed Agency

EITAN WILF

In this chapter I theorize the role of nonhuman entities not simply in extending human agency but rather in providing humans with the training ground to cultivate basic dimensions of human agency understood to be lacking in the specific ethnographic contexts I examine. In doing so, I aim to provide a window into a relatively under-theorized dimension of the idea that agency is distributed across the human/nonhuman divide. I draw on fieldwork I conducted in a number of ethnographic contexts: a US academic jazz music program, and two US research institutes in which jazz-improvising computerized algorithms are developed. In these ethnographic contexts human creativity constitutes a problem—a scarce resource—which people try to address and resolve in different, though conceptually relatable, ways. Broadly speaking, a recurring problem in all of these contexts is that of the predictability of people's purposes or intentions, which prevents them from being creative, in other words, from following a culturally specific normative ideal—a Romantic modern one—that opposes standardization of purposes. In one of these contexts, an additional problem is that of people's inability to reliably execute via appropriate behavior whatever purposes or intentions they have, whether creative or not. In all of these contexts such problems are understood as lack of creative agency, and a prevalent solution is the use of contextually meaningful contingency produced by and harvested from different nonhuman entities (Wilf 2013).

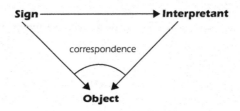

Figure 21.1 A Peircean Semiotic Framework.

I will use a Peircean semiotic framework to theorize distributed agency as a property that is semiotically mediated across the human/nonhuman divide (Peirce 1955). In such a framework, semiosis consists of three elements (Figure 21.1): a sign (whatever stands for something else); an object (whatever a sign stands for); and an interpretant (whatever a sign creates insofar as it stands for an object). In a semiotic process, a sign stands for its object, on the one hand, and its interpretant, on the other hand, in such a way as to make the interpretant stand in relation to the object in a way that corresponds to its—in other words, the sign's—own relation to the object (Kockelman 2005).

In the first ethnographic site I examine, the crisis of creative agency concerns the failure to align private purposes with public actions. The site is a US academic jazz music program, Berklee College of Music in Boston, which is part of the growing academization and institutionalized professionalization of jazz training that have culminated in the establishment of hundreds of academic programs that grant various degrees in jazz performance (Wilf 2014). As an improvised form of music, jazz consists of the real-time generation and execution of "musical ideas," as it were. To function well, players must be able to flawlessly execute their constantly emerging ideas with their instruments and respond to the musical cues provided by their band members in the course of performance. Canonical definitions of "creative thinking" in jazz focus precisely on the need for mature jazz improvisers to "attain *a perfect unity of conception with the body*. The artist becomes intensely focused on thoughts in the language of jazz, and as they come—one upon the other—*they are articulated as instantly as conceived. No lead time separates conception from expression, and the gap between intention and realization disappears*" (Berliner 1994:217; emphasis added). At stake, then, in this particular sort of framing, with its particular ethnopsychology of intention/action, is the skill to execute one's real-time musical ideas with one's instrument, to match private auditory representations with public action.

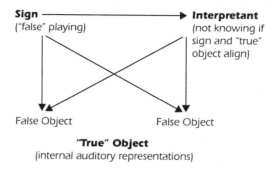

Figure 21.2 Determining Sign-Object Relations: Problems of Execution.

To cultivate this skill, players need to condition their playing bodies through intensive listening and playing in real-time performance situations rather than through the mediation of the written score. However, because of specific transformations in jazz's conditions of existence, it has become more difficult for students to train themselves in live performance situations. Specifically, the dwindling demand for jazz since the 1950s has resulted in the gradual disappearance of performance venues in which neophyte musicians can inform their competence with listening and apprentice with experienced practitioners in real-time performance situations. The educators and students I worked with argued that although students try to compensate for this shift by orchestrating independent sessions, they do so less than before because they must compete over limited rehearsal space or hold sessions in their apartments, which poses significant practical limitations (Wilf 2014:202–209). Even more important, these sessions, when they do take place, do not make up for the loss of opportunities to apprentice with seasoned musicians. Such apprenticeship has gradually given way to abstract, formalized, and rationalized training in the hundreds of academic programs that have come to function as the pillars of the jazz world over the last few decades. The educators I worked with argued time and again that as a result of these institutional transformations—the shift of jazz training from the clubs to the classroom where standardized, printed pedagogical aids have become a key mode of acquiring knowledge—students fail to cultivate the skill that would allow them to execute their real-time, emergent musical ideas with their instruments (Wilf 2014:189–199).

At stake here is a form of reduced agency that concerns one's reduced flexibility in determining sign-object relations (Figure 21.2). If we understand a note played by a musician as a sign whose mediated object for an intended listener is supposed to be a specific internal auditory representation, then

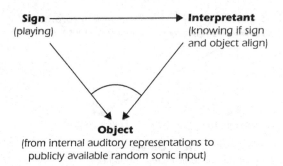

Sign ————————————▶ Interpretant
(playing)   (knowing if sign
                              and object align)

Object
(from internal auditory representations to
publicly available random sonic input)

Figure 21.3 Determining Sign-Object Relations: Addressing Execution.

students have reduced flexibility in terms of their ability to determine this kind of sign-object relations. They have a hard time mediating to others via signs—in other words, via their playing—objects, that is, specific musical ideas. They often end up playing other (that is, "false") notes than those they intended to play, thereby mediating to their listeners false objects (that is, false intentions). This is a problem of execution (Enfield 2013:104–112). Think of it in terms of an agent not being able to engage in purposeful behavior.

To enhance this specific dimension of flexibility, the students I worked with often turned to contingency produced by nonhuman entities. They engaged in gamelike interactions in which they competed with one another over who was better able to match with his or her instrument random environmental sonic stimuli. During my fieldwork it was not uncommon to see students hanging out in class until a sound such as a car horn would infiltrate the classroom from the street and immediately prompt them to try to match it with their instruments, and then to engage in debates about who managed to match it first and whether it counted as an accurate and satisfying match. Indeed, one evening, while approaching Inman Square in Cambridge, Sara, a vibraphone student, and I heard a car horn next to us and immediately tried to match it by whistling. Because each of our whistles represented a different pitch, Sara ordered me to hurry and ask the driver sitting in the car to honk again so we could establish who was right. (She was.)

I suggest that two related things happen here. First, these random sonic stimuli come to function as public proxies for internal auditory representations whose execution students can practice (Figure 21.3). In other words, the environment becomes a training ground for cultivating one's ability to determine sign-object relations. The relatively contingent nature of these stimuli is crucial because it simulates the unpredictable dimension of jazz improvisation as an emergent communicative event that requires musicians to respond to and execute unpredictable musical input. Note, then, the turn to nonhuman entities not for the purpose of extending human agency—which is underdeveloped here—but for cultivating it, to begin with, in the sense that the replication of an external pitch is a form of practice in executing an internal auditory representation on one's instrument, in other words, in being able to engage in a specific form of purposeful behavior.

Second, the public nature of these random sonic stimuli makes the assessment of another person's ability to determine sign-object relations publicly available for everyone present. Whereas normally it would be difficult for me to know if another person has the skill to determine sign-object relations because my ability to access the objects in this case—in other words, his or her specific internal auditory representations—and compare them to the signs this person gives off—that is, his or her playing—depends on this person's skill to mediate these objects for me, to begin with, now it is easy for me to ascertain whether he or she has this skill or not because these representations have become public: their place is now taken by publicly available sonic stimuli, which allows me to assess if there is an indexically iconic relation between these stimuli and the person's playing. An indexically iconic relation between a publicly available random sound and a note played by another person immediately after in an attempt to match it—this relation itself now becomes a sign that mediates for me this person's ability to determine sign-object relations. These gamelike interactions are thus metasemiotic: they concern the semiotic mediation of one's ability to semiotically mediate, in addition to being a training ground for cultivating this ability.

A second dimension of students' reduced flexibility and agency, which I recorded during my fieldwork, is that of planning: deciding which sign-object relations are to be created in the first place (see Enfield 2013:104–112). Because of their training, which is heavily mediated by textual artifacts of standardized patterns of improvisation, many students find it hard to come up with creative musical ideas to begin with, regardless of their ability to execute them with their instruments in the real time of performance (Figure 21.4). Here the focus of attention is not *execution*, but *what* to execute. Teachers often described their students as mere "button pushers" and "pattern players," using tropes that connote the mechanical valves of an engine to describe this lack of creative agency (Wilf 2014:167–169).

To address the problem of standardized ideas in many jazz pedagogical settings, James, a computer scientist, who is also a semiprofessional jazz musician, developed computerized algorithms that purport to improvise

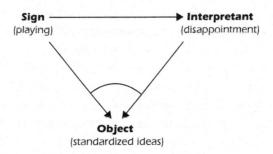

Figure 21.4 Determining Sign-Object Relations: Problems of Planning.

jazz in response to the real-time improvisation of a human player. The music generated by the algorithms is played by a humanoid robot marimba player. It is an interactive system, that is, "sociable," in that it produces music in response to the music produced by the human musicians interacting with it in real time.

In an interview I conducted with James in his lab in a major US institute of technology, he attributed the added value of his system to the fact that it generates musical ideas that humans could never generate by themselves. Different kinds of algorithms—mainly Markov models, genetic algorithms, and fractal-based algorithms—generate music using complicated calculations that incorporate both stochastic and deterministic (nonlinear) processes into their logic. Contextually meaningful contingency is a key part of their logic, what allows them to introduce the novelty that human players presently lack. By *contextually meaningful*, I mean that the contingency generated by the algorithms and played by the robot is not meaningless. Rather, the music makes sense because it is generated in the context of specific tunes and their harmonic progressions, as well as in response to the musical ideas of the people playing with the robot. It is patterned meaningfulness in which current notes make sense given past notes and relative to genre-based conventions. James's hope is that by playing with this system, which generates new creative ideas, people will be inspired to modify their own repertoire of hitherto standardized intentions (Figure 21.5). Playing with this system is thus supposed to help people to cultivate their ability to plan more interesting or creative sign-object relations, and thus to increase their flexibility and agency.[1] Motivated by the widespread discontent about standardization in the field of jazz education, as well as the significant market for jazz pedagogical aids, some of the scientists I worked with discussed the commercial possibilities of integrating the algorithms they developed in different jazz pedagogical technologies that would allow students to improvise with these technologies and receive real-time musical input

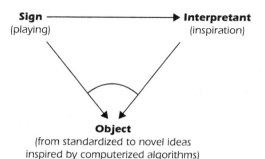

Sign ⟶ **Interpretant**
(playing)   (inspiration)

Object
(from standardized to novel ideas
inspired by computerized algorithms)

Figure 21.5 Determining Sign-Object Relations: Addressing Planning.

based on the "falsifiability" of who they are in terms of their improvisation style, in other words, to receive musical input that would not align with their standardized style of improvisation. As in the case of the turn to publicly available random sonic stimuli, the motivation for turning to computerized algorithms is that they are nonhuman entities that can function as sources of contextually meaningful contingency. This contingency is not used to extend human agency—which is lacking, here in the dimension of planning rather than execution—but to provide the training ground for its cultivation, to begin with.

To add another dimension to my argument about the role of contingency in the semiotic mediation of distributed agency across the human/nonhuman divide, note that there are numerous ethnographic contexts in which contingency produced by and harvested from nonhuman entities is mobilized as a resource for increasing one's flexibility and agency by reducing those of other humans. Consider some forms of mechanical divination, a practice that has long been studied by anthropologists. Mechanical divination—in other words, the use of aleatory processes to divine hidden events and causes—is frequently used to reveal group members' malicious intentions presumed to be responsible for different kinds of harmful incidents. In many contexts in which mechanical divination is performed, people often attribute to other people's ill intentions what many modern subjects would attribute to coincidence. Danger emanates from the increased agency of one's group members to surreptitiously orchestrate harmful incidents while maintaining the appearance of innocence.

To reduce the flexibility of one's group members, which can be articulated as flexibility in a specific dimension I will soon explain, people turn to contingency produced by nonhuman entities, and they do so in the form of mechanical divination. For example, the Azande divinatory practice called the "poison oracle," famously analyzed by E. E. Evans-Pritchard (1991), has been discussed as an "aleatory" mechanism individuals use to find out who has bewitched them or intends to do so (Du Bois 1993:58). In this practice, poison is administered to a fowl after asking a yes-or-no question. The fate of the fowl—whether it lives or dies—provides the answer to the question. The advantage of this mechanism is that "the meanings arrived at are determined by something other than a volitional, human act" (Du Bois 1993:54). This feature allows the poison oracle to function as a reliable or unbiased "method of revealing what is hidden" (Evans-Pritchard 1991:120), namely, the malicious intentions of one's group members, with which this agonistic cultural context is overflowing.[2] Although individuals do not explicitly treat the poison oracle as a randomizer but rather assign it mystical properties (Evans-Pritchard 1991:147–151), the administration of poison to fowls does, in fact, amount to the production of a randomizer. To ensure that it acts as such, "as soon as the poison is brought back from its forest home it is tested to discover whether some fowls will live and others die under its influence" (Evans-Pritchard 1991:158). A poison that systematically kills all fowls or has no effect on any of them is tantamount to a die that falls on one face time and again: it is not a proper randomizer in that, all things being equal, it is not governed by or involving equal chances for each of the actual or hypothetical members of a population; its outcomes are known in advance. Here, then, as in the contexts I discussed before, contingency produced by and harvested from nonhuman entities is mobilized as a cultural resource, only this time for reducing, rather than increasing, agency.

I suggest that this form of mechanical divination is supposed to have its effects in a specific dimension of another person's flexibility and agency, namely, "subprehending," in other words, the ability of a person to effectively anticipate the interpretants of his or her behavior (see Enfield 2013:104–112). This is because ill intentions in these ethnographic contexts are often (though not always) masked, dissimulated, and hidden behind behavioral signs that mediate for other people benign or even good intentions (Figure 21.6). In other words, the flexibility and heightened agency of a person who ill intends against other people often find expression in his or her ability to have one purpose but to deliberately give off signs that mediate another purpose for other people. Such a person can effectively anticipate and orchestrate the interpretants his or her publicly available behavior will create and cause other people to experience by effectively concealing his or her true purpose and mediating a false one. Such a person has mastered execution, planning, and subprehension.

Mechanical divination, in turn, undermines this person's ability to subprehend because it reveals the true purpose—in other words, the true

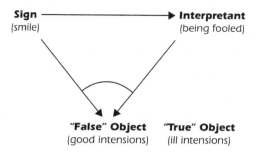

Figure 21.6 Anticipating Interpretants: Strategically Subprehending in Witchcraft.

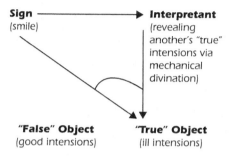

Figure 21.7 Diagnosing Interpretants: Undermining Subprehending in Witchcraft.

object—that lies behind his or her publicly available behavior—that is, behind the signs he or she publicly gives off (Figure 21.7). Mechanical divination allows concerned people to experience interpretants of the publicly available behavior of an ill-intending person, which are different from the interpretants this ill-intending person intends his or her publicly available behavior to create. It is a form of diagnostics that determines actual intentions from evinced intentions, allowing people to gain theoretical agency (knowledge) over that which reduced their practical agency (actions) and thus to try to ameliorate their situation.

To conclude, it is typically understood that humans are more agentive than nonhuman entities because they are more flexible in the various dimensions of agency discussed above. However, as I have argued in this chapter, in some ethnographic contexts humans face the problem of reduced flexibility in terms of their ability to compose their behavior, in the sense of both execution and planning. They might consequently try to capitalize on the capacity of some nonhuman entities to function as sources of contingency that can be used to cultivate flexibility in these two dimensions. Although my ethnographic focus is a very specific form of human agency, namely, artistic creation as understood by a specific group of artists, it can be extended to other, often more mundane, forms of agency. For example, one can think of the use of the "random shuffle" function on an iPod as a case in which contextually meaningful contingency is produced by and harvested from a nonhuman entity (a computerized shuffling algorithm) as a way of avoiding standardization of planning—here the choice about the order of songs one is going to listen to. And one can think of the "random oscillation" function of a tennis ball machine as a case in which contextually meaningful contingency is produced by and harvested from a nonhuman entity as a way of improving one's ability to execute one's purposes in a real-time situation.[3]

At stake here is not the extension of human agency by nonhuman entities, as when I use a bike to cover a greater distance, but the use of nonhuman entities for cultivating and enabling basic dimensions of human agency, to begin with, in particular, the generation of novel purposes and the means to execute them. Such a use can have different orientations depending on culturally specific factors. Humans can use the contingency produced by nonhuman entities to increase their own agency and flexibility, as in the cases of the jazz school and the jazz-improvising computerized algorithms, or to increase their own agency and flexibility by reducing those of others, as in the case of mechanical divination. In all of these examples, semiotic mediation emerges as a key mechanism underlying the distribution of agency across the human/nonhuman divide, and as a condition of possibility for its proper analysis.

NOTES

1. At the time of my fieldwork these algorithms were a work in progress and not always successful in achieving their goal. I remember many instances of playing with the system they animated and being uninspired by its responses to my own (frequently uninspiring) improvisations. Lack of inspiration typically resulted when the system generated responses that were either too predictable or too unpredictable (Wilf 2013:614–615).
2. At the same time, "A Zande does not readily accept an oracular verdict which conflicts seriously with his interests," and "apart from criminal cases, there can be no doubt that a man takes advantage of every loop-hole the oracle allows him to obtain what he wants or to refrain from doing what he does not want to do" (Evans-Pritchard 1991:163).
3. As one tennis training machine manufacturer puts it, "Random oscillation is where the tennis ball machine replicates a match situation by shooting balls randomly around the court. Rather than groove a particular shot, this allows a player to . . . practice shots in a more realistic environment." See http://www. spinshot-sports.com/Knowledge.html, accessed April 5, 2015.

REFERENCES

Berliner, Paul. 1994. *Thinking in Jazz: The Infinite Art of Improvisation.*
Chicago: University of Chicago Press.

Du Bois, John W. 1993. "Meaning Without Intention: Lessons from Divination." In *Responsibility and Evidence in Oral Discourse*, edited by Jane H. Hill and Judith T. Irvine, 48–71. Cambridge: Cambridge University Press.

Enfield, N. J. 2013. *Relationship Thinking: Agency, Enchrony, and Human Sociality.* Oxford: Oxford University Press.

Evans-Pritchard, Edward E. (1937) 1991. *Witchcraft, Oracles, and Magic among the Azande.* London: Clarendon Press.

Kockelman, Paul. 2005. "The Semiotic Stance." *Semiotica* (1–4): 233–304.

Peirce, Charles S. 1955. "Logic as Semiotic: The Theory of Signs." In *Philosophical Writings of Peirce*, edited by J. Buchler, 98–119. London: Dover.

Wilf, Eitan. 2013. "Sociable Robots, Jazz Music, and Divination: Contingency as a Cultural Resource for Negotiating Problems of Intentionality." *American Ethnologist* 40(4): 605–618.

Wilf, Eitan. 2014. *School for Cool: The Academic Jazz Program and the Paradox of Institutionalized Creativity.* Chicago: University of Chicago Press.

PART NINE

The Place of Agency

CHAPTER 22

Place and Extended Agency

PAUL C. ADAMS

This chapter explores a few of the ways in which place participates in distributed agency. Drawing on geographic theories, literature and philosophy, I offer *emplaced* action as action that transcends the taken-for-granted boundaries of mind and body. This perspective breaks from the natural attitude (Husserl 1982:5) since we commonly think of ourselves as autonomous actors. According to a long tradition, we think of place as a simple vessel or site for agency while neglecting the ways in which place profoundly affects what we are able to do.

According to Aristotle, place is a container with interior boundaries larger than what is contained. Newton understood place as a subdivision of space and also as a location. Descartes developed the notion that everything can be situated relative to a coordinate plane. These models share a focus on location, since an area includes all locations that are contained within given boundaries, and locations can be easily defined as positions in an X-Y grid or a three-dimensional volume. Place is still understood quite often in these classical terms as a geometrical phenomenon, namely a location or a bounded space, but when we pause to reflect on *lived* place, we find much more than a container, area, or point. We discover a manifestation of self that seems profoundly internal, yet perplexingly "out there" (Tuan 1977).

The elements of place associated with distributed agency are revealed by the phrase *to take place*—a phrase suggesting that place is temporarily seized and claimed by action rather than being separable from action.

We also say that actions are *undertaken* or *carried out*, implying that places are fields for the externalization of knowledge, expectation, understanding, and other elements of self. Combining these phrases, action seizes and appropriates places while necessarily externalizing phenomena and qualities originally perceived as internal.

FOUNDATIONS OF EMPLACED AGENCY

As Robert Sack has argued, the intimate relationship between person and place is reciprocal: "Places need the actions of people or selves to exist and have effect. The opposite is equally true—selves cannot be formed and sustained or have effect without place" (1997:88). To offer a few concrete examples: an orator is subject to the visual and acoustic properties of a lecture hall; a soldier fights on a battlefield structured in terms of sight lines, slopes, and cover; a chemist needs a laboratory that permits the isolation and recombination of precise amounts of various elements; an artist's studio provides tools and space for making objects of aesthetic value. I offer the term *emplaced action* to designate action involving place in an integral fashion. Emplaced action integrates the concrete and the abstract, the subjective and the objective, the local and the global. All actions involving people are emplaced, although not all emplaced actions involve people.

Geographers increasingly follow Doreen Massey (1993) in conceptualizing places as constellations of flows rather than bounded areas. In analogous fashion, people can be understood as extensible beings who both sense the world at a distance and act on distant places, dynamically extending themselves outward through space-time (Adams 1995, 2005). Thus, emplaced action is not contained action. Rather it links near and far aspects of the world in particular ways that fluctuate from moment to moment. The orator speaking in the lecture hall incites a protest in a public square, against a war fought in a distant country, according to orders signed in a legislative chamber, involving a chemical weapon developed in a laboratory, inspiring an artist cloistered in a studio, whose painting will circulate from gallery to gallery. Every phase of action is linked to other actions through places, and places connect actions to other actions in particular topologies and configurations. Some of this action is physical, like fighting and painting, while some of it is verbal, like orating and legislating. In either case, human action becomes extensible through space by virtue of its active appropriation of place.

To think of place in this way requires us to "get back into" place (Casey 1993), to recognize ourselves as fundamentally geographical in nature.

Scholarship is needed that breaks down the methodological, epistemo-logical, and ontological boundaries, splitting apart the various domains of emplaced action—physical/material, social/ethical, cognitive/discursive (Sack 1997). Such theorizations of place-based agency are indebted to Martin Heidegger whose concept of *Dasein* (being-in-the-world) posited that the objects encountered in daily life are understood with regard to their usefulness in relation to particular purposes and actions. On this account, a place is "something to which our direct intervention gives rise"—a phe-nomenon in which we are involved instrumentally (Casey 1997: 247, 250). *Dasein* indicates a realm of possibility where things are inconspicuous and unobtrusive as long as they can be perceived in terms of their uses in each particular place. Moved to a new place, an object changes with regard to its meaning whether we consider the transmogrification of Marcel Duchamp's infamous "Fountain" (a urinal turned 90 degrees, signed then shown in a gallery) or the more subtle shift of a steel coffee can when it is emptied, removed from the kitchen, and reused in the office as a pencil holder. The dependency of action on place is exposed when our expectations about things clash with preexisting notions of a place-based material/social/symbolic order. Such dislocations reveal the classic, location-based formu-lations of Aristotle, Newton, and Descartes as merely "the shrunken resi-due of place" (Casey 1997:251).

PLACE AND FLEXIBILITY

Places bring flexibility to agency regardless of their scale. Consider the workshop of a man who sells handmade furniture and takes temporary jobs in construction, who is also rebuilding an old sailboat and struggling to keep his vintage BMW motorcycle running. His workshop contains drills, sanders, clamps, and levels; grease for the motorcycle; epoxy for the boat; and many other tools and substances that enable various projects. Or consider the studio of a sculptor. Her time there is spent cutting, chiseling, sanding, brushing, polishing, and so on—but always with help from the worktables, tools, materials, and light in the studio. Both workshop and studio function as complex translation machines, turning bodily capaci-ties into forces far more energetic and diverse than the human body could produce on its own. This emplacement in turn lets people not only act on things, but also become the selves they imagine or wish themselves to be.

Similar arguments can be made about other places. Houses, for exam-ple, foster different types of subjectivity. Geographer Yi-Fu Tuan calls the house "an architectural embodiment of social structure and values" because it "contains, concentrates, and focuses the human psyche" (1982:52). In *Segmented Worlds and Self* (1982) he explains that the typical European home from the Middle Ages was a hall-like structure, lacking clear-cut distinctions between public and private space, whereas in contrast a modern European or American home has many gradations between public and private, including places to sequester oneself as well as various semi-public places for entertaining and socializing. Modernization involved increasing segmentation of both the self and the domestic environment, since elements of self derive from domestic routines, the potent symbolism of the home, and the spatial coordination of life within the dwelling place (Bachelard 1964). Each dwelling functions as a particular kind of "megabody" (Casey 1997:291), transforming, magnifying, and blending the agency of particular selves.

Moving to a larger scale, the city can be seen as a machine where people are "all being shot backwards and forwards ... to make some pattern" (Woolf 2002:24). The spatial organization of the city combines with variable demands on people's time, levels of access to transportation, and rules about who can be where at what time. Hägerstrand's time-geography (1970) frames these observations in terms of coupling constraints, capability constraints, and authority constraints. People inhabit particular space-time "prisms" (Carlstein 1982) that limit where they can go and what projects they can join.

Emplaced urban action includes people who have legal or conventional claims to the places they occupy, as well as immigrants, vagrants, tourists, and others whose rights to place are disputed. Therefore urban emplacement includes ideas about who belongs in any given place, and conversely who is "out of place" as members of certain groups are symbolically linked to threats such as pollution, disease, indecency, abnormality, criminality, and disorder (Cresswell 1996). Such labels suggest that some people are able to *act with* the urban environment while others are mainly *acted on* by that environment. Material and symbolic boundaries work together to shape the collective agency of the city, forming what geographers refer to as the socio-spatial dialectic (Soja 1980) and suggesting that places are complex tools for producing social stratification. Virginia Woolf's essay *A Room of One's Own* (2002) demonstrated that the creative output of women remained hidden from the world precisely because women had been denied private places to call their own. Luce Irigaray (1993) provided an interesting complement, showing how women's bodies have been appropriated as places, through externally controlled intrusions and appropriations. "Intellectual freedom depends upon material things" (Woolf 2002:88), and these things include both places and emplaced bodies.

In short, place is implicated in action because it offers not only material resources such as a workbench or drawing table, but also social scaling tools ranging from bedrooms to houses to city streets, and symbolic resources such as white picket fences, welcome mats, and "No Loitering" signs. These processes enhance the flexibility of agency across a wide range of scales, though not to the same degree for all occupants, suggesting the need to consider broader implications of agency distributed in place.

PLACE AND ACCOUNTABILITY

This brings us to the second key ingredient of distributed agency—accountability. To broach this discussion we need to consider what geographers call "sense of place," a feeling of "identification with a place engendered by living in it" (Agnew and Duncan, 1989:2). A strong sense of place is an affective bond, which Tuan evocatively calls *topophilia* (1974). Environmental psychologists carefully parse the differences between place meaning and place attachment (Manzo and Devine-Wright 2013) but geographers tend to view these as complementary aspects of the same phenomenon. In any case, we are dealing with issues including attachment to one's home and attitudes of nationalism, as well as the surprisingly intimate connections between these variously scaled senses of place (Morley 2000; Smith 2012).

When we love a place we are inclined to justify actions in terms of the place's (perceived) meaning, and this framing of accountability radically alters the calculus of right and wrong. For the love of my home I may set mousetraps and install a security system. These actions may require adjustments of my ethical system if I like mice (just not the ones in my walls) and if I believe the destitute deserve public assistance (just not from my refrigerator). The house *needs* to be maintained, I may argue, and it is home maintenance (not greed) that justifies the use of locks and mousetraps. The same logic can be inflated to justify what Mike Davis calls the "security-driven logic of urban enclavization" (1990: 223, 244), which militarizes city life with gated communities, "bum-proof benches," closed-circuit surveillance systems, and so on (Davis 1990: 235, 248). Such acts of exclusion by the urban environment are treated as a form of care—for the city—rather than as a calculating refusal to care—for people.

Moving up the scale even further, we can see the most extreme expressions of territorial defensiveness in patriotism, militarism, and the hardening of state borders. Uncomfortable moral questions about the innocence of individuals can be avoided by situating guilt at the level of a foreign state, then asserting the right of one's own state to carry out punishment on that foreign state. The nation is to its territory as the self is to the human body, and this parallel is so strong that bodies and nations symbolically overlap. Righteous indignation subsumes human casualties. People learn to identify the nation as an immense megabody in which their personal agency can be aligned with the agency of many other people and take on superhuman proportions while absolving individuals of accountability for causing suffering and death to members of that set of humans labeled "the enemy." Popular culture can make this idea strikingly literal through nationalist superheroes like Captain America, a graphic "rescaling icon" internalized by children to form "a bridge between collective identity and the individual" (Dittmer 2007:401). This cartoon literalizes the body politic, a notion that dates from the 15th century and is evident in Hobbes's writings. In modern critiques such processes of internalization and externalization are linked to bio-power (Foucault 1978). Not only is agency distributed to a place, but personal interests are deemed to be subordinate to a "national interest" that is equated with enforcing certain geographical boundaries (Newman and Paasi 1998). The needs of this collective body may be imagined/imaginary (Anderson 1991), but they guide militaristic and nationalistic actions that destroy hundreds, thousands, or even millions of real human bodies.

SUMMARY

Place's agency is evident through the proliferation and diversity of place-based actions. Place also displays agency by absorbing accountability such that people can act directly against the interests of others without the normally attendant sense of guilt for having caused another's suffering. Topophilia is the common strand between these complementary aspects of emplaced action, as "home" distributes agency and accountability at many scales. Whereas a workshop or studio is reassuring in its homey familiarity and homely usefulness, a gated community demonstrates the exclusionary defense of home and a military front seems like the bold advance of an idealized homeland.

REFERENCES

Adams, P. C. 1995. "A Reconsideration of Personal Boundaries in Space-Time." *Annals of the Association of American Geographers* 85(2): 267–285.

Adams, P. C. 2005. *The Boundless Self: Communication in Physical and Virtual Spaces.*
Syracuse, NY: Syracuse University Press.

Agnew, J. A., and J. S. Duncan, eds. 1989. *The Power of Place: Bringing Together
Geographical and Sociological Imaginations.* Oxford/New York: Routledge.
Retrieved from http://www.eblib.com.

Anderson, B. 1991. *Imagined Communities: Reflections on the Origin and Spread of
Nationalism.* 2nd ed. London/New York: Verso.

Bachelard, G. 1964. *The Poetics of Space.* Translated by Maria Jolas.
Boston: Beacon Press.

Carlstein, T. 1982. *Time Resources, Society and Ecology: On the Capacity for Human
Interaction in Space and Time.* London: Allen & Unwin.

Casey, E. S. 1993. *Getting Back into Place: Toward a Renewed Understanding of the
Place-World.* Bloomington: Indiana University Press.

Casey, E. S. 1997. *The Fate of Place: A Philosophical History.* Berkeley/Los
Angeles: University of California Press.

Cresswell, T. 1996. *In Place/Out of Place: Geography, Ideology, and Transgression.*
Minneapolis: University of Minnesota Press.

Davis, M. 1990. *City of Quartz: Excavating the Future in Los Angeles.* London/
New York: Verso.

Dittmer J. 2007. "America Is Safe While Its Boys and Girls Believe in Its
Creeds!": Captain America and American Identity prior to World War 2."
Environment and Planning D: Society and Space 25(3): 401–423.

Foucault, M. 1978. *The History of Sexuality. Vol. I: An Introduction.* Translated by
R. Hurley. New York: Pantheon.

Hägerstrand, T. 1970. "What About People in Regional Science?" *Papers of the Regional
Science Association* 24: 7–21.

Husserl, E. 1982. *Ideas Pertaining to a Pure Phenomenology and to a Phenomenological
Philosophy: First Book.* Translated by F. Kersten. Dordrecht, the
Netherlands: Kluwer.

Irigaray, L. 1993. "Place, Interval: A Reading of Aristotle." In *An Ethics of Sexual
Difference*, translated by C. Burke and C. G. Gill. Ithaca, NY: Cornell
University Press.

Manzo, L. C., and P. Devine-Wright, eds. 2013. *Place Attachment: Advances in Theory,
Methods and Applications.* London/New York: Routledge.

Massey, D. 1993. "Power-Geometry and a Progressive Sense of Place." In *Mapping the
Futures: Local Cultures, Global Change*, edited by J. Bird, B. Curtis, T. Putnam,
G. Robertson, and L. Tickner, 59–69. London: Routledge.

Morley, D. 2000. *Home Territories: Media, Mobility and Identity.* London/
New York: Routledge.

Newman, D., and A. Paasi. 1998. "Fences and Neighbours in the Postmodern
World: Boundary Narratives in Political Geography." *Progress in Human
Geography* 22: 186–207.

Sack, R. D. 1997. *Homo Geographicus: A Framework for Action, Awareness, and Moral
Concern.* Baltimore/London: Johns Hopkins University Press.

Smith, S. 2012. "Intimate Geopolitics: Religion, Marriage, and Reproductive
Bodies in Leh, Ladakh." *Annals of the Association of American Geographers*
102(6): 1511–1528.

Soja, E. W. 1980. "The Socio-spatial Dialectic." *Annals of the Association of American
Geographers* 70(2): 207–225.

Tuan, Y.-F. 1982. *Segmented Worlds and Self: Group Life and Individual Consciousness*. Minneapolis: University of Minnesota Press.

Tuan, Y.-F. 1977. *Space and Place: The Perspective of Experience*. Minneapolis: University of Minnesota Press.

Tuan, Y.-F. 1974. *Topophilia: A Study of Environmental Perception, Attitudes, and Values*. Englewood Cliffs, NJ: Prentice-Hall.

Woolf, V. (1929) 2002. *A Room of One's Own*. New York: RosettaBooks.

CHAPTER 23

How Agency Is Distributed Through Installations

SAADI LAHLOU

ACTION IS DISTRIBUTED

Artifacts will help, support, or guide users in their activity through their culturally constructed properties. This idea emerged in various forms in history (Leroi-Gourhan 1965); philosophy (Simondon 1969); psychology (Gibson 1950, 1982, 1986; Uexküll 1925; Vygotsky 1978), design (Norman 1991), cognitive science (Pea 1994), and so on. Hutchins (1995), observing jet pilots, demonstrated that what flies the plane is not pilots alone but the whole cockpit, including instruments, checklists, maps, and so on. Cognition is "distributed" in its content as well as in its process. Objects that possess agency are called "actants" (Akrich, Callon, and Latour 2006), a term including acting humans and material objects alike. When describing activity emerging from subject-object interaction, some (Gibson, Norman, Latour) focus more on properties of the object, while others (Vygotsky, Uexküll) start from the subject. This chapter proposes a larger systemic view.

Over the last two decades, I analyzed human activity recorded from a first-person perspective, with "subcams"—miniature video cameras attached to glasses of volunteers performing their usual activity, at work or elsewhere. With participants we analyzed their recordings to make explicit their cognitive processes and the various elements involved in their action (Lahlou 2011, 2014).

In doing so, it appears obvious that *action* is distributed and its determinants as well. For example, in the activity of preparing breakfast, we can observe that, as Mother sets the table, Father goes to buy croissants, Coffee-Machine brews Coffee, Bottle contains Orange-Juice, Alarm-Clock wakes up Daughter, while Thermostat maintains House warm, and so on.

To clarify the distribution of agency, let us look in detail at the determinants of action.

INSTALLATION THEORY

When you manage to cycle in heavy traffic, this is the result of *simultaneously* using the affordances of the road; of mobilizing embodied skills; of protection by the traffic rules that prevent cars from driving you off the road. Society has constructed the built environment (the road), trained you to embody skills (cycling, traffic sign reading), and runs control institutions (police, traffic lights, rules of the road). On one hand these three layers guide and scaffold your individual behavior, enabling you to safely reach your destination. On the other hand they make you a predictable road user to others, so we all together co-construct a "normal" traffic flow at societal level. The same mechanism that nudges and empowers you is also a mechanism of control at aggregate level.

The urban street is an "installation"; this installation is not located within the physical world only or inside your nervous system alone; it is distributed in the built environment, in educated and disciplined bodies, in institutions and their enforcing agents. Our everyday environment is built by humans; centuries of gradual construction have produced "installations" such as kitchens, conference rooms, or cockpits that make activity simple, so simple in fact that even novices can perform satisfyingly. Barker described of such setups as "behavioral settings": "stable, extra-individual units with great coercive power over the behavior that occurs within them" (Barker 1968:17). But we must also include the individuals in the installation.

Installation theory considers how societies guide individual activity by constructing "installations," in which individual subjects operate. Subjects are moved by individual motives and intentions, but an installation has a momentum of its own. An installation is "a socially constructed system locally guiding a specific activity, by suggesting, scaffolding and constraining what society members can/should do in this specific situation" (Lahlou

2015). Installation theory is a theory for nudging, but also for more intrusive control.

As for most important phenomena, a plethora of concepts and theories have been proposed in the literature, for example, "affordances," "disciplining institutions," "structures," "assemblages," "environments," "niches," "infrastructure," "channels," "codes," "norms," "habitus," and so forth. Installation theory tiles three layers of determinants that were so far separated by disciplinary approach, even though in practice they operate as a bundle. The various components of an installation are not located in the same medium; they emerge visibly as a functional unit only when they locally assemble in action; as a bundle they were gradually constructed in practice, and only as a bundle can they be understood. The example of the road above illustrates this: the installation is not limited to the visible setting of the pavement; it includes the representations and driving skills of the participants, as well as the institutions that regulate the traffic. Each is meaningless without the others.

Within an installation, behavior is funneled *simultaneously* by (a) affordances of the physical setting, (b) subjects' embodied competences, and (c) social control. What characterizes human installations is their intentionality. Their design fits a specific purpose: they support a project of activity. Humans make installations for all kinds of activities: roads, houses, armchairs, hospitals, cradles, graves, and so on.

Individuals do have free will (e.g., they chose to get into the traffic), but their agency is limited. Clearly, installations have a momentum of their own. Installation theory considers that humans usually act in such settings (roads, homes, restaurants, hospitals, etc.) where activity is channeled by the cultural installation. Depending on how we want to see it, we can consider that individuals use installations as instruments to reach their goals; or that installations use individuals to produce an outcome. For example, the traffic installation (roads, signs, lights, traffic rules, police, etc.) uses drivers to produce smooth transport at societal level; the roller coaster or the night club uses Albert as "a client" and as "a participant" to produce "experience" for users, and profit. Both perspectives are valid to a certain extent.

In other words, while Hutchins noted the environment contains mediating structures that process parts of the cognitive operations necessary to complete tasks, Installation theory considers more radically that our environment contains constructed "installations" which coproduce and funnel activity with the human actors as components. It must be clear here that installations are not just the context: individuals are part and parcel of them. Society does not only install physical artifacts, it also installs interpretive structures (the manual) in individuals so the physical layer is used "as it should." For smooth traffic, drivers should know how to drive their vehicle and there should be rules that are enforced. And this is indeed the case: society has set up systems to embody competences in individuals (e.g., driving lessons, license) and sets of rules of the road, with an enforcing body (the Police). These are neither independent nor accidental: the three sets of determinants are obviously part of one single societal project: smooth traffic. In practice, what the subject can do is the remaining intersection of what is objectively possible (affordances), subjectively possible (embodied competences), and socially enabled (social control). Amazingly, while this is common sense, the three layers tend to be studied independently by different disciplines. In the study of accidents, though, it becomes clear that problems occur only when the loopholes of the various layers of defense of the system combine (Reason 2000).

Installation theory has two aspects. The first is an operational framework to describe the determinants of activity. This framework, above, is simplistic, with three layers of components; it can be used for analysis and for change management. It is practical because the layers indicate where one can act to change the system.

The theory's second aspect addresses the evolution of installations. It describes the interactions between the components of the model, and genetic, functional, and historical mechanisms that produce sustainable systems. During education individuals will internalize not only various representations and practices, but also social rules. Foucault (1975) described how this embodiment of social rules makes individuals "docile bodies" and as a result each actor becomes his own controller. Other society members will also encourage and control others into behaving (from smiling or frowning to giving directions or orders); societies also have specific control forces (e.g., Police) to ensure enforcement. The rules themselves may be reified into artefacts which can become actants. Embodied interpretation systems (e.g., mental representations of objects) and physical objects themselves are taken in a chicken-and-egg reproductive cycle, with dual selection operating in each of the two forms (embodied and material). Institutions are in charge of designing, operating, maintaining, and evolving the installations; they monitor the dual selection process that make the installation a single, coherent, functional unit. In this short chapter we will use only the first part to provide a framework distinguishing three types of agency.

Installation theory considers three types of components that determine action: affordances in the physical context, embodied competences of the subject, and social influence—direct or through institutions. Affordances afford;

competences enable, and rules empower and control. The combination of these three layers generates a limited tree of possibilities for action at every step; so actors are funneled into the very activity the installation is designed for.

At a *physical level*, objects have affordances that both limit some behaviors and call for some others. Gibson considers that objects immediately display their affordances to the senses. For example, a door handle signals how it can be handled and turned (Norman 1988). Uexküll placed more emphasis on the interpretation by the subject, considering the object provides "connotations for activity" (Uexküll 1925). Unless one is in the wilderness, we are surrounded by man-made objects, which, as stated above, carry some intentionality and affordances by human design. The environment has been planted with physical installations.

The physical level can be used by Humans because they have *embodied competences* to interpret these affordances and perform action. In practice we learn and embody new affordances. Someone who never used a fancy door handle (e.g., electric button) could stay trapped in the room even if the door is not locked. Representations of common objects, material or not (doors, hospitals, democracy, etc.), are shared by the population: they are "social representations" (Moscovici 1961; Abric 1994). Social representations are the World's user's manual. As we see with the example of the door, "interpreting" is not only a matter of chaining ideas to perception, but also chaining *action* to ideas. Interpreting a door includes the motor action to open it—or close it. Just as the physical environment is planted with physical installations, the minds and bodies of Humans are an *embodied layer* that has been installed with representations and motor skills; as a combined result of biology, education, and experience.

Finally, we take into account what others do and want us to do (or not do). Others can influence us by force or menace; most often on our own behalf we are influenced by imitating others or anticipating consequences of our actions. Social psychology experiments show interpersonal or group influence in laboratory (for extreme cases see Haney, Banks, and Zimbardo 1973, or Milgram 1963); in real life influence is often mediated by institutions, and the expected behaviors come in the form of rules. There lay the third, *social layer* of installations: its components are distributed over "other people." This level can hamper and control as well as empower and support. It is the most diverse in form since influence can come directly from individuals or from groups, and can be mediated by institutions and rules.

Let's take again breakfast in the family: Father brings four Croissants; Croissants have affordance as "food." Children will interpret these as edible; they know how to eat them. The institutional rules of the family are that Croissants should be shared equally, one per person, so if Son wants to take an extra one, other participants will prevent him from doing so. Another example in a hospital installation: a cancer patient may afford several treatments among which the competent doctor will make a choice; but hospital rules will force the doctor to ask the patient's consent.

In short, Installation theory states action is supported and guided at three levels: affordances planted in the environment, competences embodied in the subject, other people and institutions. It suggests that sustainable behaviors are the ones that are simultaneously supported by and compatible with these three layers altogether. Agency, as the potential for action, is therefore distributed in these three layers.

HOW AGENCY IS DISTRIBUTED

Activity is a process that gradually transforms one state of things into another. We can consider that agency, for a subject who has a goal ("a representation of a specific desired final state"), is the capacity to reach the goal in the conditions given.

The final state is the result of a series of actions performed in a distributed way, by the subject and a series of actants: other people and objects. From the perspective of the subject, these actants can be resources or constraints, depending whether they support or hamper the process of reaching the goal. Agency of a subject, as the capacity to reach a goal, is a function of access to resources and liability to constraints.

We highlighted three layers of determinants: physical affordances, embodied competences, and social control. In that framework, what does agency mean? Capacity to reach the goal in the conditions given translates into capacity to use the necessary components in the three layers above.

Moreover, as we saw that many contexts were constructed as "installations," having access to an installation that is designed to reach the goal provides agency for that goal. This is a first finding: *capacity to use (i.e., entitlement and competence) an installation provides agency for the goals supported by this installation.* But not everything is an installation; many goals will not match exactly with the available installations; some components will be general enough to be used across the board; and so on.

Let us then look more generally at agency as the capacity to mobilize the necessary components of activity.

Material agency is access to the resources in the physical layer. It includes direct and indirect access and control over affordances. For example, I can use my kitchen, my car, and the roads in my country.

Access to resources is not enough. The subject must be able to use them in a relevant way. The subject's *embodied agency* is the set of embodied education, experience, and more generally psycho-physical capacity to interpret. It includes mental representations, motor skills, memories of past experience that can serve to interpret situations, and so on. Note that these competences can be used for the subject's goals, but also to contribute to other people's goals, as shown above.

Activity is constrained by other people. They define and enforce, usually collectively, rules in their local domains of control. When operating in these domains, subjects must obey local rules, or face the consequences. Social agency is the capacity to deal with social forces. This capacity is often the result of the subject's history in that specific community, especially his or her status and roles[1]. From a subject's perspective, social identity (belonging to various communities) provides access rights to some commons (protection, support, common resources). It also makes one subject to those rules and accountable to the communities, for good or bad. Being an inhabitant of a village may grant access to common meadows for one's cattle, local clubs, hospital, and so on. Being a national of a country provides access to public services, infrastructure, and so on. Family, town, country, organization, religious community, party, professional body, and so on enable their members to access resources and provide support through rules of use. They also forbid certain behaviors.

Finally, in some cases restrictive laws do not apply to trusted members of the community: top managers have no fixed and controlled working hours, some government heads are immune to laws during their mandate, and so on.

We can call *institutional agency* the agency granted to the individual by a community that provides support for action. Institutional agency is about what behavior is authorized or forbidden, and this agency is mediated by an institution at the moment of acting (an institution is a stable common set of rules in a community). The various layers of agency are not independent.

While this triple layered analysis may appear commonsensical or too encompassing in theory, it is handy in practice. Key here is that an installation work as a bundle: sustainable performance requires agency in the three realms *simultaneously*. For example, having a car and a road is not enough to drive from point A to point B: one must also know how to drive, and drive on the right side of the road; otherwise one may face serious problems. By separating the various levels of agency, the installation framework facilitates the analysis of cases where agency is contested, hazardous, and so on, and also provides handles to act—to empower or to restrict.

One can be surprised here not to find "power," as the capacity to force other people to perform behaviors, in our analysis of agency. In fact power can appear as brute force in embodied agency, as economic power in material agency, as institutional power in entitlement. Cognitive authority is one variant of power active in social influence. The classic approach of financial capital, cultural capital, and social capital (Bourdieu and Passeron 1990) seems to map the three levels of agency outlined by Installation theory: access to material goods, embodied skills, and social support.

Finally, we should note that agency is a situated notion: it is agency to do something specific; it is goal-dependent and context-dependent. Agency to make a pair of shoes is different from the agency to vote a law or to feed a village.

In sum, we saw three main forms of agency: *material agency* (access to affordances—direct or through the proxy of social entitlement); *embodied agency* (interpretative competences, where interpretation involves motor skills as well as cognitive); and *social agency* (often mediated by an institution, including capacity to evade local rules). Robust agency must combine the three layers. In practice we can consider the palette of these three layers to improve a given situation. By distributing agency over the layers, we can design interaction and foster or hamper different types of behavior. In doing so we can empower (or control) groups or individuals and support political or organisational change. Because such approach can be very efficient, and will partly rely on nonhuman actants that have no moral concerns, we must be especially cautious and ethical in the design process.

ACKNOWLEDGMENTS

This chapter benefited from a residency at Paris Institute for Advanced Study (France) as a EURIAS senior fellow, with support of the European Union 7th Framework Programme for research (grant agreement no. 246561), and from constructive reviews from Paul Kockelman and Nick Enfield.

NOTE

1. Stoetzel (1963) defines role as the set of behaviors that can be legitimately expected from the subject, and status as the set of behaviors the subject can legitimately expect from others.

REFERENCES

Abric, J.-C. (1994). *Pratiques sociales et représentations*. Paris: Presses Universitaires de France.

Akrich, M., M. Callon, and B. Latour. 2006. *Sociologie de la traduction: textes fondateurs*. « Sciences sociales ». Paris: Mines Paris, les Presses.

Barker, R. G. (1968). *Ecological Psychology: Concepts and Methods for Studying the Environment of Human Behavior*. Stanford University Press.

Boltanski, L., and L. Thévenot. 2006. *On Justification: Economies of Worth*. Princeton, NJ: Princeton University Press.

Bourdieu, P., and J.-C. Passeron. 1990. *Reproduction in Education, Society and Culture. Volume 4: Reproduction*. London: Sage.

Foucault, M. 1975. *Surveiller et punir : naissance de la prison. Bibliothèque des histoires*. Vol. 2004. Paris: Gallimard.

Gibson, J. J. 1950. *The Perception of the Visual World*. Boston: Houghton Mifflin.

Gibson, J. J. 1982. "Notes on Affordances." In *Reasons for Realism: Selected Essays of James J. Gibson*, edited by E. Reed and R. Jones, 401–418. London: Lawrence Erlbaum Associates.

Gibson, J. J. 1986. *The Ecological Approach to Visual Perception*. London: Lawrence Erlbaum Associates.

Haney, C., Banks, C., and Zimbardo, P. (1973). Interpersonal Dynamics in a Simulated Prison. *International Journal of Criminology and Penology*, 1, 69–97.

Hutchins, E. L. 1995. "How a Cockpit Remembers Its Speed." *Cognitive Science* 19: 265–288.

Lahlou, S. 2011. "How Can We Capture the Subject's Perspective? An Evidence-Based Approach for the Social Scientist." *Social Science Information* 50(3–4): 607–655.

Lahlou, S. 2014. "Social Representations and Social Construction: The Evolutionary Perspective of Installation Theory." In *Handbook of Social Representa*, edited by G. Sammut, E. Andreouli, G. Gaskell, and J. Valsiner, 193–209. Cambridge: Cambridge University Press.

Leroi-Gourhan, E. 1965. *Le geste et la parole*. Paris: Albin Michel.

Milgram, S. (1963). Behavioral Study of obedience. *Journal of Abnormal Psychology*, 67(4, Oct 1963), 371–378.

Moscovici, S. (1961). *La psychanalyse, son image et son public. Etude sur la représentation sociale de la psychanalyse*. Presses Universitaires de France.

Norman, D. A. (1988). *The Design of Everyday Things*. New York: Basic Books.

Norman, D. A. 1991. "Cognitive Artifacts." In *Designing Interaction: Psychology at the Human Computer Interface*, edited by J. Carroll, 17–38. New York: Cambridge University Press.

Pea, R. D. 1994. "Seeing What We Build Together: Distributed Multimedia Learning Environments for Transformative Communications." *Journal of the Learning Sciences* 3(3): 285–299.

Reason, J. T. (2000). *Human error: models and management*. British Medical Journal (Clinical Research Ed.), 320(7237), 768–770.

Simondon, G. 1969. *Du mode d'existence des objets techniques*. Paris: Aubier.

Stoetzel, J. (1963). *La psychologie sociale*. Paris: Flammarion.

Uexküll, J. von. (1925) 1965. "Mondes animaux et monde humain." In *Mondes animaux et monde humain, suivi de Théorie de la signification*, edited by J. von Uexküll, pp. 1–90. Paris: Denoël, 1965.

Vygotsky, L. S. 1978. *Mind in Society: The Development of Higher Psychological Processes*. Edited by M. Cole, V. John-Steiner, S. Scribner, and E. Souberman. Cambridge, MA: Harvard University Press.

PART TEN

From Cooperation to Deception and Disruption

CHAPTER 24

Cooperation and Social Obligations

DAVID P. SCHWEIKARD

Phenomena of distributed agency are deeply entrenched in our lives as agents. We go for walks and visit concerts together, we found clubs and organizations, build research teams and political parties. Curiously, scholars of the philosophy of mind and action have only relatively recently, that is, in the mid-1980s, started devoting their attention to these phenomena. As more elaborate accounts are being put forth and discussed, it becomes clear that core issues revolve around two main foci: the intentionality and the normativity of distributed agency. Under these headings, scholars seek to understand, on the one hand, the structure of the intentional attitudes that guide joint action and by which joint action is explained. And on the other hand, they inquire into the questions as to whether agents incur, by cooperating with others, specific mutual obligations and, if they do, how these obligations come about, what kind they are, and how they are justified. In what follows, I shall provide a brief account of these two sets of challenges and expound ways of meeting them. My focus will be on small-scale cooperative joint action, which I describe more thoroughly in the next section, and the question as to whether and, if so, how specifically social obligations between the agents involved come about.

SORTING TYPES OF AGENCY

One way of sorting phenomena of distributed agency proceeds by asking how many agents can or need to be involved in the performance of an action. I shall lay out such an approach by appealing only to actions human agents normally can and do perform (together). This will serve to narrow the scope of the following reflections without denying the significance of classifying and understanding the cooperative behaviors of animals or the actions of and interactions with technical systems.

That said, it seems helpful to distinguish between actions human agents can perform on their own and actions they can only perform together. The action of going for a walk, for instance, can be performed by a single agent and by two or more agents; by contrast, actions such as playing tennis or lifting a heavy object can (under normal conditions) be performed only by two or more agents. If we call actions performed by two or more agents *joint actions*, we can capture this difference between types of action by saying that *contingently joint actions* are those that could also be performed by a single agent, and that *necessarily joint actions* are those that require the participation or contribution of two or more agents. Joint actions come in a vast variety, ranging from spontaneous and one-time cooperation to regular and highly structured collective agency. I shall return to core characteristics of joint actions in due course, although not without mentioning that it has proved helpful to treat questions of *group agency* separately from analyses of joint action (cf. Pettit and Schweikard 2006). Even though it is quite common to refer to actions performed by two or more agents as actions of a group, the design and structure of some groups raises the question whether they qualify as agents in their own right. Corporations, for instance, are complex social entities whose internal makeup and structures of decision making justify treating their ways of operating as decisively different from that of random collectives or pairs of cooperating agents. Interest in the structure of groups that may count as agents in their own right may be prompted primarily by issues of collective responsibility, but there are certainly also fundamental questions in action theory and social ontology that deserve attention.

In what follows, I shall set aside questions raised by complex social formations and concentrate instead on small-scale cooperative joint action. Prototypical cases such as two agents going for a walk together or lifting a heavy object together can be used to illustrate two central challenges in the philosophy of joint action, and in the theory of distributed agency more generally.

THE INTENTIONALITY OF JOINT ACTION

A simplified and preliminary way of formulating these two challenges posed by small-scale joint action on which I concentrate here is given by asking what is special about joint action and what joint action implies normatively. In a nutshell, the question "What is special?" refers to those elements of joint actions that set them off against parallel individual actions, and the question concerning normative implications is aimed at the mutual obligations and entitlements that may (or may not) hold between cooperating agents. The issues thus brought to the fore are the *intentionality* and the *normativity* of joint action.

Starting with intentionality, let us consider the following case. Imagine three agents (*A*, *B*, and *C*) walking next to each other in the same direction and that from what is observable it is unclear whether they or a subset of them are walking together or not; imagine further that we know that two of them (*A* and *B*) are going for a walk together, while the third (*C*) is just accidentally walking in parallel to them. With respect to this imagined case, we may ask what makes for the difference between *A*'s and *B*'s walking *together* (or *jointly*) and *B*'s and *C*'s walking *in parallel*, where *A* and *B* perform a joint action and *B* and *C* (in abstraction from *A*'s presence) perform parallel, but otherwise unrelated, individual actions. A minimal consensus about this issue among philosophers of action is best captured in John Searle's sloganesque formulation "If there is anything special about collective behaviour, it must lie in some special feature of the mental component, in the form of the intentionality" (Searle 1990:402). But how should this specific form of intentionality be described? Which specific intentional attitudes guide and serve to explain joint actions in contrast to coincidentally parallel individual actions?

Once it is accepted that the intentional attitudes that are in play in joint action cannot be simply the same as those that guide solitary individual action, a familiar move in the debate is to guard against postulating a form of group mind that hovers above, as it were, and controls the individuals involved. It seems just obvious that explaining joint action does not call for such a postulate of a supra-individual entity. What is required, instead, is an account of how exactly the intentionality characteristic of joint action differs from ordinary individual intentionality; put differently, what is sought is an answer to the question "What is collective about collective intentionality?" (cf. Schweikard and Schmid 2013). In short, the specific jointness or collectivity of the intentionality in play can rely in its content, its mode, or its subject. I take this last "or" to be inclusive and shall go on to sketch a *relational* account of joint intentions that takes all three aspects to take a specific collective form.

In order to intentionally guide their joint walk, *A* and *B* in our previous example both have to intend their joint walk, in other words, their joint walk has to be represented in the *content* of their intentions. On a first approximation, they each need to form intentions of the form "I intend that we go for a walk" (cf. Bratman 1999: ch. 5; Bratman 2014), since if each intended only to go for walk, this could already be fulfilled if each walked completely independently of the other. Capturing what makes their walking a case of intentionally walking together in this form, however, attracts a number of problems. Thus, one may hold that intentions of the form "I intend that we ... " contradict the otherwise plausible assumptions that one can intend only one's own actions, those one can control or whose performance is up to oneself (cf. the discussion in Bratman 1999: ch. 8). These worries can be deflected by arguing that the intentions in question are different from ordinary intentions to do something, in that their formation and enactment are dependent on all individuals involved forming structurally analogous intentions. A may not be in a position to fully intend, control, or settle deliberation concerning a joint walk with B, but if the walk is to be a joint walk, then it seems plausible to require that each refer to it in the content of their intentions. Both these intentions are, in other words, adequately formed only in relation to, and in combination with, the respective other. But accepting this "collectivity condition," as Raimo Tuomela (2005) has termed it, calls into question whether the subject place of the verbalization of the intentions can plausibly be rendered in the first person singular. Intentions of the form "I intend that we ... " then appear to be circular in that their formation presupposes the "we" they are meant to constitute (cf. Bratman 2014: ch. 2).

One way of avoiding this problem lies in postulating that the relevant intentions not only have a collective content, but that they also stand in a specifically collective *mode*, the we-mode. Tuomela (2005), for instance, takes intending in the we-mode to capture individuals' "intending as a group-member" as opposed to their "intending as a private person." On his account, individual agents who shift to the we-mode thereby take the respective group's perspective and form corresponding contributory intentions. A theoretically less demanding approach restricts the adjustment called for earlier to the modification that the individual agents involved intend in the form "*We* intend that we. ... " This does not appeal to a different form of intending—we-intending (Tuomela) or primitive we-intentions (Searle 1990) but only to a pluralized verbalization of the intentions in question. By thus intending in the plural, cooperators such as A and B refer to themselves and each other using the plural indexical "we," which in the context at hand is correctly used only when it picks out a plurality each of them represents. Their intentionally guiding the joint walk thus requires that A and B each form and enact intentions of the form "We intend that we go for a walk."

But whose intention is the intention that guides the joint walk? Who is the *subject* of this intention? Having set aside the postulate of a mysterious supra-mind that could be the subject of this intention, we should be drawn to the conclusion that the intending individuals *together* form the subject of this intention. With respect to both the content and the mode of the intentions of the individual agents involved, we noted that (1) collectivity has to feature in both of these aspects, and (2) it has to feature by high-lighting the relations between the agents involved. In a two-person case, only both of them can give sense to their each intending the joint activity and to their using the first person plural indexical "we" in verbalizing these intentions. And if it takes two to set up these interrelated intentions, then the same two, together, should be viewed as the subject of the intention that guides the joint walk.

This result calls for (at least) one immediate clarification regarding the number of intentions involved. I have referred to the individual agents' intentions and to the intention that guides the joint walk, possibly as if those were simply on a par. If we view as intentions only such mental phenomena that are had and embodied by individual agents, then only the participatory intentions of the individual agents qualify as intentions. This individualistic picture runs the risk of losing sight of the analytic and explanatory task set out at the beginning of this section. On the other hand, if we allow all structures of attitudes that guide and explain actions to be intentions, then specifically related intentions, such as those of cooperating agents, can play that role together. In line with the latter understanding, we can call the structure of interrelated attitudes that guides *A*'s and *B*'s joint walk the *joint intention* whose subject *A* and *B* are together.

Strictly speaking, the analysis of joint intentions should not be limited to the actual intentions regarding the joint activity, as these will typically be accompanied by further intentions and beliefs on the part of the agents involved. In these respects it seems plausible to demand that the agents' further intentions, for example, other goals *A* may have in mind in relation to the walk with *B*, do not conflict with their joint endeavor; that they each exhibit a sufficient degree of readiness to follow through with their endeavor; and that they each are aware that what and how they intend together is out in the open between them. Requiring an elaborate form of common knowledge among the participants may seem inadequate or overly intellectualized in some contexts, but a weaker "no conflict"–condition regarding their awareness and understanding of the situation may nevertheless be necessary for the attitudinal nexus to adequately provide guidance.

Returning to the laxly formulated question as to "what is special?" about joint action, the answer suggested by the relational account just sketched is that joint action is defined as being guided by a specific complex of interrelated attitudes of the individual agents involved. This complex of attitudes, the action-guiding *joint intention*, is in the main constituted by the participants' intentions of the form "We intend that we ... ," and its subject are the participants together. Understanding the one guiding attitude (the joint intention) and its subject as being thus constituted by specifically interrelated individual attitudes and by interrelated individual agents, yields a particular perspective on what it means to say that agency is distributed. The claim that interrelations between individual attitudes are characteristic of cooperation and distributed agency leads to the question as to whether these phenomena also characteristically involve normative relations between the agents involved. This is the question we turn to in the next section.

THE NORMATIVITY OF JOINT ACTION

When it comes to the normativity of joint action, the interesting question is not whether any mutual obligations exist between the agents involved, but whether it is characteristic of joint action that the agents have or incur obligations to each other precisely in virtue of acting together. According to Margaret Gilbert's account, such specific mutual obligations are fundamental to phenomena of joint action (cf. Gilbert 2014). Gilbert claims that such obligations are implied by the fact that in getting together to perform a joint action, agents enter (what she calls) a "joint commitment," which she characterizes as an irreducible, shared practical attitude the agents create by agreeing on the pursuit of a joint endeavor, which is described as an attitude of the group that is possibly discontinuous with the intentions of the individual agents, and which can be annulled only unanimously. If two agents are thus jointly committed to act together, each is *obligated* to the other to do his or her bit and each is *entitled* to the other's contribution or to rebuking the other in case of noncompliance. Gilbert's view is that joint commitments form the basis of jointly intentional action and that the inherent obligations and entitlements, which are not understood as moral but as social normative relations, are fundamental to all kinds of joint action.

The problem with this account is certainly not that it is never true that agents cooperate on the basis of binding mutual agreements, or that it is inconceivable that cooperators sometimes treat each other as if a contract existed between them even though their agreement was nonverbal. But some authors have remained unconvinced by some of the aforementioned details of the account and by the view that normative structure that comes with joint commitments is indeed fundamental to all kinds of joint action. For instance, below the level of highly organized group agency, and unless a somehow emergent subject of the relevant intentional states is appealed to, it does not seem plausible to claim that the intention that explains a joint action can diverge from the participatory intentions of the individual agents involved. And the feature of joint intentions Gilbert terms the "concurrence criterion" (2014:106–108), which is meant to capture that joint intentions can only be modified or annulled unanimously, also seems too demanding to be a general feature of joint action. For even if a degree of unanimity, a shared belief as to what they are doing together, is required to keep the cooperators on track, as it were, it would seem exaggerated to hold that in all cases of joint action one participant is entitled to hold all others to the original joint commitment. Gilbert's view thus represents phenomena of joint action as in principle akin to scenarios in which agents have entered a contract or exchanged promises, with all the normative implications involved by that. Without disputing that some cases exhibit that sort of normative structure, it seems doubtful that all cases are like that and thus that joint commitments are essential to joint action (cf. Bratman 2014: ch. 5).

Do we have to conclude that joint action generally does not involve mutual obligations? Or does joint action imply a weaker sort of normative relationship? Against proponents of the view that only certain kinds of joint action involve mutual obligations, such as Michael Bratman (2014), others have suggested to regard practical attitudes such as *reliance* (Alonso 2009) or *trust* (Schmid 2013) as grounding normative interpersonal relationships and as being fundamental to joint action. The normative bonds grounded in these attitudes can be described as weaker than the relationship Gilbert conceives of in terms of joint commitments. The unifying idea behind accounts that refer to reliance or trust is that if one agent forms (and exhibits or expresses) this kind of attitude regarding one's partner's contribution to a joint action, the other is led to form and endorse the same kind of attitude. To illustrate this, assume that A and B are in a position to move the piano across the room, where this is something neither can do alone, but perfectly doable in unison. Assume further that each of them not only intends to move the piano, as in the analysis outlined in the previous section, but that in addition each of them relies on the other doing his or her bit, in other words, push at his or her end of the piano (cf. Alonso 2009). Or assume that each of them, besides intending to move the piano, trusts that the other will in fact push at his or her end (cf. Schmid 2013). The relevant contention put forth with these accounts is that, characteristically, cooperating agents create mutual obligations—or, in other words, give each other normative reasons to contribute—by forming attitudes of reliance or trust regarding the other's contribution. Thus, in our example, A's relying on (or trusting) B to push his or her end of the piano creates a reason for B to do so, and vice versa; let us assume that this reason is comparatively strong, so that it corresponds to an obligation for B to contribute. Obviously, not all instances of reliance or trust can generate reasons and obligations in this way, but under normal conditions, and especially in cases of mutual reliance and mutual trust, in which the attitudes can be understood as mutually reinforcing, the generative effect seems to occur. And it should be emphasized that the obligations in question are not moral, but only social obligations, which means that their force is explained by reference to the particular social situation, including the attitudes and relations that feature in it, and not by reference to more general moral principles or norms.

However, the question remains whether it is necessary to posit the presence of a different kind of attitude as fundamental in order to explicate a basic normative relationship implied by joint action. Defenders of accounts that refer to reliance or trust seem to answer in the affirmative, but an account that builds on the notion of an individual *social commitment* can confine the conceptual resources to fulfill this task to attitudes more closely related to the intentions and beliefs that accompany joint action. Abe Roth (2004) has developed a variant of such an account, but I shall conclude by outlining the main elements of a different variant. These regard the conceptual resources made use of in this account, the way it explains the normative relationship involved in joint action, and the connection it draws between commitments and obligations.

First off, talking of commitment in relation to intentions does not introduce an additional type of attitude; it rather highlights another element of the structure of intentional activity. In the case of joint intention, this amounts to making explicit that the socially oriented intention of the form "We intend that we ... " implies a specific type of commitment, a social commitment. Whenever an agent intends to do something, they commit, inter alia, to choosing means appropriate to their end and to avoiding anything that could render their attaining that goal impossible. Building on this, we can say that when an agent intends a joint action, as in the cases considered above, they assume a social commitment that regards both (1) their own contribution to the joint action and (2) the other agent(s) involved. The first aspect of this commitment captures the aforementioned implication of intending; the second reveals the social orientation of these practical attitudes and corresponds to the relational structure of the occurrences of "we" in "*We* intend that *we*. . . . "

Now, if we require that joint action be guided by an intentional structure constituted by intentions of the form "We intend that we . . . " on the part of each agent involved, and if we understand this as implying that each undertakes a social commitment to the joint activity and to the other(s) involved, then we are led to accept that joint action involves a kind of normative relationship. The normativity in play here encompasses both the norms that govern the performance of intentional activities and the social norms that govern attitudes toward other agents. Being committed to another agent, as implied in joint action on this account, does not presuppose an agreement, but it can arguably be construed as being of consequence for the respective other. For this kind of social commitment, in conjunction with the commitment to contribute to a particular joint action and especially when made explicit, gives the addressee a reason to contribute. In the familiar case, if A signifies that they are committed to B to move the piano with B, then this gives B a reason to move the piano with A, very much like attitudes of reliance and trust can be reinforcing by inviting the respective other to rely and trust. The temporal asymmetry of this example is no precondition for this generation of reasons to be in place.

The last element of this brief outline of an account that certainly needs further elaboration and defense regards the connection between social commitments and obligations. Assuming a scenario in which two agents each undertake a social commitment as specified in the previous paragraphs, what becomes decisive is that each gives the other a reason to cooperate with them. Unless they have a specific practical authority vis-à-vis the other, which we can exclude from the typical case of joint action, an agent cannot create an obligation for another. Each can, however, and especially in the symmetric case in which both are socially committed or at least disposed or ready to cooperate, change the other's normative situation to the effect that each agent is obligated to at least respond to the other's commitment, or event to contribute to the joint action. As full-blown agents, they are required to be susceptible to the reasons that apply to them, and in the social case, this requirement is extended to comprise responsiveness to others' commitments. Once the translation of this talk of reasons into talk of obligations is granted, we have at our disposal a conceptually conservative account of the *social obligations* involved in joint action. These obligations pertain to responses to others' commitments and to engagement in joint action, where the force of the latter part of such an obligation is supported by one's own social commitments.

This concludes the brief portrayal of some characteristic intentional and normative structures of joint action from the perspective of the philosophy of action. How exactly these outlines of a relational account of joint intention and an account of the normativity of joint action in terms of social commitment and social obligation extend to other types of distributed agency will have to be left to other studies. And the plausibility of the reflections presented here may well depend on, or be supported by, a synopsis with other perspectives on similar phenomena represented in this volume.

REFERENCES

Alonso, F. M. 2009. "Shared Intention, Reliance, and Interpersonal Obligations." *Ethics* 119(3): 444–475.

Bratman, M. E. 1999. *Faces of Intention: Selected Essays on Intention and Agency.* Cambridge: Cambridge University Press.

Bratman, M. E. 2014. *Shared Agency: A Planning Theory of Acting Together.* New York: Oxford University Press.

Gilbert, M. 2014. *Joint Commitment: How We Make the Social World.* Oxford: Oxford University Press.

Pettit, P., and D. Schweikard 2006. "Joint Actions and Group Agents." *Philosophy of the Social Sciences* 36(1): 1–22.

Roth, A. S. 2004. "Shared Agency and Contralateral Commitments." *The Philosophical Review* 113(3): 359–410.

Schmid, H. B. 2013. "Trying to Act Together: The Structure and Role of Trust in Joint Action." In *The Background of Institutional Reality*, edited by B. Kobow, H. B. Schmid, and M. Schmitz, 37–55. Dordrecht, the Netherlands: Springer.

Schweikard, D. P., and H. B. Schmid. 2013. "Collective Intentionality." *The Stanford Encyclopedia of Philosophy* (Summer 2013 Edition), edited by Edward N. Zalta. http://plato.stanford.edu/archives/sum2013/entries/collective-intentionality/.

Searle, J. R. 1990. "Collective Intentions and Actions." In *Intentions in Communication*, edited by P. Cohen, J. Morgan, and M. E. Pollack, 401–415. Cambridge, MA: Bradford Books, MIT Press.

Tuomela, R. 2005. "We-Intentions Revisited." *Philosophical Studies* 125:327–369.

CHAPTER 25

Deception as Exploitative Social Agency

RADU UMBRES

When we deceive others, are we using them as tools? After all, when we deceive, we use others as means to our ends, irrespective of their intentions and welfare. But I argue that such a view is only superficially valid once we consider the mechanisms of deception as a form of social agency. A more insightful understanding of deception must account for the interlocking of agency between deceiver and deceived at several levels, based on uniquely human meta-representational capacities.

The idea that deception means using humans as tools has widespread intuitive appeal. Often, people deceived by others feel "used" or "played with" or "powerless," attributes better fitting an inanimate object than an active, intentional agent. One of its guises, manipulation, strongly evokes a puppeteer handling the mechanics of a tool-like puppet. In slang, a "tool" is an individual deemed too slow-witted to realize that he is being taken for a fool. The link between deception and tool use has even more presti-gious advocates. Immanuel Kant opposed any form of lying (even when the lie would save an innocent life) because it would contradict the first formulation of the categorical imperative (to act only in accordance with the maxim through which you can at the same time will that it become a universal law) but also, and more relevant to our point here, the second formulation—that we are to treat others as ends in themselves, and not only as means: "The one who has it in mind to make a lying promise to another will see right away that he wills to make use of another human being merely as means, without the end also being contained in this other.

For the one I want to use for my aims through such a promise cannot possibly be in harmony with my way of conducting myself toward him and thus contain in himself the end of this action" (Kant 1993:429–430). While Kant is making a moral point about deception, the liar's conduct (and hence his moral failure) toward the other evokes exactly the use of a device for one's own ends, without acknowledging the humanity of the victim.

Intuition and moral metaphysics aside, this chapter explores aspects of deception that clearly distinguish it from mere tool use and bring it conceptually closer to other forms of social agency. It is argued that deception builds upon co-opting several aspects of the victim's agency, whereas no agentive qualities are needed from a tool aside from its affordances. Moreover, although deception feeds on an asymmetry of agency, it is not merely a unilateral process. The target of deception may fend for himself in ways that are unthinkable for an object. Together, these facets reveal the entangled, reciprocally responsive agency of actors involved in deception and counterdeception.

THE COMPLEXITY OF DECEPTION

The first thing about deception that sets it apart from treating others as mere tools is its constitutive social nature. Few scholars if any would disagree with the fact that deception is a form of social agency, yet it is conspicuously absent or undervalued in major works in the philosophy and psychology of social agency. As illuminating as they are, developments in the burgeoning field of studies and theoretical proposals dealing with shared agency might suggest an unwarranted identity between "shared" and "social" agency by overlooking a vast realm of sociality. Since the point made here is a fairly general one, the umbrella-term "shared" covers many forms of social agency. They may share only a "family resemblance," including concepts such as "shared," "joint," "collective intentionality," "joint action," "common ground," "joint commitment," "group," or "collective agency" (Gilbert 1990, Searle 1990, and Tomasello et al. 2005; Bratman 2014 is an exception, but even he tries to demonstrate how types of deception may still count as shared agency).

Deception and coercion are exemplary cases of those other forms of agency that are irreducibly social but have features that set them apart from the "shared agency" family. These different forms are ontologically based on asymmetry rather than symmetry, on exploitation rather than mutuality, on opposition rather than convergence, on competition rather than cooperation, on the circulation of incomplete or misleading information and imperfectly aligned or even conflicting interests. One could hardly consider non-cooperative social agency as a rare phenomenon, and, if you doubt its relevance for human societies, consider the role of coercion in the slave-master relationship behind the building of the pyramids or the expanse of totalitarian political regimes in the past century. As for deception, we can only speculate how the crucial invasion of Sicily would have enfolded were it not for Operation Mincemeat, in which the Allied forces tricked Nazi commanders (including Hitler) that the landing target was Greece, staging a body washed up on the shores of Spain who appeared to be a dead spy-master stacked with orders carefully faked by the British.

One of the possible reasons why deception stays under the radar of scholars of social agency is the weight given to human cooperative incli-nations as the key to our species' capacity for culture and for building and abiding by social institutions. In contrast, deception figured more in the scientific mapping of cognitive capacities of nonhuman primates and other animals, especially tactical deception, which brings certain primates closer to human capacities for attending to cues such as field of vision or attention, or even reading minds. While some scholars discussed to what extent chimpanzees deploy a Machiavellian intelligence with deception as a crucial aspect of competitive interactions (Whiten and Byrne 1997), the uniqueness of human thinking was attributed to our cooperative inclina-tions unparalleled among other primates (Tomasello 2014).

The role of cooperation for human social agency could hardly be denied, but this only makes human deception an even more complex phenomenon. Compared to humans, the most Machiavellian of chimps deploys rudimen-tary ruses, just as limited as its cooperative scope. Human deception may be the opposite of human cooperation, but it is causally built upon the same cognitive capacities, exploits the same propensities for acting and thinking together, and even mimics or parasitizes cooperation to exploitative pur-poses. In fact, the cooperative aspect of human agency (in forms of trust, shared symbols, expectations, and obligations of mutuality, etc.) opens up vast possibilities for exploitation that are unavailable for less cooperative species. Because the engine of cooperation depends on the mutual good faith of parties, a deceiver may mimic a bona fide cooperator and allow the other party to (mistakenly) think that the goal of interaction is common and mutualistic, but without having the positive, shared, "we" intentions of true cooperation (Tomasello 2014). In a foundational work, Nicholas Humphrey (1976) has argued that human intelligence evolved as a func-tion of social complexity. The presence of cooperation does not just make human sociality more complex in cognitive terms (in contrast with other primates). The dramatic effect is that cooperation extends the capacity of social agency to involve a huge array of flexible and interweaving processes ranging from full-on cooperation to pure competition with myriads of possibilities in between.

DECEPTION AS SOCIAL AGENCY

If we take *agency* to be "the relation between a person and a course of action and its effects" (Enfield 2013), the provisional definition of deception that I propose and evoke in empirical examples is the act of an agent (the deceiver) to manipulate information in order to use another agent's agency (the deceived) without the victim's awareness or consent. Deception is thus a form of social agency in which two (or more) actors have their individual agencies interlocked in a chain of information manipulation. To further understand the relationship, we may further unpack the concept of agency into flexibility and accountability (Kockelman 2007, Enfield 2013) to discover the kinds of asymmetries exploited by deception as social agency.

As a starting point for understanding deception, the subjective interests of the agents involved are not aligned (or not aligned enough for the purposes of the deceiver). This is important to rule out cooperation with its relatively balanced distribution of interests as a flexible alternative to deception. Unless we think of all deceivers as pathological (which they are obviously not), deception starts from an imbalance between the initiator's and the target's desires that cannot be solved efficiently through cooperation or other means. Consequently, the deceiving agent pursues a course of events that builds upon and exploits to his own advantage an asymmetry with the victim at the level of knowledge and beliefs. The epistemic imbalance is clear: the deceiver knows something more than the victim, in other words, that an act of deception is under way, that certain signs or symbols are false or misplaced, that the victim will act against its own interests, and so on. The deceiver either does nothing to correct the error of the victim or, most often, actively creates that error in order to profit from the imbalance.

Despite the imbalance, deception relies on the interlocking of individual agencies, leading to causal effects beyond the scope of any single one of them. A simpler way of putting this is that neither party brings about by itself the deception, just as it is true for any communicative or social action. On the deceiver's side, he or she must manipulate something in the cognitive environment of the deceived. On the other side, the deceived would not pursue the course of action by him- or herself were it not for the manipulation. Standing by silently while municipal workers water your plants mistakenly taking them for public property may engage someone's agency in your favor by means of misinformation, but you did not deceive anyone—the workers are simply mistaken. Contrast this with the case of, for example, a Nigerian inheritance scam, where the victim acts and (falsely) interprets the situation as a cooperative event, apparently acting jointly with the deceiver, but in reality playing into his or her hands.

In contrast, tool use may be considered a part of an individual's agency. Through its affordances, its embodied history and origin, an object may be part of the distributed agency of an individual or a collective of individuals (Hutchins 1995). The elements of the cockpit form a constitutive part of the pilot's agency in flying a plane as a ship may be part, and mediate, the social agencies of a crew. The tool becomes part of individual or social agency as long as it is engaged into cognitive and physical work by at least one human being. Deception, on the contrary, is essentially social. It takes (at least) two to create a deception (leaving "self-deception" aside), just as it takes two to have a conversation or to jointly carry an object. This creates a discrepancy at the level of flexibility, as the tool, unlike the victim of deception, may only be co-opted passively, while the deceived is induced to make choices, comprehend, and communicate. If I push you in front of a trolley (perhaps to save five people as a good utilitarian), I am not engaged in any social agency, but merely use your body as a tool for derailing the trolley. A different event happens if I persuade you that it is safe to lay on the tracks by your own volition. Between victim and perpetrator there is an imbalance of epistemic power, but they are still ultimately cognizing actors, while a tool is not. From the second perspective on agency, the proper accountability of tools is usually derived from their users. An Azande granary is the tool used by the sorcerer to kill its victim, but the legal and causal actor is the (invisible) sorcerer.

DEFENSE AND ACCOUNTABILITY IN DECEPTION

The previous section argued that deception is a form of social agency whose flexibility involves the imbalanced relationship at the level of knowledge between the agencies of two actors. The epistemic asymmetry is key to the success of deception, as the deceiver controls the event and adjusts his or her inputs according to how he or she anticipates the behavior of the victim. Yet the victim is not a simple tool, as he or she contributes with his own interpretation of facts, his or her own sources of information, and his or her own capacity for choice and control. Moreover, deception is not the automatic outcome of a single agent—the deceiver—since the target is never just a sitting duck.

Sperber and colleagues (2010) have proposed a model of epistemic vigilance that exposes the flexibility in the (potential) victim's agency. The deceiver may try to manipulate information, but the victim is not a passive recipient (a tool, one might say). Sperber et al. argue that the human mind is endowed with a set of mechanisms geared for filtering true and relevant information. Such mechanisms have evolved to avoid both intentional deception as well as unintentional misinformation from malevolent or incompetent sources. Epistemic vigilance consists of assessing a potential deceiver's reputation and subjective interests (do not trust when a man you know to be a robber tells you to go left into the woods), as well as for consistency between content and prior knowledge (do not believe that this hen for sale lays three eggs a day when no hen ever did that).

Such defense mechanisms enormously complicate the interlocking of the agencies of deceiver and deceived. Actors deploy layers of meta-representations in deception and counterdeception (I know that she knows that I know that she . . .), flexibly adjusting their choices and symbols to the other actor's inputs. Such to-and-fro is unthinkable for the relationship between a tool user and a tool, where the flexibility is only attached to the human element.

If the victim is not merely a passive element in the interlocking social agency that characterizes deception, is he or she to blame? Who is accountable for the deceptive act? What are the rights and the duties attached to deception? Here, cultural variation can enlighten our understanding of the agency behind deception. A Lebanese village society (Gilsenan 1976) abides by a rule of generalized potential deception. "Everything is *kizb*," an informant declares as a justification for a world in which people patiently plan the humiliation of others using lies and embellishment of facts, where an epistemically vigilant commoner uses a trick to reveal the dishonesty of a visiting sheikh, where everyone needs, and is expected, to lie at least a little bit to keep up pretenses of honor. Likewise, in the Romanian village I have studied for the past ten years, deception coming from people outside a circle of trust and reciprocity is an ever-present danger and makes a way of life from a heightened sense of mistrust. What makes such communities special is that the blame for being deceived often falls upon the victim. An ethic of "devil take the hindmost" applies to everyday encounters including communicative acts in which one ought to interpret the utterances of others with utmost vigilance and adequate information, lest he or she be deceived by a village competitor.

Apportioning (at least part of the) blame to the victim, villagers seem to ascertain the role played by him in the social agency underpinning deception. Had the victim been more competent, more astute, better prepared by his peers, the deceiver would have failed. In a way, the deceiver did what is expected of most people—to further his or her interests even at the expense of others, using such means as possible and useful. To try a comparison, deception flies in the air just as your inbox swells with Nigerian scam letters. One could hardly stop feeling that the unfortunate client of such scams is at least an active party to the deception with inadequate epistemic vigilance in this day and age. The same apportioning of blame is used in ritual pranks of initiation, in which the incompetence of the victim justifies and legitimates the social and epistemic power of the tricksters (Umbres 2013).

But, to return to our initial problem, why do people feel that deception involves them as mere tools of the deceivers? I conclude with a speculation about the accountability of deception. In modern, centralized societies driven by the universalistic morality of religion, or citizenship, or Kantian ethics, people do not expect fellow humans to deceive them, at least not as a rule. The norms of social interaction prescribe (at least minimally) cooperative agents, engaged in true and relevant communication. They feel obligated to speak the truth (or at least not to tell a lie knowingly) and feel entitled to the same reciprocal treatment. The social contract of everyday interaction punishes deceivers, either formally or informally, from jail sentences to social ostracism. Not all social settings, of course, require such a social norm. Strudler (2009) argues that deception is socially accepted when used as legitimate self-defense. The norm of trust[1] does not apply automatically and exhaustively in legitimate negotiation maneuvers such as communicating a false reservation price when buying a house.

In high-trust societies, the sentiment of reciprocity in truth-telling makes everyone lower their epistemic guards, leading to huge savings in the transaction costs of communication and social interaction, and furthermore to successful and efficient cooperation (compare with Keenan 1976 for a culture in which truth and relevance are not conversational postulates). But the reverse of this generalized amnesty of distrust is ceding part of our agency to others. When we trust someone, we give him or her power over our behavior, over our representations, over the flexibility of our agency. We do this in the expectation that her or she (1) will be benevolent and cooperative and (2) would do the same for us. This is why deception appears, for such enlightened altruists, as a way of using people as tools, as means to private, egoistic ends. The comparison helps us understand the way deception is accounted for in some societies, but it is misleading as a metaphor or theoretical inspiration. In deception, as in any form of social agency, it takes more than one individual to act and to be responsible for their actions.

ACKNOWLEDGMENTS

The writing of this chapter began while I was Fyssen Foundation postdoctoral fellow at Institut Jean Nicod, Paris. I am grateful to Nick Enfield and Dan Sperber for their comments on draft versions, and I thank the participants of the "Foundations of Social Agency" scientific retreat organized by the Max Planck Institute for Psycholinguistics for their suggestions.

NOTE

1. Strudler also links trust with a yielding of autonomy, and deception as breach of trust with a compromise of autonomy, lending further support to the idea that deception is a form of intertwining social agency between parties.

REFERENCES

Bratman, M. E. 2014. *Shared Agency: A Planning Theory of Acting Together*. New York: Oxford University Press.
Enfield, N. J. 2013. *Relationship Thinking: Agency, Enchrony, and Human Sociality*. Oxford: Oxford University Press.
Gilbert, M. 1990. "Walking Together: A Paradigmatic Social Phenomenon." *Midwest Studies in Philosophy* 15(1): 1–14.
Gilsenan, M. 1976. "Lying, Honor, and Contradiction." In *Transaction and Meaning: Directions in the Anthropology of Exchange and Symbolic Behavior*, edited by Bruce Kapferer, 191–219. Philadelphia: Institute for the Study of Human Values.
Humphrey, N. 1976. "The Social Function of Intellect." In *Growing Points in Ethology*, edited by P. P. G. Bateson and R. A. Hinde, 303–317. Cambridge: Cambridge University Press.
Hutchins, E. 1995. *Cognition in the Wild*. Cambridge, MA: MIT Press.
Kant, I. 1993. *Grounding for the Metaphysics of Morals*. Indianapolis: Hackett.
Keenan, E. O. 1976. "The Universality of Conversational Postulates." *Language in Society* 5(1): 67–80.
Kockelman, P. 2007. "Agency." *Current Anthropology* 48(3): 375–401.
Searle, J. R. 1990. "Collective Intentions and Actions." In *Intentions in Communication*, edited by P. R. Cohen, J. L. Morgan, and M. E. Pollack, 401–415. Cambridge, MA: MIT Press.
Sperber, D., F. Clément, C. Heintz, O. Mascaro, H. Mercier, G. Origgi, and D. Wilson, 2010. "Epistemic Vigilance." *Mind and Language* 25(4): 359–393.
Strudler, A. 2009. "Deception and Trust." In *The Philosophy of Deception*, edited by C. W. Martin, 139–152. New York: Oxford University Press.
Tomasello, M. 2014. *A Natural History of Human Thinking*. Cambridge, MA: Harvard University Press.

Tomasello, M., M. Carpenter, J. Call, T. Behne, and H. Moll. 2005. "Understanding and Sharing Intentions: The Origins of Cultural Cognition." *Behavioral and Brain Sciences* 28(5): 675–691.

Umbres, R. 2013. "Chasse au dahu et vigilance épistémique." *Terrain* 61: 84–101.

Whiten, A., and R. W. Byrne. 1997. *Machiavellian Intelligence II: Extensions and Evaluations*. Cambridge: Cambridge University Press.

CHAPTER 26

Disrupting Agents, Distributing Agency

CHARLES H. P. ZUCKERMAN

INTRODUCTION

One afternoon in Luang Prabang, Laos, I was gambling with three men over a game of pétanque. For the unfamiliar, pétanque is a game played like bocce or lawn bowling and it is a common way for people—especially men—to gamble in Luang Prabang.[1] On this day, I filmed as we played. Our game had drawn an audience of a dozen or so. The spectators lined the benches—some of them gambling, some of them just passing the time and enjoying the show. About an hour into the game, my teammate Bii began to take a shot when one spectator named Can[2] wandered from his seat on the bench and onto the court. Can then suddenly lifted his arms and screamed. Startled, Bii missed his shot. He glared at Can and barked accusatively, "You!"[3] The audience burst into laughter and Can scampered back to his seat as the two exchanged threats.

Clearly, Can was trying to distract Bii and make him miss the shot. His scream was not merely a scream but an especially aggressive heckle in a match already brimming with trash talk. A few seconds after Can's heckle, two audience members imitated Bii flinching in reaction: one man jerked his head, mimicking Bii's shaking body, while the other commented, "He was surprised, all right, he went like this," twitching his own arm to reenact Bii's flinching arm.[4]

To everyone, there was no doubt that Can's heckle had caused Bii to miss the shot, that it had affected Bii's body and surprised him in ways beyond his control. But when I watched the video recording of the event, matters became less clear. Despite my repeated viewings, the recording showed no signs of Bii flinching. Instead, the evidence that Bii was startled resided entirely within Bii's and the spectators' own reactions. Bii had responded to the heckle in a manner implying it was effective and audience members had said that the heckle was effective, that it had made Bii flinch. While Can's scream was so loud, well-timed, and explicitly addressed toward Bii that it seems unlikely the scream did *not* affect Bii's shot, we cannot know with any certainty whether it did have an effect. Put another way, it is impossible to know whether Bii would have made the shot—which he only barely missed—had Can not screamed.

There is an inevitable and irresolvable uncertainty here; one that is, in fact, helpful to better understanding agency. Acknowledging that we cannot always know *what causes what* guides us to move away from conceptualizing agency in terms of moments of causality isolated from human interpretation. The question worth asking becomes not did Bii cause Can to miss the shot, but how did Bii and the spectators make this causal relationship—real or fictive—visible? In other words, how are causal relations understood and made apparent in interaction?

In this chapter, I explore the prevalence and subtlety of attributions of agency on the pétanque court. By unpacking a video recording of a different pétanque game, I show that a player can respond to a heckle such that, through his response, he helps to frame it as effective or ineffective. In other words, I show how people can retroactively attribute and (re)distribute agency through their responses to events. I argue that we should study agency not as a static, perspective-free property of the world (e.g., "In this moment of heckling, agency is distributed across three actors"), but as part of an ongoing semiotic process through which actors ascribe agency. To put it simply, this chapter argues for an interactional approach to distributed agency that treats the "distributed" in "distributed agency" as more verb than adjective.

"TELLING STORIES", DISTRIBUTING AGENCY

In his classic essay "Response Cries," sociologist Erving Goffman has us imagine a man walking along a busy street. While walking, the man trips on a piece of broken sidewalk and catches himself. "Up to this point," Goffman writes, "[the man's] competence at walking had been taken for granted by those who witnessed him ... [but] his tripping casts these imputations suddenly into doubt. Therefore, before he continues he may well engage in some actions that have nothing to do with the laws of mechanics" (Goffman 1978:88–89). He might smirk to himself, signaling to any onlookers the uncharacteristic nature of the event, or "'overplay' his lurch," suggesting he was playing the clown. Or perhaps he will "examine the walk, as if intellectually concerned . . . to discover what in the world could possibly have caused him to falter."

These potential responses, as Goffman puts it, "tell stories to" the man's stumble. In different ways, they guide how others view the stumble's cause just as they guide how others conceive of the man, whether as "professional" or "drunkard." The man's "stories" point toward what caused the stumble and away from what did not (e.g., momentary clumsiness or inebriation). They serve to distribute and displace responsibility for the stumble.

This kind of "story"-telling abounds in interaction. People often signal what has occurred, what is occurring, and what will occur: the causes, effects, and agents that should be held responsible. While it might be tempting to dismiss these "stories" as folk understandings of agency or a cloaking of "real" causal relations, doing so would ignore the prevalence and importance of "stories" in social life. These "stories" are the means through which agency is established, communicated, and negotiated in interaction. They are often not just depictions of causality but also the evidence of it. Take Goffman's example of the tripping man "overplaying" his stumble. Where does the stumble end and the exaggeration begin? Drawing such a line—while sometimes satisfying—only lures us into the false premise that causal processes (i.e., the stumble) and attributions of causality (i.e., the exaggeration) are necessarily distinct in time and space.

That is, it is sometimes impossible or at least unproductive to distinguish the "stories" that attribute responsibility for causal processes from the processes themselves. Many of the "stories" people tell are not narratives but wordless acts—smiles, looks, exaggerated falls—that blur doing and display—actions doubling as interpretations.[5] Of course, "stories" *can* be separate in time and space from the acts they depict. For example, a stumbling man can say "That was funny" after he has tripped instead of overplaying his lurch while in the midst of tripping. "Stories" can also vary in how they attribute agency: referentially explicitly, tacitly, et cetera. As I show below, even an act as small as a pétanque player ignoring a spectating heckler can tacitly deny that the heckler is responsible for a missed shot. Ultimately, however, how one tells a "story" matters, as different methods of attributing responsibility can have different interactional effects and different consequences for how agency is distributed.

Saj jaa

What I have been calling "heckling" is what Lao pétanque players most often call *saj jaa*.[6] *Saj jaa* literally means "to apply medicine" or "to dose" and it is a local label for actions on the pétanque court that disrupt and destroy the ability of others to focus, play properly, or control their bodies and minds. The trope is that *saj jaa* can affect its victims with the same efficacy that a pill cures a headache or a dose of methamphetamines keeps one awake. Although there is a range of techniques for *saj jaa*—being loud, standing too close, bickering about the score, telling an opponent he will miss his shot, even betting—the techniques all presumably share a goal:[7] to disrupt the attention, focus, and calm of the targeted player; to affect his "heart;" and to make him lose, both the game and his cash.

All players are vulnerable to *saj jaa*, but most agree that some are more susceptible than others. The most vulnerable are said "not to have the heart for it" (*caj3 bòø-daj4*) or to be "weak-hearted" (*caj3 qòòn1*). They "tremble" (*san1 kathùan2*) in response to trash talk like "spring chickens" (*kaj1 qòòn1*) with "soft, porous skin" (*nang3 pùaj1*). Hecklers make them feel "angry" (*caj3 haaj4*) and "rushed" (*caj3 hòòn4*, literally, "hot-hearted"), and they play poorly as a result. Those better at resisting *saj jaa* are said to have stronger, more capable hearts (*caj3 khaw2 daj4*). They are tough and inured, like "experienced, older chickens" (*kaj1 kêê1*) with "tight, rubbery skin" (*nang3 niaw3*) and stay "calm and cool" (*caj3 jèn3*, literally, "cool-hearted") under pressure, allowing them to play their best. A strong heart, as one longtime pétanque coach told me, is a key trait in good athletes. Being invulnerable to *saj jaa* is, thus, both valued and valuable.

While players are sometimes said to be habitually "hot" or "cool-hearted," the terms "hot" and "cool-hearted" are also used to describe transitory emotional states.[8] People often comment upon how others appear to be feeling. Does he look "cool" and relaxed, or does he seem "hot" and distracted? Observing players' emotional states like this can provide valuable information. For example, take a moment from a money-gambling game: a player rushed his way through multiple shots and his opponents howled and heckled after each poor shot. Seeing this, one spectator remarked to his friend, "Don't bet on him, he's hot!"[9] Monitoring a player's emotions can also inform a heckler's use of saj jaa. As one man put it, a good pétanque player should observe his opponent's "heart" to map out his weaknesses and discover what kind of "dose" might best affect him.

One way a player can display his "heart" is in his responses to *saj jaa*. These responses also can display his autonomy as an agent. If a player maintains a "cool heart" in the face of medicine, he is likely to be seen as unaffected by the medicine, and thus, as a relatively autonomous agent.[10] By contrast, if he gets "hot" when given a dose of medicine, he is likely to be seen as being affected by the medicine.[11]

On the whole, *saj jaa* invites those witnessing and experiencing it to discuss and, perhaps interpret, what has happened in causal and agentive terms. Once it is clear a heckler has used medicine and that the player has perceived it, the player's next action is liable to be taken as a sign of the extent of the heckle's efficacy. His next action then becomes not merely another action but a reaction to (or, in semiotic parlance, an *interpretant of*) the heckle. This phenomenon—where a sign frames a subsequent action as a reaction—is common in discursive interaction. Let's say, for example, that someone asks you, "What's up?" and it is clear you have heard and understood her; if you stay silent, she is likely to take your silence not as simple inaction but as a cold "response," as a noticeably absent, unfilled pause and perhaps as a hint not to bother you.[12] Similarly, once it is clear that medicine has been applied and that a player has perceived it and missed his shot, questions tend to present themselves: Why was the shot missed? The general ebb and flow of the match or distraction?[13]

How a player responds to a heckle often answers these questions (whether tacitly or explicitly). Ignoring a heckler entirely is paradigmatically "cool." It can be a sign that a player is not distracted, but it can also serve as a tool for maintaining his focus. Much like taking notes during a lecture can help the note taker pay attention while also displaying focus to others, not looking at, or not responding to, a distraction can help one concentrate while simultaneously displaying concentration to others. Not ignoring the heckler, in contrast, is paradigmatically "hot." Talking to or looking at a heckler, for example, is often taken as evidence that his medicine is working.[14] Because of this, players often tout ignoring the heckler as the ideal. As one player put it, "No, [I never respond to hecklers]. [When I play], I'm not interested [in medicine]. That's me. I pay attention to [the shots I take] and that's it. I'm not interested in anything [else]."[15]

"WHO DO YOU THINK YOU ARE PLAYING WITH?"

I now turn to an example in which a player ignores his heckler and, in doing so, tacitly distributes agency. Taa, a man in his late thirties, is playing pétanque for money against Phuumii, a man in his forties. During the game, Phuumii repeatedly uses medicine on Taa, while Taa mostly ignores him. Below I present two transcripts of the event: one a more traditional interlinear transcript familiar to linguistic anthropologists, the other a more cartoonish transcript, created by loosely outlining screenshots of my video recording of the event.[16] I then walk the reader through these transcripts and show how Taa's seemingly minute actions serve to distribute agency on the court.

But first, a basic outline of the event. It is late morning and I am filming on one of Luang Prabang's money-gambling pétanque courts. Taa and Phuumii are playing in front of an audience of about a dozen.[17] The audience members are scattered at the edges of the compacted-dirt court: some lean against nearby trees, others sit on wooden benches, and a few lounge on a newly acquired couch. They watch Phuumii and Taa's game with varying degrees of focus and concern. Some are betting on the outcome and watch the game closely, while others chat casually.

Where my transcript begins, Phuumii is on the verge of defeat. He then makes a good shot and offers to bet Taa additional money. This offer to bet (Figure 26.1: 1) is, among other things, a dose of medicine[18] and Taa treats it as such, rejecting it out of hand: "Hah . . . who do you think you are playing with?" (Figure 26.1: 2), he says. Taa then takes his shot and misses (Figure 26.2: 3). His miss seems to encourage Phuumii, who now even more enthusiastically offers to bet him. Taa ignores Phuumii's offers and makes his second shot.

To summarize, during this short segment of interaction, Taa misses his first shot and makes his second, Phuumii heckling both times.

Taa's disengagement from Phuumii "tells a story to" his first missed shot and to Phuumii's heckles. The "story" is that Phuumii did not make Taa miss, that he has not gotten into Taa's heart. As is often the case, Taa tells this "story" not through explicit comments but with a series of movements, cries, and partially addressed utterances.

As mentioned above, throughout this entire segment of interaction, Taa directly addresses Phuumii only once (Figure 26.1: 2), with a softly spoken response to Phuumii's offer to bet: "Hah . . . who do you think you are playing with?" With this retort, Taa treats Phuumii's offer as a frivolous kind of saj jaa, meant to distract him and make him shoot poorly rather than put more money on the line; in reminding Phuumii who he is playing with, he dismisses and rejects Phuumii's offer out of hand. And while this response is addressed to Phuumii, there is some evidence that Taa is still not fully engaged with him. He does not look at Phuumii as he speaks but stares straight ahead at the pétanque balls.[19] Taa also speaks much more softly than Phuumii, an incongruence that suggests an interactional distance between them. This partially oriented rejection of Phuumii's offer foreshadows what is to come: Taa's complete lack of engagement with Phuumii.

#	Speaker	Transcription / Gloss	Stage direction
1	**Phuumii**	liin5 — play; khanêên2 — Point; qaw3 — take; bôô1 — NEG	*As he says this, Phuumii walks toward the other end of court, Taa steps into the spot where he will throw from.*
		"Want to gamble on this round [i.e., on who gets points this round]?" =	
2	**Taa**	bêêr4 — semen; tii3 — Hit; kap2 — with; phaj3 — who; dee4 — FAC.ONRCD	*Taa lines up to throw at the pétanque ball. He watches the ball as he speaks, smiling slightly toward the end of his utterance. He does not look at Phuumii.*
		"Hah [literally "semen"] who do you think you are playing with?"	
3	**Phuumii**	liin5 — Play; khanêên2 — Point; bôô1 — NEG	*Phuumii continues walking toward the other end of court and glances back at Taa.*
		"Want to gamble on this round [i.e., on who gets points this round]?"	
4	**Taa**		*Taa takes a shot that eventually misses his target.*
5	**Phuumii**	liin5 — play; khanêên2 — Point; bôô1 — NEG; Taa — Taa	*Phuumii begins to speak as the ball is sailing through the air.*
		"Want to gamble on this round [i.e., on who gets points this round], Taa?" =	
6	**Taa**	qoo — CRY	*Taa says this immediately after his missed shot lands.*
		"Oh!"	
7	**Phuumii**	liin5 — Play; khanêên2 — Point; bôô1 — NEG; Taa — Taa	*Phuumii forms a pointing handshape with his right hand and oscillates it back and forth, rapidly. He begins to lean in close to the already thrown pétanque balls.*
		"Want to gamble on this round [i.e., on who gets points this round], Taa?" =	
8	**Phuumii**	tii3 — Hit; nuaj1 — Ball; nii4 — DEM; haa5 — 5; daj4 — acquire	*Phuumii leans in closer toward the already thrown pétanque balls and points at the target ball. He then circles his hand around to show where the "five points" are coming from.*
		"If you knock this ball out, you will get five [points]."	
9	**Phuumii**	hee4 — CRY	*Phuumii moves back from the target ball's area as Taa winds up to take his shot.*
		"Hah!"	
10	**Taa**		*Taa takes a successful shot*
11a	**Taa**	bii3 — little.ball; paj3 — Go	*[This line co-occurs with 11b]*
		"[Knock] the little ball [out]!"	
11b	**Phuumii**	hee4 — CRY	
		"Hah!"	
12	**Taa**	qoo — CRY; jaan4 — scared; thùùk5 — hit; bii3 — little.ball; qaq1	*As he says this, Taa walks toward the other end of the court and briefly glances at Phuumii. Phuumii does not look at Taa.*
		"Ohhh, [I was] scared of hitting the little ball."	

TRANSCRIPTION 26.1

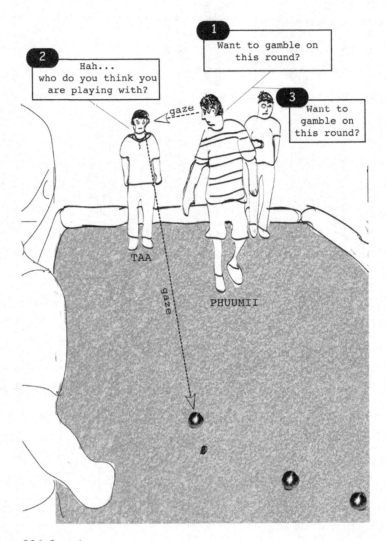

Figure 26.1 Scene 1.

From lines 3 to 11b, Phuumii addresses Taa multiple times but Taa never engages him. As Phuumii becomes more animated, Taa stares only at the pétanque balls. When Taa does talk, he seems to address the court generally, rather than Phuumii. Take, for example, his frustrated cry, "Oh!" in line 6. This cry happens immediately after the miss and is apparently a reaction to it. It suggests Taa's surprise and seems to be a kind of "self-remarking," addressed to no one in particular (Goffman 1981b:97).[20] That this frustration is not addressed to Phuumii distributes responsibility for

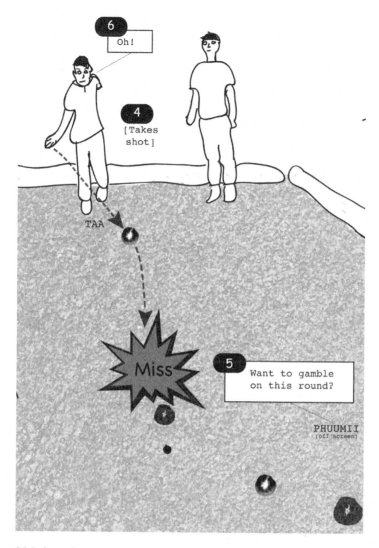

Figure 26.2 Scene 2.

the miss through a kind of negative evidence: Taa is frustrated at something for making him miss, perhaps himself, but not at Phuumii.

At every turn, Phuumii meets Taa's aloofness with exaggerated engagement. In lines 7–8 (Figure 26.3), Phuumii encroaches on the space that Taa is going to throw toward (and where Taa is looking) and points to the target ball. Phuumii's pointing gestures hover over where the pétanque balls sit, invading Taa's line of vision. Phuumii shouts at Taa and lies to him: he says

Figure 26.3 Scene 3.

that if Taa can knock the target ball off the court, he will score five points, which is not true. Phuumii floods the court with stimuli addressed to Taa, and retreats from where the pétanque balls sit only just before Taa takes his shot.

During Taa's second turn in the game (Figure 26.4), when he successfully hits the target ball, he continues to ignore Phuumii and again does several things that tacitly attribute responsibility for his initial missed shot to himself and not Phuumii. For example, as he throws his ball and it flies through the air, he and Phuumii yell simultaneously: Taa yells, "[Knock] the little ball [out]!" (line 11a), and Phuumii yells, "Hah!" (line 11b). Phuumii's "Hah!" again floods the court with stimuli directed toward Taa. Taa's shout, in contrast, works more subtly: in this situation, Taa would not want to knock the little ball, also called the jack, out at all (as this would score him fewer points than if he knocked his target ball out); he is thus shouting a kind of anti-wish, expressing what he does not wish to happen. Anti-wishes like this are not uncommon on the pétanque court and function to anthropomorphize and challenge Taa's pétanque ball as it flies through the air; perhaps akin to telling a problematic copy machine, "Jam again, I dare you."[21]

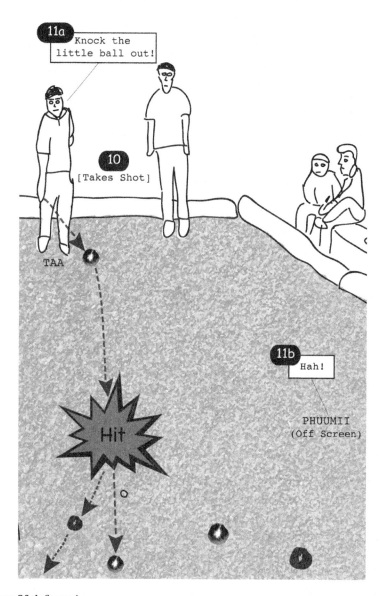

Figure 26.4 Scene 4.

When Taa does make his shot (Figure 26.5), he walks back to the other end of the court and says (line 8), perhaps a bit tongue-in-cheek, "Ohhh, [I was] scared of hitting the little ball." As he says this, and for the first time in this segment of the interaction, he briefly glances at Phuumii. Like much of what Taa has done, this utterance implies the ineffectiveness of Phuumii's

Figure 26.5 Scene 5.

doses. Even though Taa might not actually have been "scared of hitting the little ball," his utterance nevertheless functions to foreclose the interpretation that he was scared of, or even attending to, Phuumii's talk—he was scared only of hitting the little ball. This utterance also seems to explain away Taa's first, missed shot. Perhaps, it implies, Taa had missed that shot because he had overcompensated in fear of hitting the "little ball."

That Taa successfully made his second shot helps him tell a "story" about his first, missed shot. Because Phuumii heckled Taa during both shots, Taa's ability to make his second shot while being heckled implies that the cause of his first, missed shot, was something other than heckling.

In the interaction as a whole, Taa and Phuumii are talked about, and treated as, different kinds of agents. While Taa comes off as cool and in control, Phuumii exhibits a kind of frantic "hotness" aimed at sensorial overload. During my research stint more generally, I noticed that Phuumii tended toward such states; others said so as well. During this game, in fact, a number of spectators commented on the ragged state of Phuumii's heart. One man shouted out, for instance, just before Phuumii was offering to bet Taa and the above interaction began, that Phuumii's heart was "confused" and "disordered," that he "couldn't even sit still."[22] Later during the game, Phuumii was again accused of losing his cool. He had just shouted and missed a shot when a spectator called out that in using medicine on Taa, Phuumii had dosed himself instead. Like a chemist organizing dangerous chemicals and accidently spilling them on his skin, Phuumii was falling victim to his own medicine.[23] According to the spectator, Phuumii was an agent of self-destruction, "hot" and uncontrollable. Of course, ascriptions of agency and responsibility like these can in and of themselves be effectual. In saying Phuumii was "hot," the spectators were perhaps themselves "dosing" Phuumii; compare the frustration one feels when repeatedly told to "calm down" during an argument.

CONCLUSION

"Stories" are told not only on pétanque courts. Much like a man stumbling on a sidewalk can "tell a story" about why or how he tripped, people—with varying degrees of explicitness—often frame what has happened and who is responsible. This sometimes has serious consequences. As it does, for example, in a court of law, often the most ritualized and important venue for attributing agency. Take the state trial of the officers who beat and brutalized the late Rodney King, which resulted in the officers' acquittal. In the trial, the defense used a number of visual and linguistic devices to guide how people viewed the video of King's body being beaten. As Charles Goodwin (1994:621) writes, the video of the beating was framed such that "a rise in King's body [was] interpreted as aggression, which in turn justifie[d] an escalation of force [by the officers]". In this case, the defense "told a story" about the beating, and attributed responsibility for it to King, not the officers. They presented King's writhing body not as the victim of the officers' force, but as the entity with agency, in control of the situation.

If we take attributions of agency seriously, some dimensions of agency rise to the fore. First, attributions of agency are often contested. People can and often do disagree about who or what is responsible for an act, and, thus, about how agency is distributed (see Hill and Irvine 1993). Furthermore, some people may be better at telling their "side of the story," because actors have differential access to authority and the resources to represent agency (e.g., legal training, ownership of a projector, etc.—see Kockelman 2007 and Kockelman this volume for a discussion of the agency of representation itself). Would Taa's "story," for instance, be as convincing if he had not made his second shot? Second, "stories," or whatever we might want to call attributions of agency, often distribute agency differently across time and space. That is, agency and the distribution of agency are interactionally emergent, not fixed properties of things or people. Third, agency is often attributed gradiently. That is, the attribution of agency is not an all-or nothing-act; people can be held responsible to different degrees. And, fourth and finally, causality—and what we might call agency[24]—can be distributed to groups or dimensions of humans other than biological individuals and to things we might not typically consider "agents." In pétanque, for instance, players and audience members often attribute responsibility for a missed shot to a variety of things: slippery pétanque balls, stray bottle caps, poorly placed stones, bad luck, inebriation, et cetera.

Following this approach, the relevant question becomes not so much who is responsible for what, but, how does responsibility emerge interactionally, how is it distributed, and how might these distributions be negotiated and contested?

ACKNOWLEDGMENTS

The research behind this chapter was supported by a Fulbright Hays Doctoral Dissertation Research Abroad fellowship and a Wenner Gren Dissertation Fieldwork Grant. While preparing the chapter, I have received guidance and assistance in a number of ways. Versions of the paper, and the data behind it, were presented—and vigorously and helpfully discussed—at the University of Michigan Linguistic Anthropology Lab, at a Georgetown University Data Session, and at a vibrant National Capital Area Linguistic Anthropology "mini-conference" held at the University of Virginia. I would particularly like to thank Barbra Meek and Mark Sicoli for inviting me to participate in these events. Michael Lempert, Webb Keane, Alaina Lemon, Perry Sherouse, John Mathias, Meghanne Barker, Jeffrey Albanese, Kimberly Ang, Adrienne Lagman, Elizabeth Batiuk, and Dana Nichols all read and commented on drafts of this chapter in one form or another. Finally, I would like especially to thank the other conference participants and the editors of this volume, Paul Kockelman and Nick Enfield, for their support in regard to this project and beyond. To repeat the common "story": all mistakes are my own.

NOTES

1. Because of limitations in space, I am here not addressing the way in which the game fits into broader life in Laos—its sociological, economic, and historical context, its gendered dimensions, the discourses about its unseemliness, and so

on. These topics are, obviously, hugely important to fully understanding what is happening on the court. Note, too, that all of my examples come from games in which men are playing for money (as opposed to beer, which is also often gambled).

2. This name, along with all the other names of players in this chapter, is a pseudonym.

3. In Lao, "*caw4 nii4 naq1*." For transcription of Lao in this paper, I am following the system outlined in Enfield (2007).

4. In Lao, "*tùùn1 qoo1 con3 vaa1 hèt2 cang3 sii4 leej2 mùù4 kii4 naq1*."

5. See Duranti (2004:454) and Hill and Irvine (1993) for discussion of the discursive construction of responsibility and the relation between responsibility and evidence. Generally, the argument in this chapter builds on some prevalent arguments in linguistic anthropology concerning "metapragmatics" and "reflexivity" (e.g., Silverstein 1993). Others, especially Ahearn (2010), have built on these arguments somewhat differently. Note that, in contrast to some classic statements on agency from Ahearn (2001) and Duranti (2004), and in line with the work of the editors of this volume, my argument moves beyond a primary focus on grammatical categories (e.g., ergatives) and explicit framings of agency to include the alleged suburbs of language: gesture, gaze, and so on.

6. *Saj1 jaa3* is a verb, and the nominal form is *kaan3 saj1 jaa3*. For ease of reading, I will refer to it as simply *saj jaa*, without tone markers.

7. This is a slight simplification, because sometimes actions that could be considered medicine are claimed to be "only a joke." In the final analysis, what counts as *saj jaa* is, like agency, negotiated in interaction.

8. For further discussion of "hot" and "cool" heartedness in a similar context, see Cassaniti (2009).

9. Emotional moments like this shape players' reputations, but, of course, reputations are not merely an aggregate of these moments. Some moments are inevitably more lasting, salient, or important than others.

10. Or at least autonomous vis-à-vis the heckler.

11. Note that this is a simplification for multiple reasons. First, people can interpret these signs in very different ways. Second, the distribution of agency is often gradient. Players or audience members can, for example, downplay a heckler's agency by saying the heckler "joked just a tiny bit," implying the missed shot was due to the player's heart, not the strength of the medicine used. In contrast, people can characterize medicine as being so powerful that anyone would be affected. In fact, this is what happened later in the interaction between Bii and Can when Can screamed in Bii's face. The scream was so intense, people said, that of course Bii was affected, no matter the state of his heart.

12. See the concept of "conditional relevance" for further discussion (Schegloff 2007:20).

13. In regard to the ebb and flow of sports, I asked one man what he might say to calm a friend down who is feeling "hot-hearted." He offered: "Don't worry about whether or not you are going to make the shot, who could possibly make every shot in sports?"

14. Of course, players do at times deny that a heckle is getting to them—sometimes explicitly—by directly engaging with the heckler.

15. In Lao, "*bòò1 khòòj5 bòø-son3 caj3 khòòj5-qaq1 khòòj5 tang4 caj3 khaw5 tang4 caj3 tii3 lêqø-kaø-lêêw4 khòòj4 bòø-son3 . . . son3 caj3 ñang3*."

16. These "cartoons" are not meant, in any sense, to be accurate portrayals of the people involved; in fact, their main appeal, besides the ease with which they can be read, is that they preserve anonymity as the drawings look quite different from the people they represent.
17. Although each player has a teammate, neither of their teammates talk during the course of this segment.
18. That is, Taa treats Phuumii's actions as medicine, as should become clear below.
19. This is not unusual in sports, as players are generally expected to focus their attention on the game; cf. Goffman's (1981a: 134–135; 1981b:112) notion of an "open state of talk."
20. Nor is this discourse-oriented response cry generally used in situations in which one is scolding or chastising another's actions, but instead, as Nick Enfield writes, it tends to be used as "a news receipt which expresses disappointment or concern" (2007:313).
21. Players often shout commands at the balls, addressing them with directives like "Stop," "Go," and so on. For some similar themes, see Benjamin Smith's discussions of marbles and bad luck among Aymara children (2010:230; chapter 20 in this volume).
22. In Lao, "*cit2 caj3 . . . ñung3 ñaak5 leej2 nòq1 laaw2 bòø-saang1 juu1 lêq1.*"
23. In Lao, "*saj1 jaa3 khaw2 bak2 haajø-haaj4 lêq1 tuaø-qèèng tùùn1.*"
24. I do not have space to address this question here, but merely point the reader to the introductory chapters by Enfield and Kockelman of this volume and some popular arguments that deal with the possibility of nonhuman agents (Gell 1998; Latour 2005).

REFERENCES

Ahearn, Laura M. 2001. "Language and Agency." *Annual Review of Anthropology* 30: 109–137.

Ahearn, Laura M. 2010. "Agency and Language." *Society and Language Use* 7: 28.

Cassaniti, Julia. 2009. "Control in a World of Change: Emotion and Morality in a Northern Thai Town." Ph.D. dissertation, University of Chicago.

Duranti, Alessandro. 2004. "Agency in Language." In *A Companion to Linguistic Anthropology*, edited by A. Duranti, 451–473. Malden, MA: Blackwell.

Enfield, N. J. 2007. *A Grammar of Lao*. Berlin/New York: Mouton.

Gell, Alfred. 1998. *Art and Agency: An Anthropological Theory*. Oxford: Oxford University Press.

Goffman, Erving. 1978. "Response Cries." *Language* 54: 787–815.

Goffman, Erving. 1981a. "Footing." In *Forms of Talk*, edited by E. Goffman, 124–159. Philadelphia: University of Pennsylvania Press.

Goffman, Erving. 1981b. "Response Cries." In *Forms of Talk*, edited by E. Goffman, 79–122. Philadelphia: University of Pennsylvania Press.

Goodwin, C. 1994. "Professional Vision." *American Anthropologist* 96(3): 606–633.

Hill, Jane H., and Judith T. Irvine. 1993. *Responsibility and Evidence in Oral Discourse*. Cambridge: Cambridge University Press.

Kockelman, Paul. 2007. "Agency." *Current Anthropology* 48(3): 375–401.

Latour, Bruno. 2005. *Reassembling the Social: An Introduction to Actor-Network Theory*. Oxford: Oxford University Press.

Schegloff, Emanuel A. 2007. *Sequence Organization in Interaction. Volume 1: A Primer in Conversation Analysis.* Cambridge: Cambridge University Press.

Silverstein, Michael. 1993. "Metapragmatic Discourse and Metapragmatic Function." In *Reflexive Language: Reported Speech and Metapragmatics*, edited by J. A. Lucy, 33–58. Cambridge: Cambridge University Press.

Smith, Benjamin. 2010. "Of Marbles and (Little) Men: Bad Luck and Masculine Identification in Aymara Boyhood." *Journal of Linguistic Anthropology* 20(1): 225–239.

AUTHOR INDEX

Devine-Wright, P., 217
Dingemanse, Mark, 67, 74, 79
Dittmer, J., 218
Drew, Paul, 74, 75, 79
Du Bois, John W., 206
Duncan, J. S., 217
Duranti, Alessandro, 8, 267
Durkheim, E., 143

Ehrenreich, B., 152
Einarson, K. M., 175
Eisenberger, N. I., 147
Ekkekakis, P., 146
Elyachar, Julia, 193, 196
Enfield, N. J., 49, 50, 53, 63, 74, 79, 80,
    87, 95, 129, 162, 202, 203, 206, 246,
    267, 268
Erasmus, Charles J., 195
Evans-Pritchard, Edward E., 205,
    206, 208

Fantacci, Luca, 104
Fawcett, C., 174
Feldstein, S., 174
Ferllini, Roxana, 182
Floyd, Simeon, 79
Foucault, M., 25, 73, 74, 76, 218, 224
Fritz, T. H., 156

Garfinkel, H., 96
Gell-Mann, Murray, 59, 60, 62, 63
Gell, Alfred, 13, 37, 268
Gergely, G., 170
Gibson, J. J., 221, 225
Gilbert, Margaret, 60, 238, 239, 244
Gilsenan, M., 248
Gintis, Herbert, 75
Goffman, Erving, 75, 80, 254, 255,
    260, 268
Goodwin, Charles, 265
Goodwin, Marjorie H., 196
Graeber, David, 101, 104, 105, 110
Grau, Carles, 59
Grice, H. Paul, 75
Gross, S., 133
Guajardo, J. J., 173

Hägerstrand, T., 216
Han, Clara, 104, 105
Haney, C., 225
Hart, Keith, 109, 111

Heath, C., 144
Heinze, J., 132
Henrich, J., 136
Heritage, John, 91, 126
Hill, G. F., 113
Hill, Jane H., 265, 267
Hölldobler, B., 132
Honig, Bonnie, 42
Horst, Heather, 52
Hudson, Michael, 113
Huffine, Edwin, 185
Hull, Matthew, 43
Humphrey, N., 147, 245
Husserl, E., 213
Hutchins, Edwin L., 12, 221,
    223, 247

Irigaray, L., 216
Irvine, Judith T., 265, 267
Ivens, A. B. F., 132

Jaffe, J., 174
Jakobson, Roman, 196
James, J. E., 151
James, William, 18
Janata, P., 154, 155
Jasnow, M. D., 174
Jefferson, Gail, 74
Jefferson, Jon, 181
Johnson, M., 164
Johnson, R. A., 132
Johnson, S., 171
Joyce, Christopher, 181, 182

Keenan, E. O., 249
Kelso, J. A. S., 162, 163
Kirby, S., 162
Kirschner, S., 153, 155
Kitzinger, Celia, 75
Klonowski, Eva-Elvira, 185
Kockelman, Paul, 4, 7, 8, 49, 50, 53, 120,
    182, 187, 194, 200, 246, 265
Koelsch, S., 152, 154, 155
Koos, O., 170

Laidlaw, James, 13
Larkin, Brian, 50, 52
Latour, Bruno, 13, 188, 195, 196,
    221, 268
Lazzarato, Maurizio, 103
Leroi-Gourhan, E., 221

SUBJECT INDEX

Aymara language, 191, 192, 196, 268
Azande, 205, 247

babies, 161, 163, 164, 165, 173. *See also*
    children; infants; toddlers
behavioral sciences, 72, 145, 163
biology, xi, 12, 225
Bitcoin, 110, 111, 112, 114. *See also*
    digital currencies
blame
    apportioning, 45, 49, 101, 128,
        248–249
    inheriting, 9
    as an interpretant, 6
    sharing, 11
blind spots, 17
blockchain, 112
bodies, 112, 201, 222
    body parts, 144
    collective, 218
    constraints of, 60
    and control, 12
    dead, 181–188
    "docile bodies," 224
    individual, xiv, 10, 59, 63
    and minds, xi, 143, 225
    and motion, 51, 155
    physical, 13
    and selves, 129
    women's, 216
Boston, 200
British, 245
British Museum, 113
bureaucracy, 41, 42, 44

causality, 35, 36, 166, 254, 266
    causal processes, 27, 30, 33–37, 255
    cause-effect, 34
    See also accountability: causal
cellular slime molds, 64
Chachi, 68, 71, 72, 73
Cha'palaa, 68, 70, 71, 72, 75
child-rearing, 71, 103, 145, 166
children, 102, 169
    and agency, 71, 196
    and collaborative activity, 146, 173
    and family, 225
    grandchildren, 10
    parental responsibility, 103, 106
    and play, xiv, 192, 196

and social development, 175
    See also adolescents; babies; infants;
        toddlers
choice
    and accountability, 7
    adjusting, 248
    and agency, xv, 28, 43, 226
    and ants, 134
    and brute force, 60
    as human act, 20, 103, 208
    and presence of mentality, 18
Christianity, 102. *See also* God; religion
citizenship, xiii, 51, 249
coercion, xi, 131, 136, 164, 222, 244, 245
cognition, 18, 152
    distributed, 12, 221
    human, 170–174
    social, 175
coincidence, 205
coins, 109, 113
collaboration, 60
collective action, 67, 44
    collective agency, 72, 134, 169–177,
        216, 234, 244
    collective behaviors, 20
    collective mass, 44
    collectives, 72, 234
commodities, xii
communality, 141, 145
competition, 34, 112, 244, 245, 246
    for animatorship, 81, 84
    in music, 201, 202
    in sports, 146
complex networks, 64, 151
computerized algorithms. *See* algorithms
conflict, 43, 44, 135, 155, 184, 237, 245
contention, 71, 240
contingency, 22, 27, 100, 170, 199–209
    life contingencies, 104
    vs. necessity, 36
control
    agents and agency, 37, 124, 125, 224
    and the body, 119, 122, 123, 55
    controlled behavior, 7
    and deception, 247
    institutional, 51, 222
    joint, 11, 235
    and language, 62
    neural activity, 59, 60
    physical, 12

Exodus, 105
explicit negotiation, 82, 103

face, 70, 71
Facebook, 51, 52, 53, 54, 115
family, 73, 131, 186, 227
    and death, 184, 185
    and interaction, 61–62, 82–83,
        225–226
    internal dynamics, 75
    and payback, 10
feud, 10
financial crisis, 114
fission, 11
food, 18, 132, 133, 134, 146, 225
foraging, 132, 133, 135, 141, 152
force fields, 35
formal cause, 15, 17
Foucault, 25, 73, 74, 76, 218, 224
framing, 33, 99, 105, 200, 102
    and accountability, 6, 217
    and agency xiii, xiv, 15–17, 22, 32
free will, xv, 223
friendship, 63
fusion, 11, 13, 113, 128, 129

games, 191–197
gaze, 120, 128
    gaze patterning, 122, 123
    in mother-child interaction, 161,
        163–166, 174
generativity, xv
geographic theories, 213
Ghana, 61
goal-directed behavior, 7, 12, 170, 171
goals
    assistance in, 67
    and installations, 223, 226
    and intentions, 145
    interactional, 88, 94
    others' goals, 170, 171, 227
    shared, xi, 13, 65, 169, 175
God, 21, 102. See also Christianity;
    religion
Google, 110, 115
government, 10, 45, 105, 112
grammar, 79–86
Greece, 245
grounding, 63, 239
group exercise, xiv, 141–150, 156
group size, 11, 152

hardwiring, 134
help, 68, 153, 215, 221
    accepting, xi
    requesting, xii, 62, 79
    See also assistance
high-trust societies, 249. See also trust
Hitler, 245
Hobbes, 218
homo sapiens, 21
honor, 19, 248
human body. See bodies
humanity, 110, 113, 155, 244

imagination, 18, 29, 102, 191
imitation, 6, 60
immediate and mediate spheres, 36
impositions, xiv
improvisation, 199–209
independent action, 119, 227, 236
indigenous law, 10
inductive reasoning, 30
infants, xiv, 131, 143, 163–167,
        169–176. See also babies;
        children
inferential agency, 33, 35, 36, 37,
        75
infrastructure, 49–55, 111, 114,
        223, 227
    and agency, 35, 64–65
    and interactions, 32
    and the internet, 112
installations, xiv, 221–228
instigation, 26, 28, 36, 37
instincts, 21
institutions, 32, 67, 222, 223–226, 245
instrumental acts, 19
instrumental agency, 18, 19, 22,
        33, 36, 37
intentionality, xi, xiv, xv, 225
    and agency, 233
    shared, 12, 60, 234–235, 244
internet, xii, 51, 52, 53, 111, 112
interpretants, 28, 34, 206, 207, 257
    anticipation, 8
    definition, 25, 26, 27, 87
    non-anticipated, 4, 8
    Peirce, 184, 194, 200
    sign-object relations, 201, 202,
        204, 205
    and subprehension, 5–6
interpreting, 12, 43, 195, 225

revolution, xii, 20, 49–55
reward, xiii, 17, 36, 46, 112
  intrinsic, 145
  motivating, 148, 155
  and pain, 143
  psychological, 144, 146
robot, 204
rupee, 112, 113, 114, 115

sabotage, xiv
sanctions, 4, 6, 7–8, 96, 102
scaffolding, 46, 222
selectivity, 60, 63, 64, 65
self-consciousness, xv, 21, 37
semiosis, 37, 200
  semiotic framework, 200
  semiotic mediation, 199–209
  semiotic processes, 25, 26, 34, 37
serendipity, 16, 22
shared attention, 154, 173
shared intentionality, xv, 12, 60,
  238, 244
sharing, xiii, 9, 60, 105
  attention, 170, 171, 172–173
Sherlock Holmes, 187
sieving, 16, 22
signs
  and agency, 18
  as behavior, 4, 202, 203,
    206, 207
  false, 246
  in forensics, 184, 185, 186, 187
  interpretants of, 25, 28
  and objects, 188
Siwu, 61
small talk, 171
society
  agents as, ix, 13, 42, 60, 62
  compound persons, 11
  social bonding, 141–150, 151–158,
    175, 176
  social commitment, 240, 241, 242
  social cooperation (see
    cooperation: social)
  social identity, 73, 75, 227
  social insects, 131–137
  social isolation, 151
  social sciences, 50, 73, 99, 145,
    163, 166
  social stratification, 73, 75, 216

social units, 43, 64, 135, 136
socialization, 30, 53, 166, 196
soul, 120, 128
space
  for action, 191, 192, 195, 201
  bounded, 213
  public and private, 213
  and time, 35, 100, 110-112, 214, 216,
    255, 265
  urban, 50, 53
spirituality. See religion
Srebrenica, 185
standards, 19, 20, 41
state agencies, 41–47
stress, 142, 146
subjectivity, 42, 182, 215
subprehension, 4, 8, 12, 13, 206, 207
supra-mind, 237
symbiosis, 132
synchronized movement. See dance

technologies, 64
  and artifacts, xii, 196
  and communication, 52, 53, 148
  infrastructure, 51
  new, 3, 6
  See also artifacts
teleological processes, 21, 22
teleomatic processes, 21, 22
teleonomic agents, 21, 22
telepathy, 65
temporality, 100, 101, 104, 106
  asymmetry in, 241
  framing, 99, 105
  temporal regimes, 102, 103
toddlers,169. See also children
tools
  analytical, 162, 166
  the body as, 62, 247
  communicative, 174
  language as, xiv, 63
  people as, xii, 16, 243, 244,
    247–249
topics, 33, 163, 165
topophilia, 217, 218
transformation, 29, 30, 31, 216, 217
  in jazz, 201
  in life cycle, 102
  spaces transformed, 191, 192
transgression, 10

CPSIA information can be obtained
at www.ICGtesting.com
Printed in the USA
BVOW03s0320151217

502758BV00002B/9/P